WHATEVER HAPPENED
TO THE
WASHINGTON REPORTERS
1978–2012

NEWSWORK 7

WHATEVER HAPPENED
TO THE
WASHINGTON REPORTERS
1978–2012

Stephen Hess

BROOKINGS INSTITUTION PRESS
Washington, D.C.

ABOUT BROOKINGS
The Brookings Institution is a private nonprofit organization
devoted to research, education, and publication on important issues of
domestic and foreign policy. Its principal purpose is to bring the highest
quality independent research and analysis to bear on current and emerging
policy problems. Interpretations or conclusions in Brookings publications
should be understood to be solely those of the authors.

The Library of Congress has cataloged the hardcover edition as follows:
Hess, Stephen.
  Whatever happened to the Washington reporters, 1978–2012 / Stephen Hess.
    p.   cm.
  Summary: "Follows up on 450 Washington journalists first interviewed in
1978, analyzing career patterns and challenges faced by generation, gender,
minority status, news medium, and employer. Explores whether subjects rose
within their organization, moved from reporter to editor or from one medium
to another, or left journalism and if so, why and for what kind of career"—
Provided by publisher.
  Includes bibliographical references and index.
  ISBN 978-0-8157-2386-8 (hardcover : alk. paper)
  1. Journalists—Washington (D.C.)—Biography. 2. Reporters and reporting—
Washington (D.C.) I. Title.
  PN4899.W3H45 2012
  070.92'2753—dc23
  [B]   2012023187

        ISBN: 978-0-8157-2540-4 (pbk. : alk.paper)

                  Digital printing

              Printed on acid-free paper

                  Typeset in Life

          Composition by Cynthia Stock
             Silver Spring, Maryland

For my family

Beth

Charlie	Peter	James	Sara
Heidi	Mollie	Betsy	John
Eloise	Minnie	Nate	Ruthie
Tobie	Henry	Rachel	

"I find the family the most mysterious and fascinating institution in the world."
—Amos Oz

CONTENTS

NEWSWORK:
HOW I GOT THERE

Whatever Happened to the Washington Reporters, 1978–2012 is the seventh and final book in a series entitled "Newswork," which began when the Brookings Institution Press published *The Washington Reporters* in 1981. To have spent more than three decades on this project was not an accident, but it was a surprise.

When I came to Brookings in 1972 after working on the White House staffs of two presidents, my field of competence presumably was the presidency. But by 1976 I had written a book, *Organizing the Presidency,* that said all that I had to say about the presidency at the time, and so I looked around for another player in the governmental process to write about.

The press, as the news media were then called, seemed a lively topic, especially in Washington, where I had been a source for reporters. My book would focus primarily on how news operations organized themselves to cover the activities of the federal government. However, I was neither a journalist nor a communications scholar, so I would have to start by reading "the literature." What I immediately learned was that there was no literature on the Washington journalism of this era; the last book-length study was Leo C. Rosten's 1935 Ph.D. dissertation from the University of Chicago.[1]

At first I went from reporter to reporter, asking them how they did their work. What were the boundaries between competition and cooperation with other reporters? Between autonomy and control in their newsrooms? I gathered enough notes and musings to put together a 150-page report to myself. Now I knew how I wanted to begin.

[NOTES, 3/16/78] Bernard Kalb, CBS: *"The question I'd like to see* [you ask reporters]: *'Do you give any thought to your own future?' In 80 percent of cases, the answer will be no. [You] become so totally absorbed in your own job that suddenly you're 57 years old. You could give Sukarno's birthdate, but you don't know anything about your own life."*

[NOTES, 4/28/77] Martin Tolchin, *New York Times:* "Basically, report-*ers are loners. They do not work or play well with other people."*

[NOTES, 4/27/78] Don Oberdorfer, *Washington Post:* "It's very impor-*tant to understand that basically all reporters feel insecure. They are insecure with the editors, in their jobs, on their beats. This has to do with the public nature of their work—their mistakes are printed for all to see—[and with] the feeling that if they don't have a story, their rival will."*

A STANDARD QUESTIONNAIRE would not capture the way that journalists confront problems. These are people who deal in the concrete, and they can be ill at ease with abstractions. I would ask them to keep a diary for a week, filling in precise information each day, such as events attended, documents used, people interviewed (by type, not name), whether interviews were on or off the record. The results formed a tapestry of Washington newsgathering patterns. I was surprised to see the degree to which information—even about presidents at a time when the media were thought to be preoccupied with the presidency—was being filtered through Capitol Hill before reaching the public.

As I now look back on the joys of discovery and count a research victory or two, I also see my mistakes. I thought a "no names" approach would raise the response rate, so my survey was to be filled out anonymously. What I learned, to my regret, was that the reporters didn't care; in fact, some seemed irritated that they were not to be recognized in the book! I never offered the option of anonymity again.

Newswork 2, *The Government/Press Connection: Press Officers and Their Offices* (1984), also set out to examine thinly explored territory: the most frequently cited scholarly study was a 1961 survey in which thirty-eight public information officers and thirty-five journalists were interviewed.[2] My flight plan was to include a year of site observations within five agencies—the White House, State Department, Pentagon,

Department of Transportation, and Food and Drug Administration—
with visits lasting from one month to three months at each.

Here my worry was that my subjects might not speak freely with an
outsider looking over their shoulder and listening in. What turned out to
be in my favor was that I was required to get a security clearance; thus,
my trustworthiness was officially government certified. Indeed, as I was
to discover, one of my tougher tasks was to keep from being drawn into
the activities that I was there to observe.

This was to be a study of the routine—the daily work of producing
government information. But as every reporter knows, you should never
underestimate the role of chance. On January 13, 1982, Air Florida 90
crashed into the 14th Street Bridge, in sight of the secretary of transportation's office, where I happened to be observing the secretary's press
operations. On August 19, 1981, when two U.S. Navy F-14 aircraft shot
down two Libyan SU-22 fighter aircraft, I happened to be observing
press operations at the Department of Defense. Researching press operations during a crisis and up close had not been in my project outline, but
it was to become a chapter in my book. One lesson that I learned, as William Beecher, a distinguished reporter who had also served as a Pentagon
spokesman, told me, was that "half of the initial internal reporting within
government in a crisis is wrong."

Studying such common tools of communication as press releases
and briefings could not be called a stimulating experience, but trying to
untangle why officials leak information proved to be a delightful exercise
in deconstruction, which I expanded into categorization: The Ego Leak,
The Goodwill Leak, The Policy Leak, The Animus Leak, and The Whistle-
Blower Leak, complicated by some leaks serving more than one purpose.
As James Reston, the *New York Times*'s greatest Washington journalist,
liked to say, "Government is the only known vessel that leaks from the top."

In seeking the key to Newswork 3, *The Ultimate Insiders: U.S. Senators in the National Media* (1986), I quickly realized that Capitol Hill
was not a scholar-friendly place. Everywhere that I wanted to go was off
limits. Fortunately, my dear friend Pat Moynihan was now a senator and
he had a solution. He would make me a member of his staff (unpaid and
honorary); people with congressional staff credentials can go anywhere.
I now located myself in the Senate Press Gallery.

My next dilemma was how to get interviews with senators whose secretaries had no good reason for letting me see their bosses. My solution
was not to ask. Senators do a lot of walking—to committee hearings,
party caucuses, floor debates, and press conferences and then back to
their offices—and strangely, they often walk alone. My plan was to look
for them on their daily rounds and offer to tag along. Without appoint-
ments, I had conversations of various lengths with nearly half of the
United States Senate. To entice a senator was to ask this question: *"Senator, you know reporters are going to put an adjective in front of your
name. If you had your druthers, what adjective would you choose?"*
"Hard-working" was their favorite. The one senator who replied without
hesitation was Orrin Hatch (R–Utah): "Integrity, Intelligence, Guts."

[NOTES, 6/14/84] Thomas Eagleton (D-Mo.) (as we walk from the eleva-
tor in the Capitol to the Senate subway and then to his office in Dirksen):
*"I defeated a senator named Ed Long to get here. Later I convinced him
to give me his mailing list. It must have been 8,000 names. Now we probably have 700,000. We can push a button and get Vietnam-era doves if
we want to send a dovish letter. We've been captured by technology."*

[NOTES, 5/25/84] Charles Mathias (R-Md.) (standing in the corridor
outside his office): *"This place has deteriorated. It's been trivialized. The
Senate once deliberated over 50–60 issues a year; now it's thousands,
mostly technical amendments. It's stopped being a deliberative body."*
"Is this reversible?" *"No, but it should be manageable."*

[NOTES, 9/18/84] John Stennis (D-Miss.) (walking with him to the
Capitol from the Swamp Site): "Senator, you must have known great
journalists." *"I knew David Lawrence* [said almost in awe]. *I was shot*
[by muggers in 1973, outside his Washington home] *and out for six
months. When I came around, I asked an aide, 'Bring me the editorials
of David Lawrence.' That's how I was going to catch up on what had
happened. 'Oh, senator, he died a week after you were shot.'"*

ANOTHER GAME THAT I played to lubricate conversation, this time with
reporters, was "Name Your Favorite Senator." I did this usually when we
were having lunch at the press table in the Senate dining room. What
was important to me was not who, but why. Television correspondents

needed a good quote. Ann Compton, ABC: *"Goldwater, when he's having a good day."* Susan Rasky, Reuters: *"Kennedy. He's the only one foreigners recognize."* Bob Dole was the overwhelming favorite; they loved to analyze his every move as powerful chairman of the Finance Committee. As reporters spotted Dole leaving the Tuesday caucus, Jon Fuerbringer, *New York Times,* noted, "He's very good at walking away."

In Newswork 4, *Live from Capitol Hill! Studies of Congress and the Media* (1991), I was especially interested in local television because in the early 1980s the thrill of new technology had encouraged a rash of stations and media groups to open Washington bureaus; several even had Washington anchors. Network news coverage was weighted toward the Senate and its leadership, as illustrated in the previous book. But local TV news, presumably focused on House members, might shift the balance. If all politics is local, wouldn't that be reflected in local television's coverage of Congress?

My problem was how to get enough TV news programs to find out. I begged friends, relatives, and friends' friends to tape and send me a week of local broadcasts—from Grand Junction, Colorado (population 30,000), to Los Angeles and New York—and in their generosity, they produced 35 cities, 57 stations, 60 hours, 106 broadcasts, and 1,419 stories, 125 of them from Washington. I discovered, after the data were analyzed in every way possible, that only seven House members were both seen and heard in their own districts, in coverage that lasted, on average, 77 seconds. One story was about a congressman's retirement. Despite the modest returns, busy legislators were spending a lot of time seeking attention on television. Why? I think that I answered that question in the title of one chapter: "I Am on TV Therefore I Am":

> It is August 1, 1984, and I am sitting next to Senator Alan Dixon in a screening room in the basement of the Capitol. . . . [We are watching a recent broadcast from a cable station in Peoria.] A question put to him requires a delicate answer. Dixon listens to his response. He smiles, then issues a laugh that comes from deep inside him. "I got out of that pretty good," he says. Watching a man so thoroughly enjoy watching himself is an exquisite experience.

To investigate local television's overwhelming lack of interest in the legislators, my research assistant Deborah Kalb and I called 102 news directors. Only three stations claimed that covering Capitol Hill improved their ratings. The Washington bureaus, except for those of the biggest groups, started to pack up; if the hometown mayor testified before Congress, they could always buy some footage from a freelancer.

Newswork 5, *International News and Foreign Correspondents* (1996), covered a subject to which attention had been paid. But who could resist the opportunity to observe journalists at work in places such as Tokyo, Beijing, Jerusalem, Budapest, and Prague?

My methodological concern was about the value of "parachute scholarship." I had been critical of parachute journalism. I could come home with notebooks full of colorful observations, useful for narrative purposes, describing journalists and their offices and press clubs, but what would I discover that I might not otherwise? My answer ultimately was that it was a feel for a place at a moment in time. I would be seeing and interviewing all those who were there at that particular moment, noting similarities and differences while holding time constant; I would not have to wonder whether their immediate impressions had been distorted by the passage of time, as I would if I interviewed the same people later, when they might have reached different conclusions about their experiences. I would not have to wonder about the differences between posts, between the Middle East and Central Europe, between Beijing and Tokyo; I would be better able to assess what related to reporting skill and what related to language and cultural knowledge.

Early in my wanderings, veteran *New York Times* reporter John Vinocur, in Paris, warned me, *"You can't understand foreign correspondents until you've gone to a place where you're scared."* Young E. J. Dionne, in Rome, wanted me to understand what it felt like to report for the *Times* from Beirut, where *"you're hooked on your own adrenalin."* In Vienna and Prague, reporters commuted to war in Bosnia; James Graff of *Time* magazine used his fork to draw a map on the tablecloth showing the route from the airport to the Holiday Inn in Sarajevo, marking the cross streets where Serb fire was coming from. Beyond danger, there was the calculation of risk. Nicholas Kristof, the *Times* reporter in Beijing, was a risk taker of a high order, as was Bob Simon of CBS, in Tel Aviv. Kristof's expense account after Tiananmen Square included "1 bike run over by tank." Simon, who had spent 40 days in Iraqi prisons during the Gulf War, talked about "the quality of restlessness." When I observed that it had been only four months since his last crisis, he shrugged. *"Hey, we're talking news."*

"What about survival techniques?" I asked *Washington Post* reporter John Pomfret, in Istanbul, during a weekend away from Kurdistan. *"Never wash your car,"* he said. "Never wash your car?" *"If someone plants a bomb under it, you'll see fingerprints."* Sylvia Poggioli, of NPR, had strong feelings on the pros and cons of wearing a weighty flak jacket, finding that the increased safety didn't compensate for the loss of mobility. (She offered me hers to test the proposition.) Yet there were not enough responses to my often-asked question about survival to compile a handbook. NBC's Martin Fletcher, in Herzliya, as if representing the entire foreign correspondent community, computed the odds: *"It's 80 percent luck, 20 percent experience."*

I didn't meet any war lovers; I did meet a lot of fatalists. I had begun speculating about a journalist personality type in the first Newswork book: "The relationship between personality and journalism may be the most promising field of study for explaining why news is as it is."[3] The foreign correspondent brought added grist to the mill.

In Newswork 6, *Through Their Eyes: Foreign Correspondents in the United States* (2005), a new worry arose: how to analyze what was being reported when in many cases I couldn't read the language (and couldn't afford translations)? I sent an SOS to my talented colleagues in the Brookings community, and they helped ease my burden; volunteers included Josef Braml (German), Michael Calingaert (Italian), Ivo Daalder (Dutch), Niclas Ericsson (Swedish), Lincoln Gordon (Portuguese), Carol Graham (Spanish), and Tibor Purger (Hungarian).

To assess foreign correspondents' use of the State Department's Foreign Press Center in downtown Washington, my research assistant Dan Reilly spent a week there, armed with a stopwatch:

[Tuesday, February 26, 2002; 10:15 a.m.] *Nickolay Zimm arrives, works for Russian weekly magazine,* Itogi, *says before Internet FPC was much more of a gathering place for foreign media, now usually only comes in once a week to read newspapers and occasionally meet with FPC staff.* [10:31 a.m.] *Marcia Luisa Rossel finishes her story, and we strike up a conversation. She is freelance radio journalist from Peru, currently works for InterAmericano division of*

VOA. [10:33 a.m.] *Stephanio Marchi arrives, met him previously. He is a contributing writer for* Il Tempo, *an Italian daily. He does not have an office, uses FPC's newswire access, writes his articles on FPC computer.* [11:07 a.m.] *Ben Bangoura arrives, works for Internet newspaper* Guinea News Online, *has de facto office at FPC using desk in unused room.*

Reilly reported back: "FPC is a lifeline to a host of stringers, part-timers, and small media players; as good journalists as they may be, they are still bit-players on the global media stage."

Among the surprises in this study was a large group that I named "The Irregulars." Although they considered themselves foreign correspondents, they were not full-time journalists, and they did not appear among the members of the congressional press gallery. A New York bookseller, for example, wrote about opera for a Hungarian magazine; a Staten Island teacher covered art exhibitions for a magazine in Portugal. They often chose cultural topics as their subject, enriching the scope and diversity of what was being reported from America. Then there was a group called the Hollywood Foreign Press Association, many of whom also were part-timers. Often scorned by establishment journalists, they produced mostly exuberant celebrity profiles—"Nicole Kidman Is the Epitome of Class," *Solitaire* (Singapore)—and awarded Golden Globes to what they considered outstanding movies and actors. They too deserved a chapter. "Newswork" had come a long way from my seeking an alternative to writing another book about the presidency in 1977.

In the foreword to *The Washington Reporters* (1981), Bruce K. MacLaury, then the president of Brookings, wrote: "In the vast literature about how Americans govern themselves, the role of the press is often neglected. Yet the press—no less than the presidency, the judiciary, and the legislature—is a public policy institution and deserves a place in explanations of the governmental process." Looking today at the Shorenstein Center at Harvard, or the two Annenberg centers at the University of Pennsylvania and the University of Southern California, or the other vibrant places that conduct media research, it is hard to imagine the void of a generation ago. I like to think that I helped to fill that void. At any rate, it's been fun, and it's an honor to still be at Brookings—and to be able to return in Newswork 7 to the Washington reporters that I interviewed in 1978.

THANKS

Whatever Happened to the Washington Reporters, 1978–2012 has been a collective effort involving my research assistants, teaching assistants, students, and interns. Trying to track down 450 journalists who lived in Washington 30 or more years ago can be a tedious and often frustrating task. Transcribing an hour-long taped interview is no fun. Please share my appreciation for the young men and women who are listed as interviewers in the endnotes.

Joining together to do serious research has been the history of the Newswork books since the original six interns did the telephone interviewing and coding in the summer of 1978 for what would be *The Washington Reporters.* They were followed over the years by the interns who traced the adjectives that reporters put in front of senators' names for *The Ultimate Insiders: U.S. Senators in the National Media,* the interns who deconstructed tapes of local television news programs for *Live from Capitol Hill!,* and the interns who located Washington stories in foreign outlets for *Through Their Eyes: Foreign Correspondents in the United States.* I expressed my gratitude to them in those volumes, and I express it again here.

During the five years, 2005–09, when I was also a professor at George Washington University, I was blessed with three exceptional teaching assistants—Daniel Reilly, Jeremy Holden, and Michelle Begnoche—and a band of enthusiastic students. I am grateful to the university's president, Stephen Joel Trachtenberg, for that opportunity, to my colleagues in the School of Media and Public Affairs, and especially to Professor Roxanne Russell, studio manager, who created a video record of my class interviewing the journalists whose stories are the backbone of this book. Transcripts, tapes, and my notes will be given to the Library of Congress and eventually will be available to those who are interested in this subject. I am grateful for the assistance of historian John Haynes of the library's Manuscript Division.

No writer has been as blessed with a caring manuscript reader as I have been by the wise David H. Weaver of Indiana University.

This book was written in the comforting nest that the Brookings Institution maintains for me among my friends in the Governance Studies Program, all of whom know the affection and great regard in which I hold them. During this period I have also relied on very special interns: Nathaniel Lubin (Harvard), Elizabeth Krevsky (Cornell), Lynda Marlow (BBC), Samantha Barry (GWU), and Sarah Lovenheim (GWU).

Once again I am grateful to the Brookings Institution Press, publisher of the seven books in the Newswork series, and for the immaculate editing of the late James R. Schneider and of Eileen Hughes.

The book benefited greatly from the time that I was given to think about my subject from afar at the Rockefeller Foundation's Study and Conference Center in Bellagio, Italy—a gift beyond mere thanks.

STEPHEN HESS
Senior Fellow Emeritus
Brookings Institution

June 2012

WHAT WILL FOLLOW

IN 1978 I surveyed 450 journalists who were in Washington to cover national government for American commercial news organizations: half completed an elaborate sixteen-page questionnaire; half were interviewed by telephone. The findings identified the press corps by sex, race, education, types of media, and experience and (through the telephone interviews) revealed a good deal about the reporters' views on such matters as political bias and disagreements with their home office. That was considerably more information than had ever been gathered before.

Twenty-seven years later, when I became a professor at George Washington University, I recruited my students and my interns at Brookings to help me search for the 450. We tracked them down in France, England, Italy, Australia, New Zealand, and nineteen U.S. states in addition to the Washington, D.C., area. In the end we located 90 percent of the original subjects and interviewed 283 of them (interviewers are identified in the endnotes). Eighty-seven of the original subjects had died before we found them, and we relied on their obituaries for information.

This is not a "Class of '78" in the sense of identifying a group of individuals entering college together. Our respondents had an age spread of more than a half-century: Richard Strout became a Washington reporter when Warren G. Harding was president and retired when the president was Ronald Reagan; Charlotte Moulton became a Washington reporter when the president was Franklin D. Roosevelt and retired when Jimmy Carter was president; others were still working journalists when we closed the book in 2012, during the presidency of Barack Obama.

What they have in common is that at a certain moment in time they all were working in Washington. By the next day, they may have returned to the home office in Omaha or been reassigned to Jerusalem—or left journalism. Actually, eighty-one of our subjects remained journalists after leaving Washington, suggesting that our findings may help explain career patterns beyond the capital. Our group includes some prominent journalists. From television there were Ted Koppel, Sam Donaldson, Brit Hume, Marvin Kalb, and Judy Woodruff; among print journalists, there were Bill Keller, Jack Fuller, John Curley, Tom Fiedler, and Karen Elliott House, who would go from Washington to become editor or publisher of the *New York Times,* the *Chicago Tribune, USA Today,* the *Miami Herald,* and the *Wall Street Journal* respectively. Most, however, would never be known beyond their circle of colleagues or specialized audiences.

While there is rich scholarship on the basic characteristics of U.S. journalists, there is no major study of career patterns in journalism and, as we shall see, a great deal of misinformation.

Whatever happened to . . . ? We now have enough information to answer that question. How many of these 450 men and women stayed in journalism? Did they rise in their organizations? Change jobs? Move from reporter to editor? Jump from one type of medium to another—for example, print to TV? Did they remain in Washington or go somewhere else? Did they leave journalism? Why? Where did they go?

THIS BOOK IS designed as a series of discrete essays, relatively self-contained, each concentrating on some characteristic, such as age, sex, race, or place of employment, while the concluding chapter classifies career patterns.

1. "The Greatest Generation"

These veteran Washington journalists were fifty years old or older in 1978. Most of them grew up in the 1930s during the Great Depression, went off to defend the country in World War II, and returned home to complete their education, start a family, and figure out how to earn a living. They constituted 16 percent of the press corps; 90 percent were men, 1 percent nonwhite. They were entering the business of journalism—whether print or electronic—during a period in which it took incompetence for an organization not to be profitable. Nearly 40 percent of them worked for newspapers, 10 percent for television networks. Their career patterns were remarkably alike and very different from those of the journalists who came after them.

2. "The Boomers"

Ranging from twenty-one to thirty-two years of age, members of the huge baby boom generation already made up a third of the Washington press corps by 1978. With their careers in journalism, or elsewhere, still largely in front of them, they would break with the dominant career patterns set by the World War II veterans. The immediate tensions were between the mainstream culture of journalism in Washington, which was unfriendly to change, and the culture of young people raised in a time of affluence who expected more occupational freedom than their elders had.

3. The Women

Women constituted 20 percent of the Washington press corps in 1978. Confronted by bias in the industry and rough-edged behavior in its newsrooms, they went to court to challenge their employers for advancement, and they succeeded. As their numbers doubled over time, the focus of our interviews moved from discrimination to ways to balance their professional and personal lives.

4. Diversity

African Americans made up 4 percent of the Washington press corps in 1978. They tended to be young, strongly motivated, well educated, and more apt than their white colleagues to have majored in journalism, with nearly a third holding graduate degrees. They also would get some help from some employers' "affirmative action programs" along the way. A few would rise into the firmament of the national media, yet the percentage of black journalists was not rising. Why were so few talented African Americans climbing the career ladder in Washington journalism?

5. The *New York Times*

A newspaper is a pyramid-shaped organization that needs a lot of foot soldiers at the base and has room for only a few generals at the top. The climb is very steep; steepest, it is written, at the *New York Times*. While Washington is an important way station for talented and ambitious journalists on their upward trek back to New York, reporting from the Washington bureau is highly prized in its own right and sometimes leads journalists in unexpected directions. What happened to the reporters from 1978 who reached this height? If they left the *Times,* why did they leave? Where did they go?

6. The Networks

While the networks provided a few sweet spots on the morning shows, the Sunday shows, and the news magazines—notably *60 Minutes*—the livelihood of Washington correspondents at ABC, CBS, and NBC in the late seventies rested on the success of the half-hour weekday evening news programs that most Americans still watched to get the national and world news. Around the corner would come cable and the Internet, the combination of technology and economics that rearranged the television news industry. Some journalists were near retirement, but for most the pressing question would be how to adjust to the new environment.

7. In the Right or Wrong Place

Life was going to be very different if your employer in 1978 happened to be the *Washington Star* rather than the *Washington Post*, United Press International rather than the Associated Press. While it is possible to be in the right place at the right time, it is also possible to be in the wrong place at the wrong time. The role of fortuity, the degree of accident and chance in the life of a journalist, is worthy of a chapter of its own.

8. In the Niche

Nearly 19 percent of the journalists surveyed in 1978 worked for highly specialized publications of limited circulation. Just as their products differed from mainstream publications, so too did their job expectations and satisfactions. But with the infusion of prominent media companies entering the Washington niche business in 2011 and offering a more popular style of reporting and editing, past career patterns are subject to change.

9. The Gridiron Club

Every year in March they move into a downtown hotel ballroom, don outrageous costumes, add their own words—"soft-core satire"—to popular songs, and then ask the president of the United States to show up and be a good sport. This has been an annual event since 1885, when the president was Benjamin Harrison, twenty-seven years before cherry trees were planted around the Tidal Basin. Other reporters come and go, but Gridiron members, if they have a choice, choose to spend their lives in Washington; their careers, therefore, increasingly reflect changes in Washington journalism.

10. Whatever Happened to the Washington Reporters?

Here we assess the careers of the 450 reporters that we surveyed in 1978, one by one. We tally the number of those who left journalism sooner rather than later (journalism's dropouts), those who left in mid-career, and those who are lifetime journalists. Why do some leave and others stay? The results differed markedly from what sociologists and journalists themselves led us to expect, while, at the same time, created an unexpected optimism about the future of careers in journalism.

ONE

"THE GREATEST GENERATION"

WORLD WAR II ended in 1945. Rarely did these Washington reporters bring their military experiences into our interviews. All Bernard Kalb wanted to tell us about having worked on an Army newspaper published from a Quonset hut in the Aleutian Islands was that his editor was the great mystery writer Dashiell Hammett.[1] Corbin Gwaltney quickly passed over 1943: *"Went into the service, spent some time as a guest of the Germans in prison camps, and walked all over Germany. Learned a lot in the process."*[2]

Yet obituaries sometimes suggested more. When James McCartney died in 2011, the *Washington Post* wrote, "Mr. McCartney often said his interest in issues of war and peace derived in part from his experiences as a front-line infantryman in France and Germany during World War II. He was wounded in combat shortly before the end of the war."[3] Richard Boyce "[rose] in rank from apprentice seaman to lieutenant commander" in the Pacific. Jerry Baulch "joined MacArthur's staff when it was reformed in Australia in 1942 and remained until after the signing of the Japanese surrender aboard the battleship Missouri [as] MacArthur's chief news censor." Jim Free served in the "Pacific Theater, often facing enemy fire as a Beach Master, putting troops ashore." Lloyd Norman was a "reserve ensign and lieutenant on a mine sweeper in the Atlantic." David Kelso served as a "bomber pilot stationed in England [and won] five Air Medals." Daniel Gilmore was a "radio operator-gunner on a B-17 Flying

Unless otherwise noted, affiliations given in this book refer to the news organizations for which the journalists worked in 1978 and ages given were their ages in 1978.

Fortress bomber when he was shot down over Europe in May 1944 [and was] a prisoner of war until May 2, 1945." Robert Heinl "entered the Marines following college and was an artillery officer at Pearl Harbor at the time of the Japanese attack on Dec. 7, 1941. He was a member of the relief expedition to Wake Island in 1941, and saw action on both Guam and Iwo Jima." John Averill "suffered a leg wound and earned lieutenant's bars on the [20th Armored Division's] long eastward drive that culminated in the capture of Munich in the spring of 1945. But his most vivid memory was of being awakened from an exhausted sleep on the nose of a tank by a brisk blow on the soles of his boots. It was a whack from the riding crop of Gen. George S. Patton, the hard-driving leader of the campaign, who did not like his troopers sleeping on the job." James Roper was a correspondent covering the 5th Army in Italy, where he filed this dispatch in April 1945: "The people Benito Mussolini had ruled for two decades paid him their last tribute by hanging his remains head down from the rafters of a gasoline station in Milan's Loreto Square." None of the women served in the armed forces, but Charlotte Moulton came to Washington to work for the War Department.[4]

Those who had gone to college before the war often were graduates of elite institutions: Amherst, Dartmouth, Harvard, Johns Hopkins, Princeton, the University of Pennsylvania, Stanford, Yale.[5] Those whose postwar schooling was paid for by the GI Bill were more likely to go to large state universities such as the University of Oklahoma, Michigan State, and the University of Utah.[6] Two-thirds majored in the humanities or social sciences, one-third in journalism, hardly any in the hard sciences. As a scholastic profile, theirs was far removed from the stereotypes of *The Front Page,* set in the 1920s, in which high-school dropouts filled the glue pots for egg-on-vest city editors.

The returning GIs looked different from those they would be joining in the Washington press corps, according to Glenn Everett, who worked for the *Bryan Times* and other small Ohio papers: *"When I started in 1944 there were many of the older writers who had such profound prejudices that it greatly biased the copy they would write. Generally, they were much more in line with the Harding-Coolidge era than they were with Franklin D. Roosevelt's New Deal or Harry Truman's Fair Deal. They rejected everything that smacked of liberalism, and their editors applauded."* Everett, who later went into the personalized greeting card business, worried that the incoming reporters were swinging too far in the other direction.[7] My interviewing suggested that they also would be more liberal than the boomers who followed them.

Some, like Orr Kelly, came to Washington looking for a job. After attending Columbia Journalism School, he had gone to California to work at the *San Francisco Chronicle*. Then, *"in 1959 my wife and I started printing a newspaper in Berkeley, and that went until the spring of 1962, when it ran out of money. We had to decide where to go, and I just decided, 'Why not go to Washington? That's where the action is.' That was a better place for a reporter. At the* Chronicle *we ended up having to look at dead bodies every day, and after awhile you get sick of that. It's more fun in Washington."*

Kelly got a job at the *Washington Star*.[8]

The city of Washington had its own media: there were the *Washington Post* and the *Washington Times-Herald* in the morning, until the *Post* acquired the *Times-Herald* in 1954; the *Washington Star* and the *Washington Daily News* in the afternoon, until the *Star* acquired the *Daily News* in 1972; and local radio and TV stations. But young journalists were advised to go elsewhere if they wanted eventually to cover national government. Among the few places where cub reporters could get a direct start in Washington journalism were the small press services that sold stories to small papers. That was the path taken by Don Larrabee, who arrived in 1946 after having edited a weekly newspaper at an Army Air Corps base. The Griffin-Larrabee News Bureau, which sold mostly congressional news to twenty-six papers, got "five bucks a week from one paper and ten bucks from another"; it had a staff of four "overworked and underpaid" reporters.[9]

More than two of three mainstream reporters in Washington were sent by their organizations. At the wire services and weekly news magazines, a reporter moved up the ladder city by city (or country by country). Hugh Sidey described a writer's career path at *Time* magazine as going from reporting in Chicago to being deputy bureau chief in Paris to being bureau chief in Atlanta to being Washington correspondent. In Washington, the correspondent might cover the Pentagon or the White House, eventually working his or her way up to being Washington bureau chief and finally chief of correspondents in New York.[10] The actual path of correspondent Simmons Fentress at *Time* led from Atlanta

(1961) to Saigon (1966) to Washington (1967).[11] Associated Press (AP) reporter James Cary moved from Phoenix (1949) to Tokyo (1954) to Washington (1960).[12]

Newspapers also had a pecking order. Benjamin Cole joined the *Indianapolis Star* in 1944 as a copy editor and progressed to statehouse reporter, assistant city editor, and city editor before becoming the *Star's* Washington correspondent in 1949.

Darwin Olofson, of the *Omaha World-Herald,* enjoyed claiming that his transfer to Washington in 1950 was "a form of punishment." The story he told was that when he was covering the first big snowstorm of the season in Omaha, he went out "to get images of cherubic children prancing in the white flakes" but instead found them cold and shivering on an elementary school playground. So, as an enterprising new reporter, he started a snowball fight, which the children loved: *"Before I got back to the newsroom the school principal had called our executive editor and accused me of threatening the health and welfare of an entire new generation. Shortly thereafter the executive editor called me in and said he thought I would do better in an unstable environment. He was sending me to Washington."*[13]

Occasionally a move to Washington was not a promotion. Bill Steif said that his employer, Scripps Howard, was using its Washington bureau as "a dumping ground for older, higher-priced executives" from the chain's newspapers. He named names. "Nobody ever gets fired. Some should."[14] On the other hand, Knight Ridder bureau chief Bob Boyd said that a large chain had the capacity to put Washington reporters in executive positions on its papers if it felt that they had the potential.[15] The bigger the chain, the more slots for editors and publishers, said Gannett's Sid Hurlburt: *"You don't have to wait for someone to die."*[16]

Once in Washington, reporters sought better assignments as they gained seniority. An AP reporter could go from the regional staff, covering a specific state or city, to the national staff. A few moved from one organization to another while remaining on the same beat: Pentagon reporter Lloyd Norman moved from the *Chicago Tribune* (1946–59) to *Newsweek* (1959–78). Filling jobs was never a problem; *Baltimore Sun* bureau chief Pat Furgurson once interviewed seventy-five applicants for three openings.[17] But losing good people could be a problem. Recalling the squeeze that occurs when experienced reporters start to worry about sending their kids to college, Gannett bureau chief Jack Germond mourned being unable to keep "better people longer."[18]

Journalists move for the same reasons as people in other businesses do, usually revolving around personal or professional conflicts. Morton Mintz, of the investigative unit at the *Washington Post,* recalled: *"Initially,* [Bob] *Woodward and I got along very well. . . . But then Woodward and I didn't get along."*[19] David Dear commented on selling the small newspaper publishing company that he owned with his brothers: *"They pretty much brought the decision on. . . . I was only 58. I had a career ahead of me with nothing to do."*[20] Morton Paulson explained his departure from *Changing Times,* a general interest magazine: *"The magazine had changed its format completely. They began accepting advertising. The name changed to* Kiplinger's Personal Finance. *Personal finance wasn't something that I had a great abiding interest in."*[21]

"It's hard to balance the time spent with family and the time spent trying to get the news," said Bob Smith, of King Broadcasting. *"I think that's one of the challenges that journalists have, and it's not an easy one."*[22] Still, none attributed job changes to family concerns, as happened later when there were more women journalists and there was a greater need to accommodate two careers. Only one of the "greatest generation" women, Mal Johnson, of Cox Broadcasting, was married, and she began her journalism career after the death of her husband.

Most journalists who changed jobs stayed within the same type of journalism: Bernie Kalb went from CBS to NBC, Herb Kaplow from NBC to ABC. The members of this generation were essentially the last that would start their careers in the newspaper or the radio business before switching to the new medium of television. Future Washington correspondents were more likely to be groomed in local markets, particularly at CBS and NBC, networks with a stable of profitable network-owned-and-operated stations. In print journalism, reporters went from wire services to newspapers but rarely in the other direction—James Cary, for example, left the Associated Press for Copley papers—and there was a steady flow between newspapers and news magazines: John Lindsay went from the *Washington Post* to *Newsweek,* David Barnett from Hearst papers to *U.S. News & World Report.*

Some moved down in order to step up, taking a higher-ranked job at a less prestigious organization. After 15 years at the *Washington Post,*

Richard Maloy opened a Washington bureau for Thomson Newspapers, a chain of thirty-five papers, mostly in the 20,000-circulation range, at the low end of journalism's food chain: *"Thomson and Dick Maloy happened to be a perfect fit. Their management philosophy was to find a good manager and leave him the hell alone. I was perfect for them because I knew Washington but also had small-town journalism experience, which is what they wanted* [His father had been editor of the *Lorain Journal,* in Ohio]. . . . *I was told to proceed on the theory that if you don't hear from us you're doing a great job. I was never told to write or not write a story, which is fantastic. Fifteen years later they had more newspapers and I had four or five guys working for me."*[23]

Less than one in five of the mainstream reporters changed jobs after they got to Washington; the single-employer career was most common. Ben Cole retired in 1986 after nearly 40 years as the *Indianapolis Star's* Washington bureau chief. The *Omaha World-Herald's* Darwin Olofson was in Washington for 35 years, the last 14 as bureau chief. The standard postwar career pattern, regardless of whether the reporter worked for a wire service, small paper, large paper, or news magazine or for television, looked like this:

—Martha Cole, 36 years with AP, 26 years in Washington

—Louis Hiner, 40 years with the *Indianapolis News,* 35 years in Washington

—Robert Young, 38 years with the *Chicago Tribune,* 30 years in Washington

—Hugh Sidey, 41 years with *Time/Life,* 38 years in Washington

—George Herman, 44 years with CBS, 33 years in Washington.

A PAPER THAT experimented with a one-year Washington-and-back rotation for young reporters soon discovered that it was a good way to lose a good reporter. As Don Shannon recalled it, *"Those were the old days, when people didn't shift around. People tended to stay with the paper they started with, so I was with the* Los Angeles Times [from 1952] *until I retired* [in 1980]."[24]

Some even stayed on the same beat for extended periods. John Averill covered the Senate for the *Los Angeles Times* for 16 years (1964–80) and was shifted to preparing advance obituaries of senators only when a hip ailment limited his mobility. Frank Cormier, AP, had been at the

White House for 18 years when he left in 1980 because of a crippling nerve disorder. "He kept covering the White House when he couldn't stay on his feet," remembered Muriel Dobbin, the *Baltimore Sun's* White House reporter.[25] In 1980, CBS switched Bob Pierpoint to the State Department from the White House after he had spent 22 years on that beat. Asked why she had stayed at the White House for 57 years, Helen Thomas, of the United Press International (UPI), replied, *"What made me stay? Because it's the center. Everything comes to the White House. All news that affects the country or the world comes through the White House. So why not be in the center of it?"*[26]

But Fred Taylor, executive editor of the *Wall Street Journal*, believed in rotation: *"Papers that keep a reporter on the same beat until he dies are short-changing the reporter and the readers."* One of his Washington reporters *"had a low boredom threshold. We had to keep changing his beat every two-and-a-half years."*[27] Reassignments—which often came after a presidential election—could set off a chain reaction: Senate reporter to White House reporter, White House reporter to State Department reporter, State Department reporter to an overseas bureau.

Washington vacancies were filled from headquarters, if possible. Doing otherwise would create "a bad morale problem," said Cox bureau chief David Kraslow.[28] Yet it was not always possible, especially when a specialist was needed or there was a new beat to be covered. The *Washington Post* hired science reporter Victor Cohn, who had been writing about scientific developments in the Soviet Union since the 1950s, from the *Minneapolis Tribune* in 1968. The problem with specialists is that they are not easily fungible. The AP's Howard Benedict, "dean of space reporting," covered over 2,000 missile and rocket launches, but what was the agency to do with him during a long hiatus between the Apollo and Shuttle programs? Robert Heinl, the Pearl Harbor veteran, joined the *Detroit News* as a military analyst after retiring from the Marines in 1963. Some experts worked for niche publications like *Armed Forces Journal* and *Aviation Week*. Except for those at the major business magazines, specialists rarely jumped the queue into the mainstream media.

In every decade special circumstances arose that had employment consequences, usually resulting from the failure or founding of a news operation or from ownership changes. The *New York Herald Tribune* folded in 1966, the *Washington Star* in 1981. Start-ups included *USA*

Today (1982), *The Hill* (1994), and *Politico* (2007). Notable management changes took place at UPI, CBS, *U.S. News & World Report*. The reconstituting of the *Los Angeles Times* Washington bureau in 1963 followed the arrival of new publisher Otis Chandler, whose aggressive attempt to change the image of his family's rich and provincial paper centered on remaking its moribund D.C. operation. Chandler lured the nearly iconic Washington reporter Bob Donovan away from the *Herald Tribune* and gave him the money to rebuild an operation that was down to two reporters. Within a year Donovan had eleven on staff, almost all coming from other Washington bureaus, including Don Irwin (*Herald Tribune*), Bob Toth (*New York Times*), Dave Kraslow (Knight Newspapers), Larry Burd (*Chicago Tribune*), Bob Thompson (*New York Daily News*), Vince Burke (UPI), and Dick Reston (*Madison Capital Times*).

There was also a handful of journalists who created their own opportunities in this period: I. F. Stone, the muckraker who self-published *I. F. Stone's Weekly,* a newsletter, from 1953 until 1971; Thomas Schroth, who founded the *National Journal* after he was fired as editor of *Congressional Quarterly* in 1968; and Charlie Peters, who in 1969 founded the *Washington Monthly,* which sent a slew of talented young writers into mainstream journalism.

The usual career path for a Washington reporter after World War II, however, was to serve an apprenticeship in the hinterlands, developing his or her professional skills and mastering the organizational culture of the home office, and then go to Washington to put in years of service in a beat system that closely reflected the hierarchy within the federal system: White House, State Department, and Pentagon; Senate and/ or House; and the Supreme Court (plus lower courts when there were sensational trials). There would be time away in even-numbered years to cover presidential campaigns and key Senate races.

Finally, there was a matter-of-fact conclusion to a journalism career in Washington: *"I retired in 1992. I was 65 and that's the normal retirement age. So I retired,"* said Dale Nelson, who was a reporter with AP. *"I retired in the summer of 1985. I was 65, and I thought it was time to go. They were not pressuring anybody to go,"* said *New York Times* reporter Seth (Jerry) King.

There were exceptions, among them Richard L. Strout, Daniel Schorr, Alan Emory, and Corbin Gwaltney, for whom being a Washington journalist continued to be a lifelong affair. Strout was 80 years old in 1978, the oldest reporter in our survey. He had been a correspondent for the *Christian Science Monitor* since 1924 and a columnist for the *New Republic* since 1943. During the week we studied him in 1978, he filed five newspaper stories and one magazine column—4,100 words, produced in four nine-hour days and one six-hour day. Strout retired at 86 years of age and died at 92.[29]

Schorr was between Washington employers in 1978. He was to have three Washington careers: CBS (1958–59 and 1966–74), CNN (1979–85), and National Public Radio (1985–2010). As Robert Siegel told *All Things Considered* listeners on August 31, 2006, "When someone works at his trade every week, at age 75 or 80, we say, 'That's admirable.' When he does it at age 90, we say, 'That's Daniel Schorr.'" Schorr died on July 23, 2010, 13 days after giving his final NPR broadcast. He was 93 years old.

Emory was hired by the *Watertown* [New York] *Times* in 1947, straight out of Columbia Journalism School. Watertown is near the Canadian border, 70 miles north of Syracuse. Why would a paper with a circulation of 46,000 have its own Washington bureau? Emory explained: when Harold B. Johnson, the owner, raised the price from seven cents to a dime in 1951, Johnson said, *"[If you're] charging readers more, . . . you have to give them something more—how'd you like to go to Washington?"*[30] Emory covered ten presidential administrations in the years that followed. In 2000, diagnosed with pancreatic cancer, he continued writing on political issues while reporting his struggles with the health care system. Emory died that year at 78 years of age.

Gwaltney invented the *Chronicle of Higher Education* in 1966. In 1977 he had an "editorial staff of 17 full-time, 4 part-time, and 2 interns."[31] Today's *Chronicle* website lists "more than 70 full-time writers and editors, as well as 17 foreign correspondents." We interviewed Gwaltney again in 2007, when he was 86 years old:

"Are you still in the office every day?"
"No sir! I come up [to Washington] *once or twice a week."*
"From where?"
"Home. I live near Annapolis on the shores of the Chesapeake Bay, and I rise up every morning to the sun coming out of the Bay

and ask myself, 'Do I really want to drive 55 minutes into my office?' And most mornings the answer is no. So I sit at the computer and telecommute, which is perfectly acceptable. I come up, have lunch with people once or twice a week. I take a very active part in what's going on."

THERE WERE OTHER exceptions, among them Orr Kelly, Bob Abernethy, and Bernie Kalb, for whom crossing into their sixties meant discovering new opportunities.

Kelly had left the *Washington Star* for *U.S. News & World Report* in 1976: *"When I retired from U.S. News in 1986 I had to figure what to do next. I knew I didn't want to go to Florida and go fishing. I knew what I wanted to do was to be a reporter, and the closest thing I could do to that was to become a book writer. I went and got a contract for my first book, and I learned how to write books, and I've been doing that ever since. . . . It's reporting on a bigger scale, and I don't have to talk to editors every day, maybe only once a year."* Kelly had covered the Pentagon. His books are on military history. By 2008 he had written seven of them.

Abernethy began working for NBC in 1953. In Washington he covered Congress, the State Department, and the Pentagon, with a year off to study at the Yale Divinity School, because "I was just interested in it": *"At the end of the '80s there was an opening in Moscow, and I went to Moscow for five and a half years, terrific years when the Soviet Union came apart. It was just a wonderful story. By this time I was well past normal retirement age, so there was some interest expressed on behalf of NBC that I might want to consider this. But I didn't. I retired at the end of '94. I didn't want to stop working, so I had an idea for a half-hour weekly television program about religion. We added ethics a little later. I took the idea around and eventually found Channel 13, WNET, in New York. We went on the air in September of '97, almost exactly ten years ago today.* Religion & Ethics Newsweekly [PBS] *brings together wonderful things. So that's a nice thing to do. I don't know how much longer I'll be doing it, and I say that just out of recognition that I am almost 80 years old* [when interviewed in 2007]."[32]

While Kelly had gone from reporting on the military to writing military history books and Abernethy from covering Washington for a commercial network to formulating a program on religion for public TV, in 1984 Bernie Kalb switched from being a diplomatic correspondent for NBC to being assistant secretary of state for public affairs and spokesman for the secretary of state: *"I went from my very high, skeptical front row seat in the press briefing room of the State Department, took a walk of about a yard and a half, and stood behind the dais articulating U.S. foreign policy. . . . I changed cultures. Spokesmen like to believe that whatever they say ends in an unchallenged 'period,' [but] journalism lives in sentences that end in question marks. And you had this big collision between periods and question marks. And for me it was a dramatic change, so the question is why did you do it? . . . Because in a way, the job, like so many jobs, becomes repetitious, dealing with foreign policy issues as a reporter. There was a curiosity to know what went on the other side of the story. It seemed to me to be an opportunity that was tough to resist. . . . I suppose I didn't explore the outer limits of what the challenges and frustrations would be, which indeed there were. But it was an interesting exploratory journey. I'm glad I took it."*

His trip, however, had an abrupt ending. On October 2, 1986, the *Washington Post,* in a banner article by Bob Woodward, reported a White House memorandum from President Reagan's national security adviser, John Poindexter, outlining a "disinformation" campaign against Libyan leader Muammar al-Qaddafi that included planting false reports in the press. Kalb was shocked by that duplicity, of which he had no knowledge. *"My world is not disinformation. My world is precisely the opposite. And I went in to see the secretary of state* [George Shultz]. *I said look, this is not for me. I mean my loyalties, my professional loyalties, my whole upbringing is journalism. . . . You're hurting America with deception and disinformation. I'm grateful for the opportunity, but not for me."* Kalb's resignation was covered in five *New York Times* stories on October 9, 1986. William Safire observed that "Bernard Kalb joined what Dean Acheson once called 'the most exclusive club in America—men in public life who have resigned in the cause of conscience.'" Safire's column concluded, "Bernard Kalb rose above 'State Department spokesman' to become the spokesman for all Americans who respect and demand the truth." Kalb later returned to journalism as co-moderator of CNN's *Reliable Sources* program.

ALTHOUGH THE ESTABLISHED age to retire was 65, in practice "retirement" was open to a variety of interpretations. For some it meant continuing in journalism but doing so at a much slower pace, on their own terms.

"I was not going to some desert island somewhere," concluded Dick Maloy. *"I was going to stay in Washington [where I could] run down to Press Club lunches and keep in touch with old colleagues."* He also put out a small newsletter, *Hints for the City Desk,* offering "ten local story ideas per week." Don Shannon and his wife started a neighborhood paper called *Georgetown and Country.* Bill Steif, on the other hand, bought a house on St. Croix in the Virgin Islands: *"I went down there and settled in and was there about six weeks, and then the managing editor of the* Virgin Islands Daily News *called me up and said, 'How about doing some stuff?' And I did . . . and pretty soon I found there are all sorts of freelance things I could do too . . . and I've been doing it ever since."* Jerry King moved to Boston, where soon he was teaching at Boston University: *"I enjoyed teaching very, very much. . . . I really didn't want to get back into any kind of a nine-to-five situation. I didn't mind spending a lot of time, but I wanted to do it in my own choosing."*[33]

There were openings besides adjunct professor of journalism for the journalist specialist: Victor Cohn became a visiting fellow at the Harvard School of Public Health; Tom Eastham, whose long career with Hearst Newspapers included a stint as Washington bureau chief for the *San Francisco Examiner,* spent 18 years helping the Hearst Foundation award grants to college journalism students and bring high school students to Washington; Darwin Olofson became associate director of the National Press Foundation, where journalists attend seminars on such wide-ranging topics as research on an HIV vaccine and the federal court system; Howard Benedict became executive director of the Astronaut Scholarship Foundation, awarding college scholarships to engineering and science students.

Dale Nelson, after a long career with the AP, moved to Laramie, Wyoming, and got a job reporting for the *Casper Star-Tribune.* He continued to write poems, as he had throughout his Washington years.[34] *"Newspaper stories tell us about names and titles, distances and populations, fatality totals and investigations. Poems tell us about ourselves."* He wrote a book, *Gin before Breakfast,* about journalists who had been poets. In his "summing-up poem" to Washington journalism, "Forty

Years as a Reporter for the Associated Press," Nelson asks, "Did you get it right? Did the hours / Add up to anything? How should you get / The answers to your questions"? He then answers: "Look under Truth in the yellow pages."[35]

There might be disputes about the state of journalism or the future of journalism, but their craft gave journalists special talents for blending into retirement. *"We moved here to this little house in the woods in Vermont on 25 acres of woods and meadows that we had bought in 1979 and had had a small house built in 1990,"* said Jon Margolis, whose long career at the *Chicago Tribune* included being Washington correspondent-at-large as well as a sports columnist. *"I still write magazine articles and newspaper columns, although many, many fewer. . . . And I teach. I teach every fall at the University of Vermont about politics, courses that I make up. . . . What else do I do? I do a great deal of fishing, gardening, walking in the woods, reading good books, and that's about it."*[36]

TWO

"THE BOOMERS"

UNLIKE THEIR ELDERS, the baby boomers in the Washington press corps were not shaped by the experience of going to war. Only two talked of having served in the military, one of whom was Tom Fiedler, a future executive editor of the *Miami Herald,* who got his undergraduate degree in engineering from the U.S. Merchant Marine Academy. *"I went to sea as a merchant marine* [and as a member of the naval reserve] *and then later went to graduate school in journalism."*[1] Their education also differed from that of their elders: they had more schooling and more options. For some, a career in journalism was never in doubt. *"When I was 12 years old, I signed up for the journalism class at my junior high school,"* said Rich Jaroslovsky, a future executive editor of *Bloomberg News.* *"[I thought] 'My God, this is fun.'"*[2] Some were born to journalism. Jack Fuller, a future editor of the *Chicago Tribune:* *"My father was a newspaper man, and so the fact is, I had grown up with it."*[3] Others must have had doubts: twenty-three of the twenty-five journalists interviewed who dropped out of journalism before the ten-year-mark were boomers. Yet a boomer would become publisher of the *Wall Street Journal,* executive editor of the *New York Times,* and executive editor of the Associated Press. While ten boomers who were journalists earned law degrees, six of them remained in journalism; two left to practice law, one became a law professor, and the other stayed in Washington as a "public affairs practitioner," serving primarily health care companies.[4]

THE BIGGEST CHANGE between the "greatest generation" and the boomer generation was the significant increase of women in journalism, from

20 to 36 percent. Moreover, the women were as apt as their male col-
leagues to stay in journalism, and many times they were first to the story.
On network TV there were Ann Compton, Lisa Myers, Susan Spencer,
Judy Woodruff; on mainstream newspapers, Ann Devroy, Karen Eliott
House, Mary Leonard, Judith Miller, Anne Swardson. Others would star
at weekly news magazines or in niche publishing.[5]

Ann Devroy, 29, who had graduated from the University of Wisconsin–Eau Claire with a degree in journalism, was sent by Gannett to
Washington in 1977 to be the regional correspondent covering the New
Jersey congressional delegation. She was then assigned to the White
House beat in 1979, writing for a readership that was greatly expanded
by Gannett's founding of *USA Today* in 1982.[6] She was "a very, very
tough competitor," recalled Lou Cannon, the *Washington Post's* White
House correspondent. "She was more likely to be tougher competition
than the *New York Times,* and they had good reporters."[7] Devroy was
lured to the *Post* to be the political editor, a job that she hated, but one
in which she had more control over the time that she could spend with
her infant daughter Sarah, born in 1985. Devroy went back to the White
House beat in 1989 and stayed until her death in 1997 at 49 years of
age, after an 18-month battle with cancer. To David Broder, she "was the
most dogged, determined, complete reporter any of us ever saw."[8] Terry
Hunt, AP's White House correspondent, credited her with being "the
best White House reporter of our generation."[9]

THERE WERE STILL some one-employer careers, essentially spent in Washington after an out-of-town tour of duty. Walter Mossberg went from
Columbia Journalism School to the *Wall Street Journal,* spending three
years in the Detroit bureau; he then left for Washington in 1973, where
he successively covered energy and the environment, defense, international economics, and national security. *"At the end of my 18-year or
so tenure . . . I decided that I wanted to do something radically different, and I proposed to the* Journal *that we launch a technology column,
a consumer technology column that would run weekly and where we
would review technology products and explain new technologies. And
I started that in fall of 1991, and that is what I have been doing since
then. . . . I report to the managing editor in New York. I have my own
little staff, and I don't write about the government or politics or policy*

anymore. I write about—well, I assume you've read my columns—I write about computers and cell phones and digital cameras and the Internet, all of that."[10]

But for the boomers, changing employers, which was once viewed as indicating employee disloyalty or other questionable motives or circumstances that were not talked about, was becoming a way to get ahead. No journey was as fearless as that of Kim Masters, who navigated the shoals of niche publishing, newspapering, magazines, public and commercial radio, and Internet publications. She recalled that starting as a 23-year-old Bryn Mawr graduate, *"I called Capitol Publications [in Washington] and said, 'Can I work for you?' and within a very short time I was covering the Supreme Court, which I knew nothing about. . . . I then went through a series of jobs that I would call trade types of jobs* [Daily Labor Report, Legal Times, American Lawyer]. *. . . I was labeled as a legal reporter, as a trade reporter. . . . I went all over and tried to talk to the* LA Times *and the* Washington Post; *no one would look at me through any lens other than you're a trade reporter. So I went to the* [New York] Daily News, *and they gave me the Hollywood beat, which was a plus. . . . I was very worried again being labeled a trade reporter—that I had this expertise and it was Hollywood, and that would be it. . . . Premier recruited me. They were a new magazine. They wanted a column. It was with some misgivings because it was a movie magazine, and I thought, 'Oh, here we go again'. . . . It was a little bit leisurely to be working on a monthly. I called the* Washington Post *kind of cold and said, 'Would you want a stringer out here in Los Angeles?' They said okay. . . . So I started freelancing for them in the Style Section. . . . They brought me to Washington . . . and ultimately [I] got the gig doing political profiles . . . like the piece on James Carville. . . . However, in the middle of that* Vanity Fair *offered me a deal to do Hollywood stuff."*[11] Masters returned to Los Angeles in 2000 and has since covered the business of entertainment for many organizations, including *Time, Esquire,* National Public Radio, Slate.com, and *Daily Beast.* She has a local radio program and is editor-at-large at the *Hollywood Reporter.*[12]

Journalists did not always change jobs just to advance their careers. *"The reason I left Prentice-Hall and came over to BNA,"* recalled Jim Fattibene, *"is that the company had been bought by Simon and Schuster and they were more interested in the book trade. I was with the loose-leaf division, which covered Washington events, and that part of the company was sold off.*"[13] Ira Allen, who had been reporting from the White House, watched the downward slide of UPI and left. *"I would have liked to stay a little longer, but the writing was on the wall."*[14] As for life in network radio, remembered Becky Bailey, a news anchor at Mutual Broadcasting, *"the management kept changing, so every time you survived a management, you considered yourself a survivor."*[15]

WHILE PREVIOUSLY ALL careers had been in one type of journalism, print or electronic, boomers were starting to cross the media tracks. Lisa Myers describes her unplanned move from a newspaper to a television network: *"I never at any particular point decided that I was going to be on television. I was invited to do a couple of panels on* Meet the Press *and* Face the Nation, *which I found very nerve wracking. In fact, I could hardly breathe. I think the thing that really made the difference for me is there was a news conference. It would've been September of 1980. I was covering the Carter White House for the* Washington Star. *I hadn't been covering the White House long. President Carter may have thought I was a sweet young thing. It was the very end of the news conference, so it's usually when they look for 'softballs' or 'puffballs.' President Carter called on me, and I asked him about some allegations he'd made about Governor Reagan having injected racism into the presidential campaign. The president basically blew me off and said, 'Look, I never made such an allegation,' or something like that. . . . I stood there and re-asked the question. At that point he totally denied that he had ever said such a thing. After that news conference, Leslie Stahl ran over to me and said, 'Tell your parents to watch tonight.' On all the evening news shows there I was asking some questions to the president and him basically providing a not terribly straightforward answer. Then, of course, the networks rolled the tape of him saying exactly what I said that he said. So that was the moment that propelled me into television. It wasn't any grand plan on my part. It was a totally unscripted moment. I got offers after that, but the* Washington Star *gave me a big raise and I was interested in covering the Reagan White House, so I stayed there until the* Star *folded* [in 1981], *and then after that I went to work for NBC."*[16] Myers became the network's chief investigative correspondent.

FOR SOME BOOMERS, life in news gathering was merely a fling, "a short-term adventure."[17] Macculloch (Cully) Irving, 23 years old, graduated from Yale in 1977. He first had a nonpaying internship with Ralph Nader, then spent a year in the Washington bureau of the *Hartford Courant* and another year as an aide to a Connecticut congressman; he went on to law school and a career practicing real estate law in New York. For him, being a reporter was "a really fun job."[18] Jonathan Bernstein, 26, and Steven Parkhurst, 22, were also passing through Washington. After service in the army, Bernstein got a paid internship with muckraking columnist Jack Anderson in 1977. Nine months later he was offered "a disgustingly large amount of money" to report for the *National Enquirer.* He resigned in 1980: *"I got to a point where no amount of money would motivate me* [to stay]." He answered a Playboy Enterprises ad for a public relations manager. *"It was a year when Playboy was in a lot of crisis. They lost their casino license because of some tie-in with the mob."* Bernstein went on to specialize in crisis management. *"It's the PR equivalent of firefighting or fire prevention. The prevention side, we help clients assess their vulnerabilities to crisis. . . . On the response side, if a crisis occurs, it's helping them manage communications, primarily during the crisis situation."*[19]

Steven Parkhurst came east from the University of Washington, *"went on unemployment for a while, which was magnificent. I spent most of my time* [in the Library of Congress]. *. . . During that time I would fill out my minimum number of letters so that I could earn my unemployment income and say I was looking for a job. One of them responded. It was Newhouse. I went to work for* [Newhouse News Service] *for more than three years. . . . After that I decided I had a few thousand dollars in the bank so I just kind of up and left, between personal issues and wanting to see the rest of the world."* Parkhurst was to settle in Livorno, Italy, near Pisa, where he became an administrator at Child and Youth Services, a child care center on a U.S. Army base. *"All that journalism does, basically, along with several other disciplines, is it teaches you how to think. It gives you an opportunity to test out your ideas on paper and then listen to life and get a chance. And that's what I've done."*[20]

For Mary Lord, 24 years of age, an internship in 1975 turned into a serious journalism career. *"Here's the deal. Harvard does not offer majors or concentrations in journalism. . . . I also did not work for the*

Crimson *and wasn't an English major. . . . I ended up getting my degree in East Asian Studies. My whole life I was thinking I was going to get a job in Japan. . . . But I was a stringer for* Newsweek *on campus because my mother was the head of the Radcliffe News Office, where all these journalists went. When I started fumbling around she told me, 'You can't do nothing,' so I applied for an internship with* Newsweek *but didn't get it. . . . So when I applied for a second summer I got it and landed in Washington, not because I had any passion for politics, but because that was where my then-boyfriend at the time was. . . . I landed in Washington the summer after Watergate in a dynamic bureau full of incredibly smart, seasoned reporters, many of whom needed to take a summer break for the first time in three years. . . . So here I was, this reporter who had my run of the town; I covered stories, totally green, wet behind the ears. . . . It was a wonderful introduction. So I stayed put . . . and it just became my career."* Lord later switched to *U.S. News & World Report,* with which she spent several years based in Tokyo.[21]

WHEN BOOMERS EXITED journalism, their most likely destination was the federal government. Russell Dawson, 29 years old, had been a geography major at the University of Maryland. After covering waste management for a specialized publication, he went to work at the Environmental Protection Agency. *"The EPA job was terrific. Working for the administration was challenging. I had a role in every major announcement that was made from 1985 to 1989: Radon, asbestos in schools, reauthorization of the major environmental laws."* He later joined a Washington public relations company.[22] Becky Bailey, 24, joined Mutual Broadcasting's Washington bureau in 1975 and remained there until 1998. She then got a job as a congressional press secretary. *"I loved my time on the Hill, found it fascinating. . . . I must say, as a press secretary, it's awful to say, but I feel like I get a lot more respect, day to day, than I did as a journalist. . . . I was amazed that when I would say, 'I'm press secretary to Congresswoman Louise Slaughter,' the respect I would get as opposed to 'I'm a radio reporter.'"* Most of the former journalists worked in public affairs/press offices. However, William Lanouette, a *National Journal* correspondent, continued to practice a form of journalism when he joined the Government Accountability Office in 1991 to report on science and weapons policy. *"Because you're representing the legislative branch and the legislative branch is supposed to have oversight on the executive and because you're nonpartisan, you can work on anything. It's been a satisfying 15 or 16 years."*[23]

Rarer still, as Strobe Talbott noted, was "for a working journalist to go straight into a [government] policy job." In 1993, after 21 years with *Time* magazine, Talbott became ambassador-at-large and special adviser to the secretary of state for the newly independent states of the former Soviet Union. *"When I realized this was really going to happen, I found the prospects pretty scary because I had spent virtually all of my journalistic career studying the policy process and diplomacy, and I knew enough about it to know it was very difficult. . . . The actual transition was a pleasant surprise. . . . I found that journalism trains you to be on the lookout for situations and their complexity—what makes things tick, how systems work—to ask the right questions, to inform yourself in a fairly short period of time about complex situations, and also to express yourself."*[24]

Still, there were other paths out of journalism. Kathy Patterson, 29, who had been a Northwestern journalism major, was working in the Washington bureau of the *Kansas City Star.* During the week of our survey in April 1978, she was reporting on emergency farm legislation that had been passed in the Senate and defeated in the House and on farmers' reactions to it as well as on a Kansan who was testifying on criminal code revision. She left the paper in 1984 to get a master's degree in English literature. *"I needed a mental break."* After a year in Chicago "for my husband's job," she returned to Washington. When no newspaper job opened up, she was hired by the American Public Welfare Association and worked there for nine years. *"My kids were in elementary school in D.C., and I got involved as a parent on some school funding issues. I came quickly to appreciate that the school would never be in good shape until the city was in good shape."* Patterson became the only one of the 1978 respondents to seek full-time elective office. She served three terms on the Washington City Council, then was defeated when she ran for council chairman. *"I initially wanted to become a journalist to try to make a difference in people's lives, and I think going to a policy job where I worked on policy that affected low-income families was not inconsistent with the work I had done as a journalist. And then running for public office was fully consistent because I was trying to change public policy."*[25]

Edward Alwood, 28 years old, was a reporter on WTTG-TV. In April 1978, he was reporting on the White House reaction to the Senate vote in favor of a treaty to transfer control of the Panama Canal to Panama; a court hearing that involved the FBI director; and a dog ordinance in Alexandria, Virginia. He left journalism after 14 years in 1987. *"Once you get past the novelty of being a journalist, even in TV, you begin to live for the next big story because that's where the excitement comes from. And the time frame between the next big story was getting longer and longer for me. And the novelty had worn off. And another part of it had to do with age. . . . I wanted some stability. CNN was the type of organization that would move you around a lot. . . . Going into public relations* [for 8 years] *and staying here in Washington gave me some anchors in my life that I was looking for. Also I got some good advice. A friend told me I would not have the creative outlet in public relations that I had in journalism and I should consider writing a book. And that's how, while I was researching a book on gays and lesbians in the news media, that was how I got into academia. . . . That book ended up getting published by an academic press, and that's what led me to go back and get the Ph.D.* [from the University of North Carolina], *and that led into teaching. That's my progression."*[26] Alwood is a professor of journalism at Quinnipiac University.

Doug Lowenstein became a reporter for the *Dayton Daily News* in Cox Newspapers' Washington bureau in 1976, when he was 25 years old. In April 1978, he was doing a profile of the chairwoman of the Equal Employment Opportunity Commission; a 1,500-word piece on neighborhood revitalization in Baltimore; and a hard news story on President Carter's countercyclical revenue-sharing plan. *"I'd gotten to know Senator Metzenbaum of Ohio from covering him, and I mentioned that I was sort of becoming disenchanted with journalism . . . and Senator Metzenbaum said 'Why don't you come work for me?'"* Lowenstein moved to the Senate, where he stayed from 1982 to 1986, eventually becoming the senator's legislative director. He then joined *"a new business practice in Washington . . . a sort of merging of people who had political campaign experience with people who had journalistic experience, with the notion being that this wasn't about lobbying, it was about framing and shaping issues and communicating issues both to the decisionmaker community and also to the media."*

His next move came in late 1993, when he was 43 years old. *"There had been a great deal of controversy about violence in video games. The industry began to figure out that it needed to organize itself in some coherent way. Unlike the movie industry or the music industry, which had long-standing representation in Washington, the video game industry was very new and had no exposure to Washington, and suddenly they were under attack with bills to create federal systems to rate video games and so on."* Lowenstein created what became the Entertainment Software Association, representing a $30 billion industry, and he served as its president for 13 years. In 2007 he founded another advocacy organization in Washington, this time for the private equity industry. *"To be able to do that again at that stage in my career, now I am 55–56—I really didn't think I would have that chance again. And to do it for an industry that had emerged as one of the most important industries in the world was kind of a 'daily double' opportunity. . . . It was doing something that I really loved, which was doing another start-up, and doing it for an industry that was frankly playing on a stage that was bigger than any stage I'd ever had a chance to play on."*[27] One compilation of association executives listed Lowenstein's income in 2010 as $1.3 million. In 2011 he stepped down as president of the Private Equity Council, e-mailing that among the "reasons why [was that] now was the time to go." Turning 60 and experiencing back pain were other reasons.[28]

IT ONCE WAS considered unthinkable for a journalist to go into government or lobbying and hope to return to journalism. While some jumped the barrier with the help of personal connections, eventually news organizations began to see advantages in bringing back reporters who had acquired an inside perspective. Rod Kuckro worked for two congressmen and returned for a long career in specialized publications, such as *FCC Week, Oil Daily,* and *Platts. "It's easy to get seduced by the whole Hill culture, but I didn't overstay my welcome there. I learned a lot about the inner workings of how stuff gets done. When I went back to reporting, I felt much more comfortable making judgments."*[29] Bob Gettlin said that after reporting for the *Washington Star, Hartford Courant,* and other papers, *"[I] was at a point in time in my career where I was sort of looking to do something different. So I left journalism and went to what they sometimes call the dark side, public relations."* He became director of communications for lobbying groups, first the Council of Insurance Agency Brokers, then the Conference of State Bank Supervisors. *"I found it challenging. I liked being on the other side of answering questions [from] reporters rather than asking them. There's a certain aspect of journalism that's sort of voyeuristic. You know, you're always from the outside of the door looking in. Besides the money aspect, I just wanted to see what it felt like to be on the other side. It was a good experience. I don't want to do it again."* After three years on the "dark side," Gettlin returned to journalism in 2001 as managing editor of the *National Journal. "I like being back in the calling, so to speak."*[30]

THE "GREATEST GENERATION" reporters stayed in Washington, sometimes even after they retired; half of the boomer reporters left Washington, 20 percent having been reassigned by their employers. Robert Cunningham had a long career at *The Record* (Bergen County, N.J.), with a Washington interlude from 1977 to 1983. *"I enjoyed reporting, but after six years in Washington it seemed like the stories were coming back around at me again. And it was the same old, same old. So I went back to Hackensack to take an editing job and stayed there basically until I retired two years ago* [in 2005]."[31] Robert Cullen left Washington to become Moscow correspondent for *Newsweek,* then did not want to be reassigned. *"In view of the fact that* Newsweek *wanted me to go back to New York and my wife didn't want to go [and] I didn't want to go, freelance seemed like the best alternative."* Many books later, including five novels and seven volumes on the psychology of golf, Cullen was teaching English in the Prince Georges County (Maryland) public schools in 2007.[32]

Moves always mixed personal and the professional reasons, in different proportions. Lucy Knight, a young niche reporter: *"I found Washington to be an unfriendly town. I was single, and I think that if people get married and have kids, it's different."*[33] Ellen Warren, who had been a Washington reporter for 15 years when she returned to Chicago: *"I hated working in Washington. . . . I had then, and I still do, have two children, who I preferred to raise in the Midwest, where it wasn't as all-consuming as to whether our children got into Sidwell Friends and on and on and on, and whether you got invited to dinner by Alan Green-span, and who you took to the White House Correspondents Dinner. . . . I was just content to return to Chicago. So I left covering the White House to cover metropolitan news in Chicago and have always been happy that I made that decision."*[34]

Patricia Mochel moved from Metromedia Radio News to get a TV job in Baltimore. *"I was the first person to have a child, to be pregnant on the air there, and my child turned out to have a disability. My son turned out to be autistic, and I did a lot of therapies with him at home. . . . I think I've learned to be a really good mother, and, frankly, I think I'm a better person. . . . But I look at people that I've known—Katie Couric, she was an intern in my office in Washington. I look at Katie and I think, 'I wonder if [I] could do that now?' I've been off the air since 1984. I will tell you that I still have dreams of being in television. . . . I do volunteer work, I volunteer in the local jail, I help teach meditation, I teach yoga to old people for free. My life is pretty full, but I wouldn't mind going back to the days when I looked great and was sparkling brilliant."*[35]

WHEN CONFRONTED WITH a choice, reporting or editing, the elder journalists were more likely to choose reporting. Jim McCartney returned to Washington from "running a big staff in a major metropolitan area" as city editor of the *Chicago Daily News*. It was *"a crucial decision. I enjoyed reporting more than I did trying to herd a bunch of cats in the city room."*[36] Boomers were more apt to choose management. Merrilee Cox went from reporting for UPI Audio in Washington to being a news director for ABC Radio in New York, a trip that she described as *"a fabulous, amazing run for 23 years at ABC."*[37] Bill Choyke moved from reporting to management by way of a fellowship program at the University of Virginia for journalists who wish to earn an MBA. *"There are some wonderfully satisfying moments as a reporter in Washington and some wonderfully satisfying moments here* [as business editor at the *Virginian-Pilot* in Norfolk]. *I think one of the most critical factors you have to face once you decide to move is that unless you move up to the highest levels of a newspaper, the financial gains are not as attractive. . . . As you get older, you want to have more control of your life—financial issues are part of that."*[38]

Rich Jaroslovsky was hired by the *Wall Street Journal* at 21 years of age and sent to the Washington bureau at 22, where he was White House correspondent for four years. The direction of his career changed when he was 40: *"I got, out of the blue, a call from somebody within the company who I had not met, who said, 'Look, I've been charged with the task of figuring out should the* Wall Street Journal *be online. . . . I need a newsperson to figure out what a* Wall Street Journal Online *would look like.* [This was 1993.] *Because nobody had any clue, including me, as to what 'online' or an online edition of the* Wall Street Journal *might mean, we literally were ordered to figure out what those words meant."* Jaroslovsky became managing editor of the *Wall Street Journal Online.* *"It was the most fun that I have had in journalism professionally; it's the most fun I've had since my college newspaper days."*

THE WASHINGTON EXPERIENCE of three of the seven boomers who rose to exalted heights in their organizations proved to be marginal, at best, to their success; they would have risen just as high had they never set foot in the capital. When the *Baltimore Sun* sent Anthony Barbieri, who ultimately became managing editor, to Washington in 1976, he stayed two years but "frankly didn't much care for it." He went on to Moscow to continue his long career on the paper.[39] Tom Fiedler of the *Miami Herald,* ultimately the executive editor, was the paper's lead reporter on Jimmy Carter's presidential campaign in 1976. He then went to Washington when Carter was elected because "I was a known quantity around Carter's people." After Carter's one term, the paper "sent someone else to cover the White House," and Fiedler returned to Miami.[40] Jack Fuller, who ultimately became president of Tribune Publishing Company after being CEO of the *Chicago Tribune,* recalled, *"[I] went to law school with the intention of being a journalist. In fact, in my little* [application] *essay, that's what I started out with: 'I have no intention of practicing law.'"* But the tyro reporter with a law degree had a unique opportunity in 1975 to be special assistant to the U.S. Attorney General: *"If you were a lawyer, you'd die for a job like this."* He left the *Tribune,* rejoining the paper's Washington bureau in 1977, and stayed almost two years before going back to Chicago to prepare to become editor of the editorial page. *"I had soured on being a Washington correspondent. . . . I'd still be writing about national affairs [but] I'd be doing it in an opinionated way rather than in a neutral way. That was attractive to me."*[41]

Washington experience, on the other hand, was a necessary step on the career ladder of the other four who rose to the upper echelons of their organization: Bill Keller (executive editor, *New York Times*); Karen Elliott House (publisher, *Wall Street Journal*); Jonathan Wolman (senior vice president, Associated Press); and Roy E. Bode (editor-in-chief, *Dallas Times Herald*).

In 1978, Keller was not yet employed by the *Times.* Having graduated in 1970 from Pomona College with a degree in English literature, he went to Portland to work on *The Oregonian,* a Newhouse paper, which sent him to Washington in 1974. The Newhouse bureau resembled a confederation of papers interested primarily in how Congress affects their own circulation areas, with only modest national coverage. It was "a hip-pocket organization," according to Dean Reed, the bureau chief.[42] No media company that large—there were thirty Newhouse papers—cast so small a shadow in the Washington establishment.

Keller would have a steep climb. His important next move, in 1980, was to *Congressional Quarterly Weekly Report,* a magazine of minute circulation read mostly by scholars and journalists. Yet it had already served as a platform for young reporters like David Broder and Elizabeth Drew, allowing them to be noticed by those who take government seriously. Key people in the *Times* Washington bureau were impressed by Keller's enterprise and creative insight into lobbyists and interest groups. Still, he would need more daily newsgathering experience in Washington than he got as a Newhouse regional reporter. In 1982 he went to the *Dallas Times Herald,* a paper that went beyond covering the Texas congressional delegation, with reporters at the White House and the State Department. Such distinctions may be finely drawn, but they are clearly understood among mainstream journalists. So Bill Keller was now equipped to move higher, and in 1984 he was invited into the *New York Times* bureau. Two years later he was off to Moscow.[43]

Karen Elliott House needed to climb only one rung. She went from the University of Texas at Austin, where she graduated with a degree in journalism in 1970, to the *Dallas Morning News;* after 13 months spent covering education, she was moved to Washington. She was hired by the *Wall Street Journal* in 1994. *"One of the stories I did that, I think, made the* Journal *want to hire me was during Watergate. There was a young man named Bud Krogh who worked at the White House, who was one of the low-level people that got in trouble and got sentenced to prison. The day he was leaving the court I called up the White House and asked to speak to him. Of course if you're from the* Dallas Morning News, *no one wanted to talk to you. But my picture happened to have been on the front page of the* New York Times *standing behind him, so I said to him, 'I'm that woman whose picture is in the paper standing behind you and I want to talk to you about how you tell your children you're going to prison.' He said, 'Well, I don't know that I want to talk,' and he put me off. That evening I was driving down 17th Street past the White House at night with my boyfriend, and I saw him walking and I screamed, 'Stop the car!' And I got out of the car and just went up to him and said, 'I'm that woman that called you today, and I want to talk with you.' He said, 'Well, I'm taking my last walk around the White House.' So I just started walking with him. We walked down 17th Street, down past the Ellipse and around the Ellipse, and back up again, with me sort of quizzing him the whole time. I mean, 'Last walk around the White House'— that was a great phrase from the beginning. Then he talked about how he used to run out there, and then he got into how his children had seen him on TV and what he was going to tell them. You know, if I do say so myself, it was a great human interest feature. The* Dallas Morning News *ran it. I think the Dallas bureau chief of the* Wall Street Journal *saw it. Anyway, I went to the* Wall Street Journal.*"[44]*

There were no turns in the road for Jonathan Wolman, just a basic decision on whether he wanted to be a reporter or an editor. The AP sent Wolman, who studied philosophy at the University of Wisconsin–Madison, to Washington in 1975 as an urban affairs reporter after an initial out-of-college posting in Detroit: *"No, I wasn't so interested in making the move. That was more AP's idea than my own. I was enjoying my assignment in Detroit and had really just started an assignment as Michigan news editor when Washington came calling. . . . I was there in one way, shape, or form from 1975 to 1998. Long time. But it was a terrifically interesting period to be doing Washington journalism. . . . As is so often the case, I was a reporter and enjoying that and was asked to come into editing, and it turned out I enjoyed that too. And I did the back and forth a couple of times. In 1979 I made the turn for what became the rest of my career, which is I had been a national writer based in Washington at that point and I came into the bureau as assistant news editor, and I've been an editor ever since. I suppose it's logical to think that I might be a better editor than reporter, but we'll never know. . . . New York, as you know, is AP's headquarters location, and as Washington bureau chief, which I was for ten years, you are one of the senior managers in the news department. So it's logical that one of the places to look when you are thinking of top editing jobs in New York is Washington. And there I was."*[45]

Roy E. Bode, 29 years old, of Andrews, Texas, also was in Washington in 1978: *"It had always been my ambition. I worked my way up there by working for a little daily paper called the* Tulsa Daily World *and then graduated to Washington through finding a job with the* Arkansas Gazette, *a defunct paper now, but [it] was one of the icons of Southern journalism. . . . That would have been 1972. . . . While the* Gazette *was focused on the people in Washington from Arkansas, there were a lot of interesting people: Fulbright, John McClellan, Wilbur Mills, all from Arkansas. So there was a lot of power concentrated in the delegation from this small state. It made the position much more enticing and much richer. I was very young, just under 23 years old. . . . [In 1977] I was hired as the bureau chief of the* Dallas Times Herald. *There were three people in the bureau. I worked there for two years. The bureau had expanded to four people and a part-time receptionist. . . . I felt at the close of the '70s that I'd seen everything that could happen in Washington, and I was ready to go back to Texas. Management would be more interesting, so that's where I went. . . . MediaNews Group bought the paper in 1986. I went from associate editor at the* Herald *to editor of two small newspapers in New Jersey, which were owned by Dean Singleton's MediaNews Group. The papers in Patterson and Passaic were merged into one paper. . . . I was there for a couple of years.*

"The Dallas Times Herald *again changed hands when Singleton sold it, and it was bought by an individual who asked me to return as editor-in-chief. I was there until the paper closed in '91. At that time I had to make a decision. . . . There were no other newspaper editing jobs available in Texas, and I was at home in this part of the country and that was where I wanted to be. I had a call from the president of the University of Texas Southwestern Medical School, which is the flagship*

medical school of the University of Texas. . . . I accepted his offer and stayed there until 2006 as VP for Public Affairs. In that role I felt like it was not so much public affairs as running a news bureau since most of what we did there was cover medical and scientific research and clinical treatments. . . . I was 57 and was thinking I've got to get back into the newspaper business if I'm ever going to do it. It really was my first love, and I started out in this business at 14 years old in a small twice-weekly paper where I grew up in West Texas. . . . And I thought this whole newspaper media world has changed so much, and I've gotten so old and cranky, that the only thing I can do is work for myself. So that's what I did. In February 2006 my wife and I bought four small papers in central Texas outside the Austin area. We bought these papers from a large media group. We sold our ranch outside of Austin and moved down to Marble Falls, and we go to work here everyday. We are local owners, and these papers are integral parts of their communities. It's journalism like it used to be in many ways before Wall Street took it captive. That's what we do today."[46]

THREE

THE WOMEN

CHARLOTTE MOULTON WAS 65 years of age in 1978, the oldest woman in our survey. She grew up in Dorchester, a Boston suburb, graduated from the School of Secretarial Studies at Simmons College, and came to Washington in 1940 to work as a secretary at the War Department earning $1,400 a year. A year later she arranged a transfer to another secretarial job in the public relations office. Soon, she said, *"I was editing a news summary for the top people in the War Department. . . . [Then] I went to United Press in 1942 to work the morgue. Do you know what a morgue is? It's a file room where they keep their newspaper clippings.* [She also ran the telephone switchboard on Saturdays.] *I moved up by making a pest of myself and telling the bureau manager that I wanted to be a reporter.* [She started reporting on April 3, 1944.] *I got the beat that was the lowest on the totem pole, a combination of Interstate Commerce Commission, Federal Communications Commission, and the Post Office Department. I didn't know anything about reporting. I'd never written a news story. I just had to learn it. And the only reason I was able to do that was because men were being called to military service, and they absolutely had to have women. They didn't want them, you know, but they had to have them."*

In September 1949, Moulton was named the wire service's Supreme Court reporter, ultimately becoming a legend in what was to be a long line of women who would make their mark on this beat. *It was not a particularly popular beat—I mean you had to spend a great deal of your time reading Supreme Court cases, briefs that came in. That was the way you prepared for the time when you were going to file your stories. You had to read all this stuff, and I think it's probably fair to say that most of the young men who were starting in the business then, you know, they liked to run around Capitol Hill and talk to congressmen and interview people and all that, and they weren't particularly interested in sitting at a desk and reading a great deal of the time. It was confining."*

She retired in 1978, after covering the Supreme Court for nearly 30 years. *"I was 65. And I was ready to retire. . . . I got darn sick of working."* Charlotte Moulton died 26 years later, at 91 years of age.[1]

The single biggest creator of jobs for women journalists in the nation's capital—besides World War II—was Eleanor Roosevelt. The president's wife decreed that only women could cover her news conferences.[2] The *New York Times* at first resisted assigning a woman to its Washington bureau and instead sent a reporter from New York each time she held a press conference.[3] Leo Rosten's 1935 study of the Washington press corps lists only three women, one of whom was the correspondent for the Communist Party's *Daily Worker.*[4]

At the end of the war the boys came home, and their employers were required by law to give them their jobs back. The United Press retained only three women: Moulton, Eileen Shanahan, and Helen Thomas. According to Shanahan, *"Charlotte was kept on for the right reasons. She was covering the Supreme Court . . . and reporting rings around a whole series of Associated Press reporters. . . . They were afraid to fire her. As for Helen and me, one might think, given our successful subsequent careers, that we too were kept on because of our perceived excellence. Not so. Nobody else wanted those lousy jobs rewriting the news from the local papers for the radio wire, with a choice of working either 5:30 a.m. to 2:30 p.m. or 3:00 p.m. to midnight."*[5]

WOMEN TRYING TO break into mainstream journalism in the 1960s experienced variations of the same story. Deborah Howell, a 1962 graduate of the University of Texas: *"I had a job on the AP, which was canceled before I got there because they decided, and I have a little letter that says, 'We're not going to hire any more women in the Texas AP.' And there were no laws, so I couldn't do anything about it except try to find a job off the women's pages."*[6] Judy Woodruff, who graduated from Duke University in 1968: *"My spring break I went to Atlanta. I interviewed with all three affiliate news directors. Two of them barely gave me the time of*

*day. The third, the ABC affiliate's news director—this was a station that
was doing one newscast on the weekend—he said, 'I could use a gopher,
a newsroom secretary. You can answer the phone and pick up some of
my mail.' I worked for them a year and a half. The last six months they
hired me to do the 11:00 Sunday night weather. It was like a Cinder-
ella story. During the week I would come in and be the secretary in the
newsroom, and then on Sunday night I would come in at 6:00, and for
five hours I would pore over the weather wires, and then I learned how
to do the weather reports.*"[7] Nina Totenberg, who was trying to get a job
in Boston, was asked whether she was planning to have any children or
was told "We have our woman." *"That was my favorite—'We have our
woman.' That was all the time. 'We have our woman.'"*[8]

Alicia Shepard, a George Washington University student, nabbed a
real journalism job in Washington when she graduated in 1978; she then
moved on to California and Japan. She remembered the Washington of
that era: *"I didn't realize in 1978 that I was a pioneer. There were so
few women reporting. It reminded me, in retrospect, of Japan. If I were
walking down the street and saw another American, I would cross the
street to talk to them. And that's what it was like as a female journalist in Washington in the late 1970s. It was intimidating. It was mainly
middle-aged white men who had worked for their hometown paper most
of their lives and then came to Washington and joined the Gridiron
Club. Because I had lived out of the country for five years I had a foreign
correspondent's perspective when I returned [in 1993], and one of the
first things I realized was that it was getting harder for middle-aged white
men to find new jobs because news organizations were finally starting to
embrace diversity.*"[9]

ARRIVING AT DIVERSITY was a painful process. Women journalists had
to resort to suing their mainstream employers for gender discrimination
under Title VII of the Civil Rights Act. Eileen Shanahan was part of a
1974 class action suit against the *New York Times.* She had gone from
United Press to the *Journal of Commerce* to the Washington bureau of
the *Times,* where she covered economics and tax policy. The pretrial discovery process measured how far she had been left behind: although she
was twelfth in seniority, she was nineteenth on the salary scale. *Boylan* v.
New York Times was finally settled in 1978; the *Times* admitted doing no

wrong but promised to do better. In another landmark suit, the Associated Press was sued in 1978; five years later, its female employees were awarded more than $800,000 in back pay.

Jo Thomas, who graduated from Wake Forest University in 1965, was a prize-winning reporter at the *Detroit Free Press;* she joined the Washington bureau of the *New York Times* in 1977 as part of a new national investigative reporting team: *"They hired people who had reputations as being pretty good investigative reporters, all guys except for me. I'm pretty convinced that the 1974 women's class action law suit against the* Times *was the reason why I was hired because they were under a lot of pressure to add women to the staff. Being a woman had everything to do with my career path. . . . I found out when I got to Washington that the guy who had been hired at the same time I had been hired had nowhere near the experience and was the same age [but] was making twice as much as I was."*

Eventually Thomas would report on British army death squads in Northern Ireland, on Castro's Cuba, and on the Oklahoma City bombing. *"Certainly during my career at the* Times, *from 1977 until 2002, if you were a woman and tried to be a real reporter, your job was a hundred times as hard. I've had to fight editors my whole career, and I often felt that they thought a pretty young woman couldn't possibly get the stories I was getting. The sort of suspicion of women investigating these types of things was pervasive all along."*[10]

But the struggle for diversity in the newsroom eventually began to pay dividends for some. Lisa Myers went from the *Washington Star* to NBC in 1981: *"Particularly in newspapers it was an asset, because at that time newspapers were looking for women because they were organizations of white males. I think it probably didn't hurt coming up in television to be a woman at that time because the trailblazers had gone before and basically opened the door, which allowed more of us to walk through and succeed."*[11]

ROBIN SPROUL, WHO became Washington bureau chief of ABC News in 1995, remembered that when she got her first job in 1975 *"there were a couple of women correspondents, 'news nuns' as we called them back then because most of them had no families."*[12] Family rarely came up as a factor in career choices in interviews with male reporters of this generation. Bob Pierpoint remarked, "I was fortunate in that I had a very competent wife who managed to take care of the family while I was traveling around the world,"[13] and Don Shannon observed that "those were the good old days when I think families just had to sort of go along."[14] But "family" was a keyword with female reporters. "I'm not married. I don't have children," explained Lisa Myers, "that makes it a lot less complicated than it is for a lot of my colleagues."

Those who felt that family considerations did not affect their job decisions tended to present themselves as focused and career driven. Georgie Anne Geyer, on assignment in Guatemala for the *Chicago Daily News* before coming to Washington, wrote in her memoir, "The sacrifices one makes to be a foreign correspondent—husband, children, the house with the view of the lake, the comforts of normalcy, and the reassurances of conformity—seemed, quite simply, irrelevant."[15]

For some, unwavering commitment was part of a drive to achieve new heights for women, not just a personal career goal. That drive was most apparent with African American women journalists. Mal Johnson went from the civil rights movement in North Philadelphia to reporting for a local TV station in 1965 to helping found the National Association of Black Journalists; she went on to a long career with Cox Broadcasting in Washington.[16] *"I was like the second wave,"* said Judlyne Lilly, *"so it was really important to women like myself to get the career going and to have family considerations later."*[17] Lee Thornton earned a Ph.D. at Northwestern in 1973 and began her journalism career the next year at CBS: *"I started teaching broadcast journalism at Howard in 1983 and ended up teaching there for 14 years, eight of which were [as an] adjunct. Then I went on tenure track at the associate professor level. The University of Maryland came looking for me to apply for the Richard Eaton Chair in Broadcast News, and I won out over a lot of competition. I've been there ten years* [in 2007]. *From Howard and Maryland, my students are absolutely everywhere. If I have a legacy, they are it. That's as good as it gets for a career. It's amazing. . . . My family life had no bearing on my career decisions."*[18]

MOST OF THE women, however, talked of their careers as spiked with serious consequences for their family. Jean Heller, a *Newsday* reporter in Washington in 1978 who later worked in Michigan, Wyoming, and

Florida, remarked: *"Journalism can take a huge toll on your family because of the frequent odd hours and long days, and lots of journalists don't put down roots anywhere because they move every few years."*[19] That pattern was most apparent at the major newspapers, news magazines, and TV organizations whose correspondents often rotated through Washington on their way to foreign assignments. *"The strains on the family,"* said Richard Roth in 2007, *"are enormous. . . . My divorce should be complete very soon now, so I guess that kind of speaks for itself. . . . There's a large amount of ambiguity, difficulty, adjustment to odd hours and unscheduled travel that the family of a network television correspondent has to adjust to."*[20]

"I quit cold turkey, September 1, 1979, when our first child was born," said Carol Falk, who in 1969 was one of the first women hired to be a writer at the *Wall Street Journal*. *"I've edited school and church newsletters, but I never went back to work for pay. I'm not a freelance type."*[21] Yet for many journalists with children, part-time or freelance work was the only way to employ their professional skills in the time that they had available. Washington was a good city for part-timers. Nancy Koran, a writer for specialized publications, described the transition: *"In February of 1983 my first child was born, my son, and at that point I explained to my editors that I would like to continue to write part-time and that* Oil Express *was not an appropriate assignment because it was a very intense beat. . . . I finished my maternity leave, and I came back. . . . After several months they acquired a publication that was for telecommunications, and it was a bimonthly. So because its deadlines were farther apart, and it was a smaller publication, I did that, working 20 hours a week. . . . I wrote until just before the birth of my daughter, in December of '85. With my additional child-rearing responsibilities, I left the company, and I did a stint of freelancing."*[22]

Being a "trailing spouse" was a common career pattern. "My husband got a job in Washington, and I came along," said Judy Rutter, who was with *U.S. News & World Report* in 1978.[23] It was most often the wife who did the trailing, but not always. NBC moved Carole Simpson from Chicago, and her husband *"didn't have a job when we came to Washington. We talked about whether we should do this or not, and he knew this was my dream. . . . I appreciate his giving me that opportunity. He could have stayed where he was, and we were happy in Chicago."* And

Don Campbell, a veteran political writer for Gannett, registered more relocations than any other person in our 1978 survey, joining his wife, Julia Wallace, when she assumed editorships in Salem, Oregon; Phoenix, Arizona; Atlanta, Georgia; and Dayton, Ohio.[24]

Some debated the relative merits of marrying another journalist. Said Michael Putzel, talking about his wife, Ann Blackman, *"It's wonderful to come home and say, 'You'll never believe what happened at the office today,' and know your spouse will know exactly what you're talking about."*[25] But for Patricia Fanning, the conflicting schedules of two journalism careers became a "double whammy." The marriage did not survive.[26]

For female journalists with children, every aspect of professional decisions was influenced by family considerations. Relative merits of reporting or editing? Measured in regularity of hours per day. Of working different beats? Measured in days away from home. Of working for different news organizations? Measured by family-friendly reputation. Of covering different types of news? Measured by whether the news was produced monthly, weekly, daily, or hourly.

"The first year of my daughter's life I traveled a lot," said Anne Davenport of ABC News. *"I found myself on a March 15—it happened to snow on the Ides of March, which is my husband's birthday—on a plane. I was traveling with Al Gore and Dick Gephardt to New Hampshire and then Iowa because Gephardt was announcing he was pulling out of the race [and] that Gore would be able to run. . . . The weather's crummy. I left my baby at home and my husband on his birthday. It was not fulfilling then."*[27] Davenport later moved to the *PBS Newshour.*

Washington might be a great career destination in journalism, but was it a great place to raise children? Mary Kay Quinlan of Gannett News Service, a president of the National Press Club, related that *"my husband and I, from the time we were first married, talked about not wanting to raise kids in a metro area, both of us having been from smaller communities. The pace of life and the city life of Washington can be taxing on people, and we didn't want our kids raised in that kind of an environment, where kids sometimes get short shrift."*[28] She and her husband relocated to Omaha, where she began a teaching career at the University of Nebraska. Other journalists appreciated the benefits of having their children grow up in the heady atmosphere of the nation's capital. *"We talk about interesting things at the dinner table,"* said CNN's Gloria Borger.[29]

IN TELEVISION BROADCASTING, the upward spiral for women dates to ABC's hiring Barbara Walters as co-anchor of its evening news program in 1976. Walters had long been associated with "soft" news at NBC's *Today* show, and the move did not please Harry Reasoner, her co-anchor. She was followed at the networks' Washington bureaus by reporters born in the 1940s (then in their early thirties) who arrived from local stations—in Philadelphia, New Orleans, Richmond, Minneapolis—and eventually won prized assignments: Rita Braver, Connie Chung, Ann Compton, Candy Crowley, Andrea Mitchell, Jessica Savitch, Susan Spencer, Lesley Stahl, Judy Woodruff. For five years Woodruff reported from Atlanta, first for WAGA-TV and then for NBC: *"In 1975–76 Jimmy Carter, who I knew well from Georgia politics, was running for president. I kept saying to NBC, 'These people are serious; they really think they are going to win.' NBC said sure, sure. They finally said all right, go do a profile of Jimmy Carter. . . . They just wanted to keep me quiet. Carter started to win. He did well in Iowa and New Hampshire, and suddenly he was the wonder boy, and I was there. . . . Two years after NBC hired me, I was the third string at the White House in 1977."* Diane Sawyer was the outlier. She worked as an assistant to the White House press secretary from 1970 to 1975, then went to California to help Richard Nixon write his memoirs, which were published in 1978. At that time she joined CBS as a political correspondent.[30]

Perseverance was rewarded for some.[31] *"You know, business trends young,"* said Crowley in 2005, *"and none of us are getting any younger."*[32] But five years later, after nearly two decades as a CNN political correspondent, Crowley was made anchor of the network's Sunday morning program, *State of the Union.* Woodruff was elevated to an anchor chair when PBS reformatted its one-hour evening news program in 2009. Compton, who in 1974 was the first woman assigned by a television network to cover the White House on a full-time basis, was still at the White House in 2010, still working for ABC, reporting for its radio network. *"My technique for [raising] the kids was to get them all into college,"* said Compton; *"I didn't need to rush home anymore at night for dinner."*[33] Crowley agreed: *"Once they hit college you can write checks from any hotel in America. So they don't physically need you there."*

When the *Tyndall Report* measured the "most heavily used reporters" of 2002–09, Andrea Mitchell was ranked number 1; Lisa Myers, 6; Anne Thompson, 9; Martha Raddatz, 12; Betsy Stark, 15; Lisa Stark, 19; and Sharyl Attkisson, 20. Still, there was a glass ceiling in New York, where the network news programs originate. Linda Douglass, who was stationed in Washington during 1993–2006, looked back on her years at CBS and ABC: *"Both of my bureau chiefs were women, and both were incredibly smart, talented people. But they still took their orders from New York, which was dominated by men. . . . When a woman would occasionally cycle through the evening news show producer ranks, she was usually in charge of features, not hard news. At the management level in New York, the people who are our real bosses, the managers who discussed editorial matters with correspondents were almost always men. Some of the executive producers of morning news shows and magazine shows were women."*[34]

Our 1978 survey was of commercial news organizations; it did not include National Public Radio, where women made up 41 percent of the reportorial workforce by 1988, creating what Nina Totenberg called "an old-girl network." Starting with Susan Stamberg, the co-host of *All Things Considered* for 14 years, and Linda Wertheimer, co-host for 13 years, they influenced the voice of NPR's coverage in important ways. Legal affairs correspondent Totenberg arrived in 1975. Although the Supreme Court is a beat best explained in print, Totenberg, a college dropout, was able to capture the drama of court decisions for listeners through her exceptional narrative skill. Cokie Roberts became congressional correspondent two years later, bringing to NPR an inbred capacity to explain the nuances of Capitol Hill, where her father had been majority leader of the House of Representatives.[35] Chuck Bailey, a legendary Minneapolis journalist who was their editor at NPR in the early 1980s, recalled, *"One of the things I enjoyed so much about supervising so many women at NPR was that they told you what they thought, how they felt, and what they were angry about. There's a premium in journalism on not revealing your feelings. It's a corollary of objectivity, the disinterested approach to the story we're working on. But we all know we have feelings. Men just suppress them.*"[36]

FOR THE NEWSPAPER reporters, who were in their thirties in 1978, the climb was steeper, more frustrating, and often less rewarding than for their counterparts in the electronic media. While television added cable opportunities, newspapers were locked in a rite of mergers, reorganizations, and foreclosures. When her paper folded in 1991, Cheryl Arvidson became the communications director of the Blue Cross, Blue Shield Association. *"I left journalism because there was a major newspaper depression going on. Not only was I a victim of that, but I had spent six years running a major news operation as* [the *Dallas Times Herald's*] *bureau chief, and realistically, the prospect of getting a staff job in a bureau where you have a history of already being a bureau chief is somewhat slim. A lot of bosses would be hesitant to hire me.*"[37] Patricia Fanning recalled that when the *Baltimore Evening Sun* stopped publishing in 1995, *"that was the third newspaper that I had worked for that went out of business. I feel like I'm jumping from lily pad to lily pad."* Marlene Cimons, of the *Los Angeles Times,* was glad to take a buyout, as was Carol Richards, at *Newsday.* Ellen Warren, a respected *Chicago Tribune* columnist, claimed, *"If I had to do it over, would I perhaps have chosen something else? Yeah, I think I probably would have. . . . I was in pre-veterinary medicine* [in college], *so I would become a vet. That's not the answer you expected, was it?"*[38] Susan Page, *USA Today* bureau chief, noted other women who had risen to bureau chief, then added, *"That hasn't necessarily translated higher up the food chain in newspapers."*[39]

Yet there were two print journalists, 30 years old in 1978, born less than a month apart, whose careers would leave deep tracks: Judith Miller of the *New York Times* and Karen Elliott House of the *Wall Street Journal.* Both were first assigned to cover the Securities and Exchange Commission, a beat that didn't accord with their interests. House recalled, *"I went to work every day fearful that it would be my last because you had to put these filings on the ticker, and I really had no idea what the filings were."*[40] Both ultimately specialized in reporting on the Middle East. Each won a Pulitzer Prize.

Otherwise, their careers didn't look much alike. House's trajectory at the *Wall Street Journal* was a straight, ascending line: reporting on a regulatory agency in 1974–75 led to covering energy issues during an oil crisis (1975–78), which led to the diplomacy beat and world travel with the secretary of state (1978–84), which led to the foreign desk in New York, where she became foreign editor (1984–89). House then was named vice president and later president of the International Group, responsible for all Dow Jones overseas publications, such as the *European Journal,* the *Asian Journal,* and the *Far Eastern Economic Review,* from 1989 to 2002. The Dow Jones board of directors appointed her publisher of the *Wall Street Journal* in 2002, the highest position in print journalism ever held by a woman without a family claim. She was one of three candidates in contention for the corporation's CEO position in 2006; when she didn't get the job, she retired, after 32 years with the paper. Her severance package, which was thirty-eight pages long, included $1.7 million disbursed over the following 24 months and other options. Thinking back on her seamless progression from reporter to editor to publisher, *"If you want to compete with men, you have to work harder than men because men tend to see—in my day and I think [it's] still true—they see women as having 'jobs' and men as having 'careers.'"*

Judith Miller's progression at the *New York Times* was not seamless. Her initial years in the Washington bureau (1977–83) led to a plum appointment as bureau chief in Cairo (1983–87), a return to Washington as news editor and deputy bureau chief (1987–88), and then a blizzard of assignments, most often involving the Middle East and controversy. Franklin Foer, in a penetrating *New York* magazine article in 2004, described how "her ambition, her aggressiveness, her cultivation of sources by any means necessary, her hunger to be first" produced a series of stunning stories and the deep animosity of her colleagues.[41] She was at the forefront in exposing the global terrorism network, especially bioterrorism. Her downfall began with her claims that Saddam Hussein was building weapons of mass destruction, which the *Times* was painfully forced to correct. When, in July 2005, Miller refused to reveal to a grand jury the name of the source who had told her that Valerie Plame was a covert CIA operative, she spent eighty-five days in jail. Her First Amendment defense was later questioned when it was revealed that she knew that her source, I. Lewis Libby, had signed a waiver of confidentially. She said that she questioned its validity. Judith Miller ended her

28-year career with the *Times* on November 9, 2005; the terms of the separation were not revealed.

THE YEAR 1988, a decade after we conducted our survey, was a good point to gauge the magnitude of change. Going by the first names of those accredited to the congressional press galleries, we found that the number of women had nearly doubled, from 690 to 1,231. They had been a fifth of the press corps; now they were a third. The greatest gain—41 percent—was in the periodical press gallery, the seat of the weekly news magazines, newsletters, and specialized publications. Taking the proportion of women at the bureaus of *Time, Newsweek,* and *U.S. News & World Report* altogether, we found an increase from 29 percent to 38 percent. A second study painted a portrait of woman journalists in 1988 as more experienced than those surveyed in 1978, with an average of nine years in journalism, including five years before arriving in Washington.[42]

But when we measured the numbers again in 2010, there had been almost no upward movement: women constituted 33 percent of the press corps in 1988 and 37 percent in 2010. The rate of growth had virtually stopped in Washington, and exactly the same results came up nationally in a massive survey conducted by David Weaver's team and published in 2007.[43] Moreover, the same flat trend line was seen in comparable occupations. Lawyers resembled reporters in terms of working long and unpredictable hours in a traditionally male-dominated culture, and women made up half of the students in both graduate journalism programs and law schools. Yet only about a third of journalists were women, and, according to the 2000 census, only about a third of lawyers.[44]

STILL, WITHIN WHAT appeared to be a numerically static environment, there were substantial changes in the way that women in Washington described their lives. They may not have been at par with men, but there were enough women journalists who had been there long enough and at high enough levels of responsibility to change the tone of our interviews. When asked whether being a woman presented any newsroom challenge at the *Wall Street Journal,* Laura Meckler replied, *"My direct supervisor is a woman."*[45]

Discrimination and bias, the recurring themes of 1978, were now rarely mentioned. Even sports journalist Christine Brennan, after citing an issue that she called the "whoops and hollers in the locker room," added, *"I never suffered a day in my life. Not a one."*[46] When matters of gender differences were brought up, it was often at the urging of the interviewer. Elisabeth Bumiller of the *New York Times* said there's *"not as many* [women] *as there should be"* on the White House beat.[47] Lisa Meyer, AP Radio, said of covering the Pentagon, *"It's just not as easy as being a guy."*[48] The Supreme Court continued to have a love-hate effect on women journalists. Linda Greenhouse had told us in 1979 that it was a beat that *"no one wants. . . . People at the* [New York Times] *bureau say, 'I'm glad* you're *doing it. I wouldn't want to.'"*[49] (Greenhouse won the Pulitzer Prize in 1998 for her Supreme Court reporting.) It was also a beat that women loved, noted Joan Biskupic of *USA Today: "If you know your stuff you can schedule your life around it."*[50]

Beyond "family," the new keyword was "balance," repeated in interview after interview. *"I don't have kids, but I really want them. For me it's a question of how I would balance work and family,"* said Anne Hawke, of NPR.[51] *"As long as I can maintain the balance that I'm striking right now, then I'm okay,"* said Brooke Hart, of NBC's News Channel.[52] Balance often implied spousal responsibilities that differed markedly from those of the earlier generation. *"It helps that he has a more static, predictable schedule, as opposed to mine, which can be very unpredictable. And it helps because we have two children,"* said the AP's Donna Cassata of her husband, a dentist.[53] Susan Feeney, a national political reporter for the *Dallas Morning News,* and her husband, Steve Hirsh, director of special events at Fox TV, explained in 2006 that their arrangements could be complicated:

> Hirsh: *I was more often able to work my schedule around Susan. It is very rare, I think it's been twice, maybe three times that we have had to be out of town at the same time in the eight years since our oldest son was born.*

> Feeney: *It takes a lot of work, but it is basically one of the laws we have. I go one week, he goes the next.*

> Hirsh: *She's leaving on Tuesday, so she'll take the car to Dulles. I am coming home on Tuesday, I fly into Dulles, pick up the car and drive home.*

Feeney: *He is literally the king of doing half of all kids' things, sometimes more.*[54]

IF THE CAREER of one female journalist can encapsulate the trend—discrimination, family, balance—the remarkable career of June Kronholz can. *"I was the only woman in the Dallas bureau [of the* Wall Street Journal *in 1976], and it was a very macho place, you know, there were pinups around the office, and it was not a particularly, it was not a very friendly atmosphere. . . . [Five years later] by fluke, I was sent to Rhodesia to cover the end of the independence war, and I liked Africa so much that I was given the Africa beat. So I did that for a couple of years, and then I was asked to develop a beat on third world issues. . . . Then in '83 [I] came back to be the bureau chief in Boston, in '85 went to Hong Kong to be bureau chief, caught the revolution in the Philippines, [and] returned to Washington to be the deputy bureau chief in 1987."* Here her career took a unique twist.

Kronholz married an American diplomat and left journalism for seven years. *"You're going to get married when you fall in love, you really are. You're not going to decide, 'Oh, I'm going to wait 15 years to get married,' you know; you're going to do it when your heart tells you to do it. So it just so happens that I didn't get married until I was 40 and I had my children at 41 and 42. It's not because I planned it that way. That's just the way it happened."*

In 1997 Kronholz rejoined the *Wall Street Journal* in the Washington bureau. When she was interviewed in 2006, her kids were 16 and 17, and she had adjusted her work schedule to four days a week. *"We've got 'college night' tonight so I'll go home about 6:30, which is a little bit early for me. You know, you just have to set your priorities. This is a fairly family-friendly place, everybody's got kids about the same age, and no one around here will raise an eyebrow if you have to take off time to do a college tour or something like go to a kid's baseball game. Everyone recognizes that when your story's hot you work hard at it and don't watch the clock and when your story cools off, you can take some time if you need it. You just do it. It's what being a woman is all about."*[55]

FOUR

DIVERSITY

BETWEEN HIS JUNIOR and senior year at Harvard, Hal Logan interned at the *Washington Post,* and he was offered a full-time job upon graduation: *"That was in 1973, and I remained in the newsroom until 1978. I had a wonderful time in the newsroom, and I was very happy having the ability to shape a story. But what I decided after four or five years was that I wanted the ability to shape how an entire paper covered issues, and specially how the paper covers issues of concern to African Americans. I'm an African American. There were a lot of guys I knew, reporters who were very good reporters and writers, but none of us knew the first thing about business.*

"So I decided to go to business school so that I could learn how to build and run a black-oriented newspaper. I got an MBA at Stanford in 1980. . . . I figured out why it's so difficult for a black paper to be economically successful in Washington. . . . I returned to the Post *as the assistant to the publisher. I guess I could say I got very interested in the notion of publishing a paper on a screen in addition to publishing it on a piece of paper. That pretty much set the path of much of my career since then. This was 1981. I became head of electronic publishing for the* Post."

Logan moved to Dow Jones in 1984 and to Pacific Bell Directory in California in 1988 to produce an electronic version of the Yellow Pages. *"Later I had the chance to run an Internet start-up company down in Silicon Valley, which worked out pretty well.* [Vicinity Corporation provided mapping and direction services.] *The company managed to do an IPO right before the NASDAQ collapsed and later was acquired by Microsoft. . . . Of all things I've done, the work at Vicinity was the most satisfying.*

You know, the opportunity to start a brand new company and shepherd it to what became really a pretty decent success. But, you know, being in the newsroom was probably the most fun of anything I did. "[1]

CAROLE SIMPSON WAS the only black journalism major in her graduating class at the University of Michigan in 1962. *"I went to all the job interviews on campus, and every place I went I got the same story, that I had three strikes against me: I was a Negro, I was a woman, and I was inexperienced."* She became a journalism instructor and publicist at Tuskegee Institute for two years, and then she went to graduate school in broadcast media at the University of Iowa.

"Now it was 1965. A lot of people that had not been interested in me became very suddenly interested in me. This was after Birmingham and the dogs and the hoses, and it's Malcolm X and it's the civil rights movement. . . . Clearly, employers were getting the message that they should be doing something about minorities in this industry." She was hired by WCFL Radio. *"There had never been a female broadcasting hard news in Chicago before. . . . That was going to be $10,000 a year, and my dad at the post office then, where he'd worked for thirty years, was making like $5,000 a year. I remember my first paycheck, I gave to my parents: 'This is yours.' I was so proud of this. I felt like the richest woman on earth.*

"So I became a street reporter of a news department that numbered thirteen people. . . . There was great resentment among these white male colleagues of mine. I was really put through the wringer. . . . There were attempts to sabotage me. . . . I'm in the middle of the newscast, and someone hurls a giant rubber tarantula on the desk. . . . I would not allow them to fluster me. . . . Actually, it was very good training."

Martin Luther King came to Chicago. *"He was walking out* [to go to breakfast], *and he said, 'Where is she?' They pointed to me over there, and he said, 'Young lady, have you been here all night long?' I said, 'Yes, Dr. King, I'm sorry. I hope I didn't cause anybody any trouble, but I'm a young struggling black reporter, and your coming to Chicago is a major, major story, and I would give anything if I'd be able to break this story as to what you're here for and what it's about.' And he said, 'Well, if you stayed up all night. . . . ' I'll never forget. Martin Luther King gave me my first scoop!"*

In 1970 Simpson moved from radio to television: *"I felt, 'This is where the country's moving.' Television news was growing and becoming more and more important. Clearly, if I wanted to be in a mass medium that was going to have impact, television was going to be the place that I would go."*

She worked first for NBC's Chicago affiliate, WMAQ-TV, then for the network in its Midwest bureau, and in 1974 relocated to Washington: *"I was to be assigned to cover HEW, which was the Department of Health, Education and Welfare. It was not my choice of assignments. I really wanted to cover politics. But it was a way to get to Washington. I was assigned because it had to do with 'female' kind of stuff and 'black' kind of stuff. It was health care, which women certainly care about. And education, because I had a child I knew about schools. And welfare, which had to do with black people, in the minds of our employers. So I was a natural as a black female to come to Washington and cover that beat. . . . After five years there was an opening to cover the House of Representatives, and I fought and fought and fought: 'Me, how about me? I can do it.' I waged a campaign to get this assignment. I really wanted it. . . . So in 1979, I was named House correspondent for NBC."*

At the start of 1982, Simpson switched to ABC. *"They waved big bucks in front of my face. I mean, huge money, way above this little modest thing that NBC was going to give me."* She eventually became anchor of *World News Tonight Sunday*. *"I have fought racism and sexism all of my life, and* [in 1994] *I'm now getting to the age where I think ageism is going to start creeping in, and if I fought racism and sexism, you can damn well be sure I'm going to fight ageism."* Simpson's contract with ABC ran through 2004. She subsequently established scholarships for women and minorities majoring in journalism and taught at Emerson College in Boston.[2]

WARREN BROWN GOT a degree in 1970 from the Columbia University Graduate School of Journalism, and his classmates eventually steered him to the *Washington Post*. But first, following the conventional wisdom of the time, he got a job on a small newspaper, the *New Orleans State Item*, in order to work his way up to a big newspaper, the *Philadelphia Inquirer*, with a short stopover in Chicago to work at *Jet* and *Ebony* magazines. The move from New Orleans to Chicago was a response to someone at *Ebony* who said, "You're a hotshot Ivy League graduate, and you're down there in the South burying dead white people." (He was writing obituaries.) He arrived at the *Post* in 1976.

"I was hired there to their national staff. I started out covering something euphemistically called urban affairs, which was just another way of saying civil rights, you know, and labor. . . . I wasn't terribly happy there. Luckily, Frank Swoboda, who had become a business editor, gave me a chance to start writing business stories, which I found extremely interesting and much more gratifying.

"That was in 1982. And I asked if I could cover the automotive industry, and he gave me the go-ahead to do it, and gave me a lot of support while I was doing it. I literally fell in love with covering that industry. It's just to me the most fascinating thing that anybody can write about, how all of this comes together: regulations, cars, products, personalities, just the whole chemistry of everything involved in it. I came back to Frank with an idea about some columns. He was at first not terribly enthusiastic, but he was a kind of person who gave you enough rope to hang yourself or to pull yourself further up.

"I started writing the 'On Wheels' column at first for the 'Weekend' section, and I started writing the 'Car Culture' column about 2003, maybe 2004. A good friend of mine, Paul Eisenstein, a freelancer in Detroit, in the early 1980s was fooling around with something called the Internet, and a lot of other reporters ignored him. But he took it seriously. . . . and I learned from that. So as soon as the Post *had entry into Internet presentations, I was already predisposed to go full force, jumping into that, which is what I've done.*

"What I love about the automobile industry is that if it understands that you are serious about understanding what it is they are doing and why it is they are doing it, and if you come prepared and you ask hard questions, pretty soon they begin to respect you, and pretty soon they stop worrying about whether you're black or white or green or yellow. . . . I've never run into a designer, an engineer, technician, statistician, physics person, any of these people who worried about my race first. They were mostly interested in explaining the theory and making sure that I understood what they were doing. . . . You know, what impressed them wasn't the color of my skin or anything else like that, what impressed them was my continued passion to really try to figure out how all of it

is put together. And so to me the balance of my career has been like a fully paid scholarship to one of the best graduate schools in the world. . . . I don't normally think about race anymore." Brown took a buyout from the *Post* in 2009, continuing to write his column under contract.[3]

HAL LOGAN, CAROLE Simpson, and Warren Brown were among the fifteen African Americans that we surveyed in 1978. Regrettably, over time we lost track of three others, two of whom had worked for the Mutual Black Network; the third was the only black journalist to report for a niche publication, a newsletter that specialized in health policy. Two-thirds of the journalists were women, reflecting the "two-fer" phenomenon, whereby diversity-enhancing employers could claim credit for filling two minority slots with one job. And two-thirds were boomers, young enough to take advantage of new affirmative action programs. James Adams was a student at Fisk University in Nashville: *"I came to Washington one day, my brother was playing with a band at the time, and I had heard of this television internship program at WTOP, which is now WUSA, and I went by after this rock concert, [in] my shorts and vest and all this 60s, 70s kind of stuff to pick up an application. And they were actually interviewing. So I sat there for two hours. I was the last person they interviewed, and I made it past the first cut. And so then I made it past the second cut. Then I got into a program that WTOP had going on, and I spent a year there as a trainee. And out of that trainee program I got a job in Houston, Texas. And the whole idea of the program was to give affirmative action, to give African Americans an opportunity to learn this business. And I did, and I was successful."*[4] Adams's long career includes many years as co-anchor of evening news on News4, NBC, in Washington.

Almost all the blacks that we interviewed were to spend a substantial portion of their lives as journalists. The only person, besides Logan, to drop out before the ten-year-mark was Roy Betts, a 22-year-old graduate of Howard University, who spent three years as an assistant editor in the *Ebony/Jet* Washington bureau and another three years editing a niche publication on small business until it failed in 1983. He was then hired by the Commerce Department, a government agency that he had covered, and switched to media relations at the U.S. Postal Service in 1988. *"I've had the opportunity to work with leaders who have moved the Postal Service from your grandmother and granddaddy's post office to a very forward-thinking progressive postal service."* We asked him in 2007 whether he was satisfied with his career: *"Elated,"* he replied.[5]

Increasingly among boomers, a career in journalism no longer followed an unbroken line from entry to retirement. Betty Anne Williams was 22 years old when she arrived in Washington to work for the AP in 1974; she left in 1984. *"I figured that if I was ever going to try editing, I'd better get at it. So I got an offer from Gannett in Rochester, New York, at the* Democrat & Chronicle. *It was a great opportunity. I was assistant managing editor there for three and a half years."* When Gannett created *USA Today,* she moved back to Washington to become the night international editor. From 1995 to 2000, Williams was the paper's recruiter. *"The timing was bad, however. The paper was curbing its expenses and reduced its hiring, so we interviewed people but didn't hire very many. But that's journalism. . . . After that I started working for Black College Wire, which was a start-up project to help train African American students at historically black colleges and universities to become journalists. I stayed close to journalism. I can't seem to be able to escape it no matter what I do. Actually, I don't really want to escape, I say that in jest."*[6]

Williams went on to be a managing editor at the *Gazette-Star* in Prince George's County, Maryland, while also teaching journalism as an adjunct instructor at Howard. In 2007 she moved out of journalism again to become communications director at the Joint Center for Political and Economic Studies, a leading think tank in Washington focusing on issues of particular concern to African Americans.

Karen DeWitt also had a long and many-layered career in journalism, which included credits at *National Journal, Washington Post, New York Times,* and *USA Today.* She also was host of a cooking show, "Karen's Kitchen," on WETA-BETA, and she did a stint as a senior producer with ABC's *Nightline. "Journalism, particularly when you're young, gives you the license to ask anybody anything, no matter who they are. As a writer, you're on the side of angels. I became a journalist to be a gadfly. I loved it. . . . I covered wars too, and that was a thrill. I was in Nicaragua, South Africa. . . . I was on the front lines of history. I knew what was going on."*[7] When DeWitt was interviewed again in 2006, she was communications director at the Leadership Conference on Civil Rights.

THE SUCCESS OF these blacks might have opened doors to greater representation in the national media, yet African Americans probably still do not make up more than the 4 percent of the Washington press that they did in 1978. While there has been no new survey, there is evidence. Annual tabulations from the American Society of Newspaper Editors (ASNE) show a steady decline of black journalists in the nation's newsrooms. Although there has been no shortage of jobs lost by journalists in general, the percent loss is greater among blacks.[8] In television and radio, according to the director of the RTDNA/Hofstra Survey released in 2010, "Again, the percentages of minorities in television decreased from the year before. In fact, we end the decade with no gains whatsoever for minorities in TV news, and the percentage of minorities in radio news is down substantially."[9]

Perhaps the most unusual evidence can be drawn from a study by the Pew Research Center's Project for Excellence in Journalism. After examining 67,000 national news stories that appeared during President Obama's first year, it concluded: "Just 643 of those stories, 1.9 percent, . . . related in a significant way to African Americans in the U.S."[10] Not all black journalists write stories that fit in that category, but stories in that category are often written by black journalists. Barbara Reynolds, reporting for the *Chicago Tribune* in 1978, told us, *"It does make a difference in my coverage that I'm a black. . . . On an economics story, I'll be interested in how it affects minority business. Minority business keeps up the tax base in the cities, minority business restores pride, minority business is good. So minority business is important to me, although it's only a small matter in the total economy."*[11]

THE *POST,* AS the leading daily in a city with a majority black population, is the largest employer of black journalists, with most concentrated on the staff of its Metro section.[12] But there aren't many African Americans in national journalism in Washington, where their presence is top-loaded. The names that make the cut are often seen in bold type:

—Dean Baquet became the *New York Times* Washington bureau chief in 2007, earning kudos for having been fired as editor of the *Los Angeles Times* when he refused to cut jobs from his newsroom. He moved to New York in 2011, elevated to managing editor, the paper's number-two job.

—Kevin Merida was named the *Washington Post's* national editor in 2009.

—William Raspberry (1994), Colbert King (2003), and Eugene Robinson (2009), all *Post* columnists, won Pulitzer Prizes, as did Clarence Page (1989) at the *Chicago Tribune.*

—Mark Whitaker went from being the editor of *Newsweek* to bureau chief at NBC News to executive vice president and managing editor for CNN Worldwide.

—Suzanne Malveaux became an anchor at CNN after having been its White House correspondent.

For the most part, African American columnists, editors, anchors, and star reporters are found at the most influential organizations. For reasons honorable and otherwise, the TV networks and the leading newspapers, which were under the most pressure to hire minority candidates, offered more incentives, and minority candidates were attracted by them. Nor was there a shortage of well-educated candidates to choose from. As characterized by a veteran black reporter: "Regardless of ethnicity, we're Big Ten or Ivy, middle class, aspiring to upper middle class."

Network correspondents are automatically eligible for elite status. The White House chose to have President Obama tell Robin Roberts of ABC News that he was supporting same-sex marriage.[13] Yet none of the black network correspondents have reached the highest rung since Ed Bradley died in 2006, although Byron Pitts of *CBS Evening News* is starting to appear on *60 Minutes.*[14] Others have reached the weekend anchor level, such as Russ Mitchell (CBS) and Lester Holt (NBC), who also hosts *Dateline.* Talent has a way of cycling through the upper reaches: Helene Cooper came to the *New York Times* from the *Wall Street Journal;* Gwen Ifill, managing editor and moderator for *Washington Week* and an anchor on the *Newshour,* both for PBS, had been at the *Washington Post* and the *New York Times;* Michel Martin, host of *Tell Me More,* joined NPR from ABC News; the career of Juan Williams, political analyst for Fox News, included a long tenure at the *Post* and at NPR.

The millennial decade's most significant posting of an African American in Washington came in 2005 when the Tribune Company chose Vickie Walton-James to oversee coverage of its nine newspapers, including the *Chicago Tribune,* the *Los Angeles Times, Newsday,* the *Baltimore*

Sun, the *Hartford Courant,* and papers in Orlando and Ft. Lauderdale, Florida, along with a string of local television stations. Her assignment was to meld those disparate operations into a single entity. *"What we're doing is trying to meet and talk and meet and talk and meet and talk. In the process of building this new bureau, we talked about what everybody thought they needed to succeed to produce good journalism, which is one of the reasons we don't have one of those big newsrooms. . . . The* LA Times *has its space, Chicago has its space, Baltimore has a space,* Newsday *has a space, because again, while we're sharing we're also competing, and so a bullpen-type newsroom would not serve our purposes. . . . As for resources, each of the managing editors works with the bureau chiefs, and I work with all of the managing editors. . . . I think we've got a good-size bureau right now* [in 2006], *and I hope we can stay the way we are."*[15] In 2008 the company filed for bankruptcy protection, listing assets of $7.6 billion and debt of $12.9 billion. Walton-James joined NPR to supervise its coverage of the Midwest and South.

There are a small number of black Washington reporters, who, like their white brethren, are the foot soldiers tracking regional news, congressional hearings, outer Cabinet offices, and regulatory agencies. Gannett News Service, a leader for affirmative action, numbered two black reporters and an editor in its bureau of thirty employees in 2005. Ellyn Ferguson was a regional reporter for Gannett for 20 years: *"In general, I've found that from the time I started* [1987], *the number of women have increased but minorities have plateaued."*[16]

AT THE SAME time, the parallel world of black journalism devotes only modest space to national news. Once Simeon Booker produced notable coverage of the civil rights struggle for *Jet* and *Ebony,* including the 1955 murder of 14-year-old Emmett Till in Mississippi. Today, no African American newspaper publishes a daily edition; most are now weeklies. The black papers in Washington function efficiently in their own communities but rarely cross the line into mainstream reporting. Black magazines are represented in the press gallery and receive the mandatory one-on-one interview with Colin Powell or Condoleeza Rice, as do foreign journalists. *Essence* magazine sent Cynthia Gordy to Washington when Obama entered the White House, but she later switched to TheRoot.com, an invention of Harvard professor Henry Louis Gates Jr.

that is owned by the *Washington Post,* to provide commentary "from a variety of black perspectives." According to a December 2010 Pew Research Center survey, blacks get 86 percent of their news from TV (whites, 64 percent). Yet the Pew Research Center's report on African American media concludes that "black-oriented TV news programs have been rare, and few have long staying power."[17]

WHY ARE SO few talented African Americans climbing the career ladder in Washington journalism? Robin Sproul, the ABC bureau chief, has given sustained thought to this question as it relates to her company. *"Look at ABC as a pyramid, with the president of the news division at the top and the employees at the bottom. Coming in the door we had an incredibly diverse group of people. Really smart and interesting and great. We hired well. We recruited well. And somewhere in the middle of the pyramid we started to lose some of [the] more diverse, talented people, who would jump and go to other places. . . . Our highest-achieving minority employees who get to the middle find that they are very marketable.*

"That's one thing, but that's not the only thing. . . . There is a basic human tendency to be more comfortable to be with people who are like you. . . . And we would find that those minority employees in the middle would look up there and not see anybody that looked like them and say, 'You're not that comfortable with me, and I am different from you' and they would find that this just wasn't a place where they wanted to be."[18]

Terry Neal was on the fast track. Working for the *Washington Post,* he had been the only black print reporter covering the 2000 presidential campaign, and in 2002 he moved to *Washingtonpost.com. "I'm actually literally having lunch with somebody at the* Post *today about another position back at the paper,"* he told us in 2005, when he was a columnist on the *Post*'s website. *"[It's a] managerial sort of position, an editor at the paper. I'm fortunate enough that I get calls every so often saying, 'Terry, hey! Come talk to us about considering this outside of journalism. . . . ' Life is all about priorities, and the various things that you want to do. While it is appealing to me to . . . be able to use all of the things that I've learned in 15 years of journalism and help other journalists do their jobs better, the trade-off for me is I'll make less money . . . and I'll get to see my kids less. I have a 9-month-old and a 3-year-old. Now I know that journalists are usually folks that say money doesn't matter and kids and family don't matter, but it matters to me.*"[19] Terry Neal became senior vice president and director of strategic media in the Washington office of Hill & Knowlton, an international communications consultancy.

AFTER NEARLY A decade as a *Wall Street Journal* reporter, Frank James joined the *Chicago Tribune* in 1989; he had been in the paper's Washington bureau since 1995. *"When I go to press conferences in Washington, D.C., I'm often the only black reporter. I'm lucky if there's another one. This might be twenty or thirty people, and I'm the only black. It makes me ask myself, 'How could it be that in 2005 you have a press conference in Washington, D.C., a city that is majority black, and I'm the only black reporter here?' It happens a lot on the homeland security beat, but when I covered economics it happened there, privacy and technology issues, it happened there. . . . Does it have a personal effect on me? Sure, it saddens me that here we are in 2005 and I'm the only. I don't want to be the only."*[20] James joined NPR in 2009.

FIVE

THE *NEW YORK TIMES*

THE MOST COMPELLING part of the history of the *New York Times* in the second half of the twentieth century—according to Timesmen in Washington—was the fierce struggle between the bureau in Washington and headquarters in New York.[1] By rights, control belongs to who pays the bills. But in 1932 owner Adolph S. Ochs was in deep need of a Washington bureau chief, the incumbent having died unexpectedly, and Arthur Krock consented to take the job—but only if Ochs gave him total autonomy. In Washington he then reigned as "potentate," thought Tom Wicker. *"He could set out to make Joseph Kennedy the chairman of the Securities and Exchange Commission and succeed."*[2]

By 1953 Krock had turned the bureau over to James ("Scotty") Reston, fearing his star reporter might otherwise jump ship to the *Washington Post*. (Krock continued to write a column.) The new bureau chief was also a skilled bureaucratic player. He maintained a special closeness to the publisher and retained the powers handed down from Krock, including the privilege of hiring his own reporters. According to Wicker, *"A daily schedule* [of stories] *was given to New York and automatically used. The* [Washington bureau's] *complaints were solely objections to copyediting in New York or whether a story was cut from 1,000 words to 850. There is even a tale, probably apocryphal, that two* [Washington] *reporters wrote the same story and both were used* [rather than challenge the powerful Washington bureau]."

Reston's influence within the Washington establishment during the 1950s and 1960s was "impossible to overlook," wrote Joseph Kraft in a contemporary account. "On some big matters the State Department

55

informs him almost automatically, as it would the representative of a major power."[3] Wallace Carroll, a skilled editor, became Reston's news editor, the number-two position, and Reston's talented new hires soon became known around Washington as "Scotty's boys." Russell Baker, the most elegant stylist of the era, came from the *Baltimore Sun.* Anthony Lewis, who had just won a Pulitzer Prize at the *Washington Daily News,* would cover the Justice Department and the Supreme Court. The new Senate correspondent was Allen Drury, of the *Washington Star.* Tom Wicker, from the *Nashville Tennessean,* added strength to the political beat and would later succeed Drury on Capitol Hill. For economics there was Edwin Dale, from the *New York Herald Tribune.* The only one of Scotty's boys to come from the *Times* in New York was Max Frankel, a young man who had gone directly from college at Columbia University to the *Times;* a foreign policy maven, he had already reported from Vienna, Belgrade, and Moscow. This collection of journalists, Frankel later bragged, "golfed with senators, swam with White House aides, and called Cabinet members by their first names."[4]

Their subsequent careers illustrate the types of patterns at this level. Allen Drury stayed around only long enough to pen a blockbuster novel, *Advice and Consent,* which also won a Pulitzer Prize. He then left journalism to spend the rest of his life writing fiction. Ed Dale eventually entered government as spokesman for the Office of Management and Budget under President Reagan. Russell Baker, when he became restless, was given his own column on the op-ed page and became host of PBS's Masterpiece Theatre. Tom Wicker eventually succeeded Reston as Washington bureau chief. Max Frankel succeeded Wicker. Wicker got Krock's column when he was pushed out as bureau chief. Frankel rose from Sunday editor to editorial page editor to executive editor, the title the *Times* gives its editor-in-chief. Tony Lewis, the odd-man-out in the shuffle for bureau chief, chose reassignment in London. Its large number of foreign postings always gives the *Times* some breathing room in managing sticky personnel problems, with London a favored spot in the holding pattern. (It also would be on the itinerary of Howell Raines, a future Washington bureau chief and executive editor.) When Lewis returned, he too got his own column, which he wrote from Cambridge, Massachusetts.

Obviously employees of the *Times* could be on a fast, narrow, and slippery track. But there were others bidding for the services of the talented who didn't make the final cut. Wallace Carroll moved on to become editor-publisher of the *Winston-Salem Journal and Sentinel;* when passed over twice to be national editor, Robert Phelps, another number two in the Washington bureau, joined the *Boston Globe,* rising to managing editor; Walter Rugaber went to the *Greensboro* [N.C.] *Daily News and Record* as executive editor before becoming publisher of the *Roanoke Times;* after his tour as Washington bureau chief, Bill Kovach became editor of the *Atlanta Journal-Constitution.*

There also was collateral damage: others along the way sometimes suffered the consequences of their colleagues' march to the top. When Frankel accepted the editorial page job in New York, for instance, he negotiated the right to clean house. As a result, Graham Hovey and William V. Shannon were moved to the Washington bureau. (Hovey left the *Times* four years later to run the University of Michigan Journalism Fellows program; Shannon, who had written a lively book on the American Irish, was appointed U.S. Ambassador to Ireland.) The trickle-down influence of editors on reporters' careers was especially felt in Washington during the reign of A. M. ("Abe") Rosenthal, an executive editor who had never served in Washington and a man of great passions. Careers on which Rosenthal had a negative impact included those of major figures such as Ben Franklin, Charles Mohr, Eileen Shanahan, and Warren Weaver. Reporters can be left on the shelf, failing to get assignments that they know they deserve. An extreme example was when the *Times* did not give its White House correspondent a slot on President Kennedy's first European trip in 1961. (Bill Lawrence promptly resigned and joined ABC.)[5] Reporters were not fired, except for ethical lapses. In 1977 Rosenthal demanded the resignation of Laura Foreman, who, while in the Philadelphia bureau before coming to Washington, had had an affair with a flamboyant Democratic politician, Henry ("Buddy") Cianfrani. Rosenthal reportedly said, "It's O.K. to fuck elephants; just don't cover the circus."[6]

This was also a period of added turmoil on a paper that was trying to reconcile its shabby record on hiring and promoting women and African Americans with its liberal editorial page pronouncements. In 1974, women employees brought a landmark suit against the *Times;* four years later, when Linda Greenhouse arrived at the bureau, there had been visible improvement. She started with a one-year internship as assistant to

Reston, which led to a chance to try out for the Metro staff. Once she became a certified reporter, she rose to bureau chief in Albany, and she was given a *Times*-sponsored fellowship at Yale to prepare for covering the Supreme Court.

The breakthroughs for blacks, which came later, were more difficult to achieve. Gerald Boyd was an experienced Washington reporter with the St. Louis *Post-Dispatch* whom the *Times* very much wanted to hire. Nonetheless, after a job interview, Rosenthal's assistant remarked, "I really enjoyed your clips; they're so well written. Did you write them yourself or did someone write them for you?"[7] The obverse was that some inexperienced journalists were promoted too quickly.

Russell Baker saw New York as "filled with people of high ambition and dangerous cunning."[8] He could have added, "and too many editors." As economics reporter Edward Cowan put it, *"The* Times *is an organization top heavy with editors. We can get instructions from one* [New York] *desk in the morning and another desk in the afternoon."*[9] The New York complaint was that the Washington reporters were too close to the officials that they covered. Also, New York did not forgive Washington for the stories that got away, notably the Nixon presidential campaign's gritty break-in at the Watergate Hotel in 1972. Howell Raines, to become Washington's severest critic, called the bureau "a collection of savants and nerds that felt like a cross between the Faculty Club and the Junior Electrons Science Club."[10]

A serious problem was that New York and Washington editors often assigned different weights to what they considered newsworthy. David Broder witnessed that when he joined the *Times* in the mid-1960s. New York editors, he wrote, "had a certain few stimuli to which they reacted in a political story: Instances of extremism, either of the New Left or the Radical Right; political action by Southern (but not northern) Negroes; Kennedy stories of any variety. These may be the grist of political talk at New York cocktail parties, but . . . they do not begin to embrace the variety of concerns that really animate national politics."[11] (Broder quit the *Times* after sixteen months to continue his career as the *Washington Post's* chief political correspondent.)

New York was destined to win the battle for ultimate control. But first there had to be a "civil war." Tom Wicker, who replaced Reston in 1964, lacked his mentor's standing in the organization and his aptitude for infighting. In the judgment of the top editors, removing Wicker would reassert New York's control, and they convinced publisher Arthur Ochs Sulzberger of the necessity for change in 1968, a demanding year for political news. Then they made their mistake: they gave him the wrong candidate to replace Wicker. James Greenfield, a former assistant secretary of state, was an outsider who had worked at the *Times* for only seven months. Reston, still a columnist, warned that "a smooth transition to Greenfield is out of the question, and a stormy transition may be more costly than it is worth." Next he raised his level of concern, telling Sulzberger that "Greenfield was the worst idea since Eisenhower had chosen Nixon as his vice president."[12] Sulzberger withdrew the appointment. Greenfield was out, and Wicker could remain until the end of the year. For the Washington editors, it was a Pyrrhic victory; no bureau chief ever again had the power of a Krock or a Reston. Years later I asked Bill Kovach if he had ever appointed new reporters when he was bureau chief: *"No, although I twice convinced Abe Rosenthal* [in New York] *to make hires."*[13]

Rick Smith's Story

In 1978 the bureau chief was Hedrick Smith, who got the job in 1976 after one of those dream careers that the *Times* can offer its top-tier correspondents, which included crisscrossing the South during the civil rights explosions of the early 1960s, doing a short tour in Vietnam, reporting from Cairo on a wide swath of the Middle East, coming back home to be part of the foreign affairs beat in Washington, then going off to Moscow and writing a best seller, *The Russians*. But being bureau chief was an experience of a different order:

"I don't think they really thought much about what it meant to take a first-rate reporter and make him or her an executive. It was a very different experience to have grown up with a group of reporters, run with them, covered stories with them, gone to parties with them, watched them raise their kids as a peer, and suddenly be their boss, determining assignments. I don't mean just daily assignments, because usually the news editor and others handled that, but their career assignments. Whether or not they should stay working in Washington or were sent to New York; what their pay levels were; who handled some of the biggest

coverage, particularly during campaigns. I didn't have sufficient prepara-
tion for that. It was a shock to me. People complain, they gripe, they're
upset; this is a high-tension business. The bureau chief becomes a target
of that. You can hand out goodies, but you also have to take lots of
responsibility.

"The Times *then had a lot of feuding between New York and Wash-*
ington. Under Reston, Reston had been in control. When Reston left
and Tom Wicker took over, the editors in New York made life miserable
for him. Abe Rosenthal was the executive editor. He wanted to control
the whole paper. He didn't want Washington to be a separate barony. .
. . I knew what the situation was. But in terms of any kind of manage-
ment training or preparation, I would say there was none. In terms of
the power and authority, there almost always are periodically vacancies
that come up. . . . [There] was a woman named Eileen Shanahan, a
very hot-tempered but talented financial reporter who deserved to be the
lead financial reporter when Ed Dale retired. I wanted to name her. Abe
Rosenthal told me, 'Over my dead body.' He couldn't stand her.

"And the world had changed a lot from the time when Reston was*
bureau chief and I was a young member of the bureau. . . . The Times
was it *in terms of Washington coverage, which gave us all kinds of entré.*
Reston was kind of the bulletin board for the highest power players in
Washington—secretary of state, secretary of defense. . . . By the time I
took over, which was 12 years later, the power of the television networks
appealed to the media types managing the news for the White House.
. . . The Times *wasn't unimportant, but it was one of several important*
players. . . . And I think my expectations of myself, and I'm sure Abe's
expectations and the paper's expectations, were that I was going to be
another Reston. I don't think the game was there. I wasn't another
Reston. Scotty was a very unusual, very talented guy. And I'm a good
journalist, but I wasn't as talented as he was.

"Bill Kovach came in and became the non-writing bureau chief, and*
I continued as the chief correspondent [until 1985]. *. . . And I'm in my*
mid-50s. I couldn't see myself staying at the Times *to retirement. . . . I'd*
been with the Times *for 26 years.* [Smith decided to leave the *Times* to
do TV documentaries.]. *. . . I remember typing up* [a letter of resigna-
tion] *and getting ready to take it into the publisher. And I thought, 'God,*
I wonder after I jump off the high board here if there's going to be any

*water in the pool. Am I going to go splat on the bottom of the pool? Is it
going to work?' And it worked wonderfully, and I was very happy to have
done it. It was just immediately challenging. It was a brand new medium.
And it came at a time when I think lots of us need a growth spurt.*"[14]

THE BUREAU THAT Bill Kovach took over from Smith in 1978 was in need
of repair, for morale and other purposes. A young reporter, Nancy Hicks,
pointed to "the square dance crisis" in 1977 as a symbol of discontent:
"About three weeks ago, the Times *had a square dance and almost no
reporters came. Rick Smith said, 'But everybody used to come to Scotty's
square dances.'"*[15] A number of reporters were approaching retirement;
as *Times* veteran Maggie Hunter noted, *"Reporters are often disgruntled
by the time they retire because of how badly they are being used toward
the end of their careers."* (She cited the example of the great war correspondent Homer Bigart, who retired in 1972.)[16] There were several gaps
where key reporters had joined the new Carter administration and had to
be replaced from within or outside. Eileen Shanahan left to be assistant
secretary for public affairs in the Department of Health, Education, and
Welfare; diplomatic correspondent Leslie Gelb became an assistant secretary of state, with the politico-military affairs portfolio. There was the
perennial hovering of New York, viewed by former Timesman Anthony
Ripley as "management by fear."[17]

Unions struck the three major New York papers from August 10 to
November 5, 1978, and no editions of the *Times* were printed. Kovach,
however, had one unique situation to confront. Shortly after the press
operators walked out, Arthur Ochs Sulzberger Jr. reported for work in
Washington. Having a tyro reporter in the bureau who was also the publisher's son could be awkward for all concerned: the bureau chief, other
reporters, and the son. Sulzberger was a conscientious and popular col-
league during his two-plus years in the bureau. But after hours he hung
out with a small group of young staffers, forming "a kind of Brat Pack in
the Washington office," while also sharing a beach house with reporters
Judy Miller and Steven Rattner, who were "romantically involved at the
time."[18] Sulzberger Sr. asked Kovach to be a wise guide to his son, if possible. *"Kovach warned Arthur Jr. about the dangers of consorting with
such an exclusive group of friends. . . . Arthur Jr. listened politely, but he
put no distance between himself and his colleagues."*[19]

Rick Burt's Story

The choice of a replacement for Les Gelb was head-shakingly odd, but so too had been Gelb's appointment. Both Gelb and Richard (Rick) Burt had been national security intellectuals, coming from a think tank and a university: Gelb from the Brookings Institution in Washington, Burt from the International Institute for Strategic Studies in London. Burt claimed "some rudimentary journalist experience," which amounted to stringing for spare change in London and some copy editing at the *Boston Globe* while he was in graduate school. Yet Gelb's success made it possible for the *Times* to let Burt start a journalism career at the top:

"Getting into the Washington bureau of the New York Times *is a real achievement for most journalists. It's where I think everyone was very happy to be, but they also felt that they had earned it. And they weren't sure that I had earned it. They weren't even sure that I was a real journalist. . . . I was enormously lucky to [sit] next to* [State Department correspondent] *Bernie Gwertzman. . . . I remember my first encounter with him. The bureau chief, Rick Smith, said, 'We'd like you to do a kind of scene-setter, just saying* [Soviet Foreign Minister] *Gromyko is arriving and here are the issues and this is what might happen. . . .' Bernie just kind of sidled over while I was laboring on my typewriter, and he realized that I was on deadline. He actually took the copy paper out of my typewriter, ripped it out, and rewrote the first five paragraphs of the story and then gave it back to me. He had taken the third graph and put it in the lead and turned it into a really first-rate piece. He'd saved my bacon, and so I became a kind of neophyte with Bernie; I was under his wing for probably six months, and finally, just like the mother bird that pushes the babies out of the nest, I had gotten enough of the craft to be able to do that.*

"You'll remember during the Carter period there was a pretty controversial and interesting guy, Zbigniew Brzezinski. The way the situation was structured when I came to the Times *was there was a big group of reporters who covered the State Department, the political people in the White House had their White House press corps, and you had the Pentagon reporters. There was really nobody who had a relationship [with] or covered Brzezinski and his* [National Security Council] *staff. . . .* [There was a bitter struggle between Brzezinski and Secretary of State

Cyrus Vance; Vance eventually resigned.] *And I covered that. The way I covered it was developing relationships with Brzezinski and his people. . . . At one stage State Department spokesman Hodding Carter actually was quoted as saying when Zbig Brzezinski's mouth moves, Rick Burt's pen writes."*

Jimmy Carter was defeated. Ronald Reagan became president. Les Gelb returned to the *New York Times.* Rick Burt was offered and accepted the job that Gelb was vacating at the State Department, *"so we essentially had replaced each other."* Burt went on to become U.S. ambassador to Germany and then chief U.S. negotiator in strategic arms reduction talks. *"To be quite candid, when I went to the* Times, *I didn't see it as necessarily a long-term career move. I certainly didn't plan to go into government, but I didn't consider myself an ink-stained wretch. You know, the* Times *was full of these people who had been the editor of their college newspaper and wanted to be a journalist and be at the* New York Times *since they were 12 years old. I didn't entirely relate to them, and at the same time I did relate to a different group of people: the foreign policy community. I was young enough and dumb enough not to even think about long-term career planning. I just thought it was a wonderful opportunity to do something very important at a great institution."*[20]

Steve Roberts's Story

And then there was Steven V. Roberts, who could have materialized from Burt's description of "these people who had been the editor of their college newspaper and wanted to be a journalist and be at the *New York Times* since they were 12 years old":

"I ran the school newspaper in the sixth grade. The first day I went to high school, the first thing I did was go out for the student newspaper. And by junior year [I] was the editor. . . . So then when I went off to college, [I] did exactly the same thing. The first day that I arrived at Harvard in the fall of 1960, I went out for the school newspaper, the Harvard Crimson. . . . *I was also very lucky during the spring of my freshman year to get the job as the* New York Times *stringer on campus."*

Looking forward to graduation, Roberts wrote Scotty Reston asking for a summer internship. *"Reston wrote back, 'Really what I want to do is create a full-time, year-long clerkship with a young person working*

for me for a full year. Would you be interested?' I was interested. . . .
The first time I met him he was taking me around the Washington
bureau and introducing me to some of these people who became among
the greatest names of the half-century in American journalism—Max
Frankel, Russell Baker, Anthony Lewis. And Reston says, 'This is Rob-
erts. He's going to come work for me in the spring.' . . . I had one week
between Harvard and the New York Times."

At the end of Roberts's clerkship year, Tom Wicker, the new bureau
chief, wanted to hire Roberts to be a general assignment reporter. *"At*
which point New York exploded and said, 'What are you talking about?
The kid is 22 years old. We don't hire reporters at 22.'. . . Reston came
into my office and said, 'Have you heard from New York yet?' I said, 'No
boss, I haven't.' Literally, he said, 'Come with me' [and] we walked out
of 1701 K Street, where our office was, got in a cab, went to National
Airport, flew to New York, marched into the office of the managing editor,
Clifton Daniel, and Reston said, 'Are you going to hire this kid or not?'
At which point Daniel said, 'OK, OK!' That's how I became a reporter
on the New York Times *at 22. . . . You talk about career patterns."*

Roberts's career took him to New York during the difficult days of
Mayor John Lindsay's administration and to Chicago during the "police
riots" at the 1968 Democratic convention. Then he was Los Angeles
bureau chief for five years, and he spent three and a half years working
out of Athens when the Turks invaded Cyprus and democracy returned
to Greece. "[In 1978] *I got a phone call in the middle of the night from a*
man named Hedrick Smith, the newly named Washington bureau chief.
He said, 'I hear you're having trouble figuring out a new foreign assign-
ment.' I said, 'That's true, I am.' He said, 'How would you like to come
back and be one of my reporters? I'd love to have you in the Washington
bureau.' And this had been my dream since the day I walked through
that door 11 years before as Scotty Reston's assistant.

"My great dream had always been to cover Congress. . . . I remem-
ber [when] I came back to Washington [after the 1980 election], *I was*
still holding my suitcase as I walked into the bureau. The then-bureau
chief who had succeeded Rick Smith, a man named Bill Kovach, says
basically, 'Get your ass up to Capitol Hill. The new chairman of the
Senate Judiciary Committee is about to hold a press conference.' From
that day on I was the congressional correspondent. . . . I had a great

time covering Capitol Hill. I did it for six years. . . . I loved the Hill. I
just loved it." In many news organizations, that might have been how
the story ends—with a reporter working his way up to where he wants
to be. At the *Washington Post,* Helen Dewar stayed on as Senate correspondent from 1979 until her retirement in 2004. But that's not how
it played out for Roberts:

"The Times *decided they needed a change at the White House* [in
1986]. *You don't turn down the job of White House correspondent of the*
New York Times. *You just can't turn it down."* Then, with a new president taking office in 1989, the bureau changed White House correspondents again. *"I was 45 years old. I had been at the* New York Times *for*
25 years. I knew at some point I was going to run out of options. They
were not going to make me a columnist. I didn't want to be an editor. . . .
The other thing that had happened was the Times *had an exceptionally*
stupid and backward policy about television. They thought that anybody
who wanted [reporters] *on television was stealing something that the*
New York Times *owned. I was really starting to acquire a certain reputa-*
tion on television. But they were closing that off because they were very
resistant to my doing more."

Roberts quit. *"Mort Zuckerman was the owner* [of U.S. News &
World Report.] *He was looking to hire a couple of very high-visibility*
people. . . . He was willing to pay almost double what I was making at
the New York Times. . . . *And for seven years I had a very good time*
there. But again, you never know what's going to happen in your insti-
tution. There was a man named Jim Fallows who had written a book
called Breaking the News, *in which he did a whole chapter attacking me*
and Cokie [Roberts's wife] *as all that was bad in Washington journal-*
ism—elitists, took money for speeches. And overnight he became the
editor of the magazine. I went to him and said, 'I'm willing to work
with you.' And he said, 'I'm not willing to work with you.' And he fired
me. . . . I had been teaching at George Washington as a adjunct for six
years at that point. . . . And then one day the phone rang, and it was
the president of George Washington University, who whispered the two
magic words: endowed chair. So I came to teach as a full-time professor.

"My final point is, and this took years, . . . I found myself recalibrat-
ing how I got my professional satisfaction. It used to be getting stopped
in airports because people saw me on TV or read my articles in the New

York Times. *And that was a great buzz, and I still love it. But over the years I've clearly reset my clock. . . . I had lunch earlier this week with a former student who is now a Jerusalem correspondent. I'd much rather see her on television than see myself on television. . . . I'm not saying I learned that overnight. But I did learn it. So when you talk about professional evolution it's a whole different way of thinking. It's a whole different way of measuring gratification and success.* "[21]

Marty Tolchin's Story

Whereas Steve Roberts became a *Times* reporter by jumping the queue with the aid of Scotty Reston, Martin Tolchin, who for many years would be Roberts's partner in covering Capitol Hill, followed the plodding path to reporter laid down in New York, starting as a "copy boy"—in this case, a copy boy with a law degree:

"*I got a bachelor of law degree, and then I was in the service for two years, and I came out and took a VA course called 'How to Get a Job,' the burden of which was go for something that you're really interested in. So I wrote to 110 editors and had six interviews and four job offers* [in 1954]. . . . *What I was offered was copy boy jobs and mailroom jobs. I took the one at the* New York Times. *Then when you get that job* [according to the VA course], *consider it a foot in the door and make yourself useful to the people who are doing the kind of work you want to do and someday a task will come up and somebody will be on a project, somebody will be on vacation, somebody will be sick, and they will need somebody and they will look at you and they'll say 'Well, what the heck, he knows how to bring us coffee, he knows how to rip copy off the old teletype machines. Let's give the kid a break.' I followed that to a tee. It worked for me.*

"*I was a copy boy for a year. At that time if you weren't promoted after a year, you were expected to resign. But I was promoted. Not to reporter, but to news clerk, which meant I did a little writing but basically I was still a gofer, and after six months I was promoted to news assistant at the United Nations bureau, and then, three years start to finish, I was promoted to reporter. My first reporting job was on the women's page, which in those days was 'food, fashions, furnishings, and family,' and I was 'family' and reported on the economics of aging. . . . After five years*

*of that, Abe Rosenthal came in as metropolitan editor and persuaded
me to join the news staff. . . . Since I had only done features, I had a lot
of difficulty with deadlines. . . . so they put me on night re-write, which
meant 7 at night 'til 3 in the morning, days off middle of the week. . . .
After about two years of that, I was brought down to cover 'health and
hospitals,' in which capacity I wrote a series that led to a few arrests, a
few convictions, after which I was sent to City Hall as bureau chief, after
which I did politics in general in New York, and then I was transferred
to Washington.*

"*So I came to Washington* [in 1973] *as a regional reporter because,
as Abe said, in those days you couldn't get there from here. The Washington bureau was its own hierarchy and was constantly at war with
New York, hired its own people, and so the only way I could get to
Washington was as a regional reporter, which meant that I covered the
New York, Connecticut, and New Jersey congressional delegations. . . .
I did that for about two and a half years, and then they asked me if I
would like to be congressional correspondent working for the Washington bureau, and I said 'Sure, I'd love to.'*"

Except for several years covering the Carter White House, Martin
Tolchin reported from Capitol Hill until 1994. He had spent 40 years on
the *Times*, almost evenly divided between New York and Washington,
and he was about to receive an offer of a kind that might come to a
prominent journalist: the job you can't refuse. "*I left the* Times *because
a New York financier asked me to start a newspaper* [to cover Capitol
Hill]. *I turned him down several times, and he kept coming back and
kept coming back. . . . Finally I told this financier, 'Yes, I'm interested.'
It took six months to get them to give me what I wanted, which basically was a piece of the action. I would not do this if I did not have an
equity interest in this. . . . I had spent my life as a reporter. I had almost
zero managerial experience. . . . I had to find an office. . . . Then I had
to find a printer and a distributor, and then I had to hire personnel. . . .
The hardest thing was hiring an advertising staff because I just didn't
know anybody in advertising. . . . It was really quite harrowing. People
tell me two things about a start-up. You'll never work harder and you'll
never have more fun, and in both cases that's been true. I was then 66
years old when I started* The Hill, *a time when I, by rights, should have
been in a nursing home, right? It took three years [before] we made a*

profit. . . . We launched in September of '94 and just lost $100,000 that year. The next year we lost a lot of money, about $800,000. But the third year we made a modest profit, about $200,000, and now it really is a cash cow, it's raking in multi millions, multi millions, multi, multi, multi millions of dollars."[22]

Bernie Gwertzman's Story

Another Timesman "hooked on journalism," Bernard Gwertzman, had been managing editor of *Highlands,* the monthly newspaper at Albert Leonard Junior High School in New Rochelle, New York. He was also managing editor of the *Harvard Crimson.* After starting his professional career at the *Washington Star,* Gwertzman became Moscow bureau chief for the *Times,* a position he held from 1969 to 1971: *"I was recommended as a journalist who spoke Russian."* He returned to Washington as chief diplomatic correspondent: *"I stayed in that job until 1987. Then there was a turnover in the top editorial management when Max Frankel replaced Abe Rosenthal as executive editor. I was getting a little restless doing the same thing from administration to administration. I was invited to be deputy foreign editor, and after much thought, my wife and I and our two boys moved to New York. I stayed in that job until August of '89, when I was promoted to foreign editor. [When] I had been in that job for six years, [executive editor] Joe Lelyveld asked me to look at something else. I really thought at that point my journalism career was over; I had just turned 60.*

"My oldest son, James, was at Harvard and majoring in computer science. He said, 'Come look at my computer lab,' so I went into his computer lab, and he had this big machine that looked impressive to me. I had a Macintosh at home. He said, 'Let me show you something, dad.' That was the first time I had seen the World Wide Web. It showed some exhibits. It had pictures and text. As far as I knew, the Internet up until then was just text. And I said to him, 'James, if you can have text on a computer screen, why can't we have newspapers on the Web?' I said to Lelyveld, 'Maybe we should do something like this.' One thing led to another, and the Times *started a task force on online journalism. That task force put out the first* Times *website in January of '96. I became the first editor of the website* [nytimes.com]. *We hired a bunch of kids who*

were good at technology. The Times *looked down on the website as some freakish slide show.*

"*So I changed completely, from the traditional journalist to a website journalist. That was quite an education for me.* [Gwertzman was 67 years old in 2002.] *So the time came to move on. I took retirement with a buyout.*" Leslie Gelb, now president of the Council on Foreign Relations, asked Gwertzman to come to CFR as a full-time online consultant for its website. His regular foreign affairs interview column is called "Gwertzman Asks the Experts." "*I enjoyed in the twilight of my career starting Internet journalism. That was an amazing change, and it worked out well for me.*"[23]

The Stories of Jerry King and Phil Shabecoff

"Every bureau needs good utility infielders and some specialists," recalled Rick Smith.[24] Seth (Jerry) King was a utility infielder; Phil Shabecoff was a specialist. King was the Chicago bureau chief in 1977 when "*the longtime ag* [agriculture] *specialist in the bureau in Washington retired, and they asked me if I would go join the bureau and cover the Interior* [Department]. *The way the Washington bureau was run at that time was that you had assignments in these fields of concentration, but there was quite a bit of moving around. Reporters were often called on to look at things that were not exactly in their field.*" King also made the bureau's arrangements for the 1980 and 1984 Republican and Democratic parties' presidential conventions. "*I was placed in charge of all the logistical planning for the coverage of the conventions, the physical planning, housing, and so on. . . . You took a couple of months. The biggest problem always was housing because the* Times *took fifty to sixty people out there to cover the conventions.*" King retired at 65 in 1985. "*I had a very interesting, active career with the paper.*"[25]

King turned over the Interior Department portfolio to Philip Shabecoff, who for many years had been unsuccessfully lobbying *Times* editors to create an environment beat. "*It wasn't until Reagan became president and installed a couple of ideologues as heads of the Environment Protection Agency and the Interior* [Department] *that it became a hot political issue,* [and I was allowed] *to cover the environment full time.*" Shabecoff had been a foreign correspondent, and he was assigned to the White

House beat during the Nixon and Ford presidencies.[26] His environment assignment lasted 14 years. *"Some editors just didn't have a clue about the environmental stories' significance and had the wrong impression about the way I was covering it. They thought I was writing too much about what the economy was doing to the environment and not enough about how environmental regulation was hurting the economy. So they took me off the beat. And I quit."* He founded an online publication, *Greenwire,* which he eventually sold to the *National Journal.* Shabecoff was with the *Times* for 32 years. *"I guess my end was not particularly happy. But oh, I had just the best of times! I couldn't have imagined a better career."*

NOT ALL JOURNALISTS at the *Times* had the same odds of survival. Take the case of a group of hard-charging investigative reporters grafted onto the bureau to atone for its belated response to Watergate. Jo Thomas came from the *Detroit Free Press,* where she had uncovered a mafia scheme to take over the trucking business in the city. Her new job, she concluded, was not a good fit. *"The* Times *was more interested in stuff under investigation rather than investigating stuff. In other words, they loved the stories that said, 'The Justice Department is investigating this or that.'"*[27] Tony Marro called them "the faster off the mark" reporters; none stayed with the *Times.*[28] Seymour Hersh, famed for exposing the My Lai massacre as a freelancer in 1969, was in the bureau from 1972 to 1975 and again in 1979. Nor did any of the black journalists in the bureau during this period remain with the *Times.* Ernest Holsendolph became an editorial writer and columnist at the *Atlanta Journal-Constitution.* Nancy Hicks and her husband, Robert Maynard, who worked for the *Washington Post,* went to Berkeley to create an institute to train black journalists.[29]

Still, Tony Marro, who left the *Times* for *Newsday* and eventually became its editor, recalled, *"I enjoyed working there. I had a good time there. By reputation, it was an unhappy place to work. But I used to tell people that I was one of the three people who enjoyed it, and I did. I enjoyed it from the day I got there* [in 1976] *until the day I left* [in 1979]." The *New York Times* bureau in Washington had thirty slots for reporters.[30] We interviewed seventeen; of those, seven remained with the *Times* until retirement and ten went on to other places.

SIX

THE NETWORKS

As 1978 CAME to a close, the three prime television news programs were in a near tie. Of all TV viewers, 27 percent tuned to the *CBS Evening News with Walter Cronkite;* 25 percent, to the *NBC Nightly News;* and 24 percent, to ABC's *World News Tonight.* The Edward R. Murrow era at CBS had ended in 1961, when Murrow left to join the Kennedy administration. The sixties had been dominated by NBC's pairing of anchors Chet Huntley in New York and David Brinkley in Washington, but by 1968 the public's trust in Cronkite had regained the lead for CBS. Huntley retired in 1970. It became a three-way race when Roone Arledge arrived at ABC News as chairman in 1977, bringing the flair that had created the *Wide World of Sports.* The networks went from treating their news divisions as "loss leaders" to expecting them to be "profit centers," remembers Bob Schieffer: *"There's a difference in putting on the news and putting on something that's designed to attract viewers."*[1]

The 1980–84 period was characterized by fierce jockeying for position. After taking over in 1980, the new president of NBC News, Bill Small, remarked, "I didn't come to NBC to stay in second place."[2] (Small had been CBS's Washington bureau chief before moving to NBC.) Also in 1980, Cronkite announced plans to retire; CBS announced that its new anchor in 1981 would be Dan Rather; Roger Mudd, his prime competitor, asked for an immediate release from his contract; Small of NBC hired Mudd, along with two other CBS correspondents, brothers Marvin Kalb and Bernard Kalb; Brinkley left NBC after a bitter dispute with Small; and ABC's Arledge hired Brinkley to create a new type of Sunday program. Small was forced to resign at NBC in 1982; Mudd and

Tom Brokaw became co-anchors of *NBC Nightly News,* working together from 1982 to 1983, when Brokaw became sole anchor; and Mudd and Marvin Kalb became co-moderators of *Meet the Press,* working together from 1984 to 1985, when Kalb became sole moderator.

Marvin Kalb had been CBS's chief diplomatic correspondent: *"In 1975 I was out of work for eight months because of a bad back. Bill [Small] used to visit me at home. After a couple of months I said to him, 'I want you to take me off salary because I am not doing anything for your network. I am just lying here.' And he said no, that he is going to keep me on full salary. Then I said, 'Well, do it on half.' 'No, full salary until you get better.' And that was eight months. And I never forgot that. And in 1980 when he became the president of NBC and he called me and he said, 'I'd like you to come over here,' I knew that I owed Bill, so I went."* Bernard Kalb, who had a distinguished career as a foreign correspondent in Asia, went to NBC "really to be with Marvin." He called this "sibling love."[3]

IN A FINELY detailed memoir, *The Place To Be: Washington, CBS, and the Glory Days of Television News,* Roger Mudd described the floor plan of the CBS bureau at 2020 M Street, where "along the south wall of the newsroom were five cubicles, each about six-feet-by-eight, their walls covered in a beige textured paper and each equipped with a desk, a chair, a typewriter, a telephone, and a television star." This was known as "The Front Row." "The Back Row" was "a scattering of desks and chairs and mail trays. To type up a story, second stringers had to scrounge to find an available typewriter in the main newsroom."[4] Although the Washington offices of ABC and NBC did not happen to use CBS's interior decorator, all networks clearly played by the same variation on Orwell's dictum: All journalists are equal, but some are more equal than others.

In the cubicles on the particular CBS front row that Mudd described sat Dan Rather, Daniel Schorr, Marvin Kalb, Roger Mudd, and George Herman. Had there been a sixth cubicle, Mudd contended, it would have gone to Robert Pierpoint. Those with front row seats could expect to have long careers at a network unless unusual events dictated otherwise, as when Schorr left CBS after a major dispute, moved on to become the first anchor at Ted Turner's new Cable News Network and, after a dispute with Turner, moved on to National Public Radio, where he remained a commentator until his death at 93 years of age.[5] Herman and Pierpoint spent their entire careers at CBS: Herman retired at 67, after 43 years with the network, and Pierpoint at 64, after 40 years. Both started as war correspondents in Korea and ended on Sunday programs, Herman as the moderator on *Face the Nation* and Pierpoint on *Sunday Morning*. That was "a big change," remembered Pierpoint. *"I would spend anywhere from a week to ten days on a single story, and it might get 10 to 15 minutes on the air. Whereas covering the White House or the State Department, you were lucky if you got a minute and thirty seconds on the air."*[6] He was not celebrating his good luck. It's a truism among television journalists that brief appearances on a weeknight news program top long appearances on weekends, when the audiences are smaller.[7]

Only Marvin Kalb chose to leave journalism: *"I left NBC in 1987. . . . I had a very good job. . . . But I began to be somewhat unhappy with the way news was being presented, with my role in the presentation, the value system that I began to see come into play. . . . Somewhere around '86 going into '87 part of my mind already left NBC and left journalism. But I didn't know where I was going. . . . And then suddenly out of the blue comes a telephone call from Graham Allison, who was the dean of the Kennedy School at Harvard: 'You would be the perfect guy to run the Shorenstein Center* [on the Press, Politics and Public Policy],*' which at that time was just starting. And given the fact that I was sort of half out of NBC in my mind, not in theirs, I decided to go all the way. From a financial point of view it was one of the dumbest moves I'd ever made. I took a 90 percent cut in salary to join Harvard. . . . But it was a fantastic challenge, and I loved every minute of it."*[8]

THE WHITE HOUSE is the TV correspondent's ultimate beat in terms of on-air time. Explained Brit Hume: *"The main reason [is that] if you're a network . . . trying to think of a way to organize and conceive of your coverage of Washington, the simplest way to do it is to have the president be the protagonist and all of the other institutions in Washington be part of the supporting cast, or the obstacle course depending on the circumstances, and you trace the progress of the presidency. And the suspense is whether the president will do well or badly on these individual skirmishes on legislation or confirmation of nominees or whatever and how he will accumulate or spend or use his political capital and so forth. And it makes sense; it's a narrative, it's a story, it's human, so it's sort of natural.*"[9]

For some, such as Dan Rather and Sam Donaldson, being at the White House becomes a springboard to fame.[10] *"To walk down the street with Sam Donaldson was to be in the presence of a truly famous man,"* remembered Hume. Still, despite the benefits of celebrity, some reporters find the beat confining and the travel exhausting. Changes are most likely to come when presidents change and the networks give a White House assignment to the reporter who covered the winning candidate, as when Bill Plante followed Ronald Reagan into the White House in January 1981 and then returned with Bill Clinton in January 1993.[11] CBS wrongly thought Texan Dan Rather would connect better with Texan Lyndon Johnson when Johnson suddenly became president. Phil Jones was made Capitol Hill correspondent when CBS moved Bob Schieffer to the White House to cover Gerald Ford. The game of musical chairs, with one less chair than the number of circling reporters, can be awkward for the players. Yet in rare circumstances TV journalists better their careers by leaving the White House.

Judy Woodruff had been at NBC for almost nine years, six at the White House. *"I have always been the restless spirit. . . . I had learned a lot of things and I thought I wanted to try something different, and so I made the change . . . to be on the ground floor of a whole new thing in television, an hour-long news program, no commercial breaks. . . . Most of my friends told me I was absolutely nuts . . . to go to work at this little upstart that PBS has. . . . It ended up being a marvelous thing to do because* The NewsHour *took off and it became—certainly not in terms of audience numbers but in terms of influences—it became one of the most influential newscasts in the country and remains that to this day."*[12]

For Brit Hume, after 11 years on Capitol Hill and 8 years at the White House, leaving ABC was *"the easiest decision I ever made. . . . If you don't want to leave Washington, you can kind of work your way through the available beats and then you've done them all and then where do you go? . . . ABC News had nothing to offer me. . . . They would have given me some title, 'chief Washington correspondent' or some such, and along comes Fox News.* [Rupert Murdoch launched Fox News in 1996, with Roger Ailes as the CEO.]

"In late 1997, [Ailes] said to me, I want you to do a political show at six every night. . . . He said, 'I want to put it on the air in March.'. . . We were just getting started around January—we didn't have a studio, we didn't have a director, we didn't have squat. . . . The Monica Lewinski scandal broke. My wife Kim—who was a veteran producer from ABC who was hired by Fox ahead of me . . . and she was the bureau chief— walked up to me and said . . . this is the time to start your show, right now. . . . I called Roger Ailes. He said, 'We'll start it tonight.'. . . and we put the show on the air. It was called Special Report, *which was a dumb name . . . and still is a dumb name. . . . Well, it's been a bigger rating success than we ever imagined."*

AT THE STATE Department, reporters look "grave, important, and inscrutable," Russell Baker once observed.[13] If so, perhaps they acquired their polish by working first as foreign correspondents: Ted Koppel in Latin America, Hong Kong, and Vietnam; Marvin Kalb in Moscow; and John Dancy in Berlin, London, and Moscow. Barrie Dunsmore spent 30 years at ABC, 18 overseas, 12 in Washington.

While no less competitive than their Front Row colleagues, as a group State Department reporters were more collegial, possibly because in traveling with secretaries of state around the world, they had to kill a great deal of time together. John McWethy counted touching down in more than fifty countries. Kalb and Koppel, in the midst of Kissinger's shuttle diplomacy, wrote a novel together, whose cover proclaimed that in Henry Kissinger's opinion, it was "a great work of fiction."[14]

According to Dunsmore, what most affected the careers of these reporters was that suddenly "the cold war was over" and with it the narrative that had made the world outside the United States worthy of television evening news coverage. The tip that Charles Kuralt learned when assigned to cover South America was that to get on the air, "put Fidel into every lead."[15] But by 1995 Dunsmore found *"there was precious little interest in foreign affairs and international news. And I didn't really have something that was greatly desired by any of the networks at that time."*[16] So he retired to Vermont "as a relatively young man of 56."

Kalb was 56 years old when he went to Harvard. Dancy, 59, had been with NBC for 30 years when he retired in 1996. McWethy, ABC's chief national security correspondent, moved to Keystone, Colorado, at 56, only to die in a ski accident at 61. For younger retirees in good health, having covered diplomatic relations offered as many university gigs as they wanted to take during their leisure time. Kalb was delighted to welcome his old friends to Harvard: Dancy and Dunsmore each spent a semester at the Shorenstein Center. Dunsmore did a study of the potential consequences of live television coverage of war. Dancy also was a Shapiro Fellow at George Washington University's School of Media and Public Affairs, taught journalism at Duke, and for two years served as director of international media studies and visiting professor of communications at Brigham Young University.

Ted Koppel's career was of another order. Koppel was 39 years old when Iranian students took over the U.S. embassy in Tehran on November 8, 1979. ABC went on the air at 11:30 with a late-night special, *America Held Hostage,* and an outraged nation began waiting nightly for the next episode. It was Roone Arledge's opportunity to seize a chunk of time for his news division that ABC was not putting to good commercial use anyway and that belonged to NBC's *Tonight Show.* The anchor slot was given to Koppel after Frank Reynolds, the *World News Tonight* anchor, chose not to take on the added assignment. The program evolved into *Nightline,* and by Day 444—January 20, 1981—when Ronald Reagan took the presidential oath and the Iranians sent the hostages home, Koppel and his program had rightly earned a place in the history of TV news broadcasting.

IN 1978 THE Supreme Court was covered at each network by correspondents who had legal training. Carl Stern (NBC) and Tim O'Brien (ABC) earned law degrees while reporting for local TV stations, Stern in Cleveland, O'Brien in New Orleans. Fred Graham (CBS) got a law degree first and came to the network from the *New York Times.* The history of their expanding disputes with their bosses generally came down to how to fit complicated court cases into an increasingly entertainment-driven medium.

Carl Stern: *"The principal problem was what had been a reporter's business became a producer's business. . . . The principal producer to whom I reported in New York [had] very strong views as to what she thought the Court was doing, which occasionally did parallel what the Court was doing, but not all the time. . . . She would change my copy . . .*

and I'd say, 'Well, they didn't say that.' And she'd say, 'Well, it means the same thing, and people will understand it better.' . . . Frequently it reached the point where I didn't believe half the things I was saying on the air. Not that it was blatantly false, but that it was inaccurate. . . . I had this phone call from [Stephen] *Friedman* [the evening news' senior executive], *he's bawling me out. He says, 'I've had this fairness bullshit up to here. What matters is not whether we're fair in this story or fair in that story. What matters is whether we are fair overall.' Now I ask you, as a rational human being, how you get to be fair overall? It's sort of like the guy with one foot in boiling water and one foot in ice water. On average, he's comfortable? . . . It just became an entirely different business, and I was relieved to go on to something else."*[17]

Fred Graham: *"CBS changed. . . . They brought in two executives from Los Angeles, Van Gordon Sauter and Ed Joyce, to run the news division, and they had this idea that news should be what they called 'infotainment,' a mixture of information and entertainment. And Sauter has a concept that he called 'moments.' And he said, 'The way to engage the viewers is you find out in every story a poignant moment in which someone involved in the story discloses a tear-filled moment, a happy moment, anyway an emotional moment and that emotion as part of a news story will build your news viewership and your rating will go up.' . . . The problem with that was that one person's moment might not be another person's moment. So at CBS we lost the definition of news."*[18]

Tim O'Brien: *"One time I had a senior producer say to me, 'Tim, we love your spot up to this point, but where the drawings come in it really fails* [cameras were not allowed in the courtroom]. *. . . Can't you just say who won and who lost?' I said, 'That's not the idea here. We're [trying] to illustrate the significance of the opinion, and you just want to tell the story and avoid the significance of the opinion.' . . . When Carl and Fred left I had no competition. I had producers say to me, 'You know, this is a great spot and you're doing great work, but you're really shadow boxing; there's nobody else doing this on the other side. . . . I ceased to be relevant to* World News Tonight's *psyche."*[19]

Leaving was least problematic for Carl Stern. *"I was with NBC for 33 years. I left in '93, April 15; it was a Thursday. I'd reached retirement age, which was 55 at NBC."* Stern became the spokesman for the Attorney General; from the Justice Department, he went on to a professorship at George Washington University, always including a course on ethics in journalism in his class offerings.

Stern could retire, but when Fred Graham's contract at CBS was not renewed, Graham needed a new job. *"I went to Nashville, Tennessee, my hometown, as a local anchor, and I was not good at that. It was a fiasco."* However, in 1990 Steven Brill, publisher of *American Lawyer* magazine, was about to start Court TV, a cable channel that would feature live trials, and Graham became the first employee. *"It turned out that as bad as I was as a local TV anchor, I was pretty good at anchoring at Court TV,"* where he was still employed when we interviewed him in 2008.

Tim O'Brien went to CNN. *"They had been negotiating with me for some time, and the money wasn't quite right. They finally came through with a nice package, but for that money they wanted me on the air every day. . . . I was being assigned lots of stories I just found terribly boring. You know, when you start falling asleep in your own interviews, that's a bad sign. So I was not terribly happy. I was there almost three years."* O'Brien ultimately found some happiness in television as a contributing correspondent on the program that Bob Abernethy created for PBS, *Religion and Ethics Newsweekly.*

BEING A SPECIALIST required a television reporter's set of skills in addition to substantive expertise. Irving R. Levine, with his trademark bow tie and his manner of slightly stressing his middle initial, developed an almost endearing persona as NBC's chief economics correspondent.[20] Robert Bazell had been a graduate student in immunology at Berkeley, but a short detour to *Science* magazine convinced him that *"I was much more interested in journalism about science than I was [in] just practicing science."* He briefly reported from Washington, from 1976 to 1978. (He was the only interviewee who told us, *"I personally detest Washington journalists."*)[21] Interviewed again in 2007, he said, *"I asked to be transferred back to New York because I like New York and it got me away from doing the political angle on everything, and I'm still here, all these years later. My title is Chief Science and Health Correspondent for NBC, and I have been here for a long time. . . . I can't imagine anything else I would rather have done. It's a little late now to have regrets, but I really mean it."*[22]

WHERE DO CORRESPONDENTS go when the network no longer wants them or they no longer want the network? *"A man by the name of Roone Arledge had fun hiring a lot of CBS people to work at ABC,"* recalled Jed Duvall, who made the move. *"There were an awful lot of people that I worked with at both organizations. . . . Then they got tired of me and shifted me from staff to freelance. After being freelance for a little while, I was just dropped. You know, it's a good way to avoid lawsuits and those problems, just move people down to freelance and then drop them."*[23] Occasionally a network reporter jumped back and forth, as in the CBS-NBC-CBS career of Richard Roth.[24] But the brutal fact was that there were only three potential employers. Starting in 1980, however, cable television expanded the options. Moves from broadcast to cable reflected different needs. Walter Rogers wanted adventure. Bill Zimmerman wanted to get away from adventure. Don Farmer wanted to work with his wife.

Rogers was covering the Justice Department during the George H. W. Bush presidency: *"It was a really dead-end job; I knew it, [but] I couldn't persuade ABC of that. . . . So then I joined CNN, and they said, 'Would you go to Berlin?' and I said 'Yes,' and they said, 'Would you also go to Sarajevo?' and I said 'Yes,' and they then said, 'You're hired,' because they had a hard time getting people to go to war zones. Again it got back to that basic premise: I had to be willing to go places other people wouldn't go, live places other people wouldn't live, and do stories and take risks that other people wouldn't do, and I found that a pretty good formula for moving up the ranks."*[25] Rogers never returned to Washington and retired from CNN in 2005.

Bill Zimmerman, on the other hand, had had a sufficiency of travel as the ABC bureau chief in Beirut and Rome. He was recently divorced: *"[I] had custody of four kids and found it impossible to take care of them and operate as a television correspondent at the same time. . . . So when CNN called it was a very welcome opportunity which permitted me to be in a studio rather than out running around the world or the nation or whatever."*[26]

Don Farmer was covering the House of Representatives for ABC; his wife Chris Curle was an anchor at WJLA in Washington. *"CNN was going to go on air in June [1980], and they were very persuasive about getting us there. We had always wanted to work together. Finding a good compatible anchor* [team] *is hard because it's like being married. It's a very intimate relationship. You're right next to someone and looking at their left ear. So I decided to leave ABC News. Chris agreed, and we went to Atlanta and signed up. We did a show, sort of like* The Today Show *format. We stayed at CNN for seven and a half years. It was good, but it was boring.*"[27]

Besides cable, another option for network correspondents was to work as an anchor at a local station. David Garcia had spent more than 17 years at ABC, moving from post to post; he covered the Supreme Court, Congress, and the White House and was South America bureau chief, stationed in Miami. *"The powers that run the network had an affinity for moving correspondents to different locations. You felt almost like an army brat."* In 1983 his agent got him an anchor position in Los Angeles. *"I arrived in time for earthquakes and riots and forest fires and mudslides. So after 20 years* [in 2007] *I had enough of that, and now we're out in the desert."* Asked whether he ever considered leaving journalism, Garcia replied, *"God, no. Never, never, never."*[28]

Garcia's transition was successful; Fred Graham's pratfall in Nashville was more the rule. Steve Bell left ABC for KYW in 1987. *"I'm not a natural, light ad-libber. I was never comfortable with all the interaction with various people on the set. . . . I love Philadelphia, but I wasn't the greatest local anchor."*[29] Bell became a professor of telecommunications at Ball State University in Muncie, Indiana, retiring in 2007 after 15 years. Wilson Hall went from a 27-year career at NBC to WNYT-TV, a CBS affiliate in Albany, New York, and from there to teaching at the University of Bridgeport and the University of Tennessee.[30]

OTHER THAN THOSE who became journalism teachers and several who pursued unexpected second careers—such as Bettina Gregory, who got a Ph.D. in clinical psychology, and Margaret Osmer McQuade, who founded an asset management company with her husband—most exiles from television news used their experience and their Rolodex to do commercial television production, public relations, lobbying, or media training.

"I liked NBC because it was the job I always wanted," said Jackson Bain. *"When I finally got that job, it was very difficult to enjoy because it was an incredible amount of time to set aside and I had other priorities with the family."*[31] He started a business conducting *"unique workshops*

and seminars to teach executives how to take control of public speaking challenges, media interviews, congressional testimony, and all verbal communication opportunities." Richard Valeriani, after he left NBC, was similarly engaged in what he described as *"teaching people how to defend themselves against people like me."*[32]

Charles Quinn described his condition as burnout: *"The two high points of my career in journalism were covering Martin Luther King and Bobby Kennedy. I was in the room when Bobby was killed in L.A. I wasn't with Martin in Memphis. . . . I was Rome bureau chief for 3 years. . . . I quit NBC around '80 or '81. Yeah, I think I was a victim of burnout. I just got bored with the news and unhappy with the declining quality of news. . . . It's a very hard business. Unless you've got a lot of guts, a lot of determination, I advise people to stay away. . . . [If] you're a reporter, it's 7-24, and you're never free. That's one of the reasons I finally got out. Second, I got sick and tired of people ordering me around all the time. When I was younger I enjoyed it. I was on the air. I was making money. When I got older I decided that wasn't important. I wish the hell I had been a reporter covering the Twin Towers. God, what a story! Those are the kinds of regrets I have.*

"I went to work for the American Petroleum Institute, which is an organization for oil companies. They do a lot of things, research, lobby, education. I stayed with them 10 years. I'm not wild about the oil industry per se, but they're not as bad as the tobacco industry, for example, or the gun industry. All I did really was I was a conduit from the oil industry to the journalists. I didn't either defend or promote the oil industry, although I think they do a good job, basically, in getting us enough fuel to carry us around and heat our homes."[33] Bill Wordham, after 15 years with NBC and ABC, became a spokesman for the Tobacco Institute, the industry's Washington-based trade group.[34]

Ike Pappas was fired: *"It was the great upheaval at CBS. A very uncertain time. They had already fired several veterans, good people who had given their all for CBS, and I expected it. . . . March of 1987 it was, March 6. I was let go with 300 others. . . . On that day it was particularly painful for me because I was in New York being invested as an Archon of the Greek Orthodox Church—the highest lay honor they can bestow upon a layman, the defenders of the faith. And there was a big dinner in the grand ballroom at the Waldorf. There may have been 2,000 people.*

And my family came up from Washington. Jimmy Carter was made an Archon, and our paths crossed on the stage. He says, 'Hey, Ike, what's this I read in the papers about you?' And I said, 'Well, Mr. President, they dumped me.' And he looked at me with that big Jimmy Carter grin, and he said, 'I know how that feels.'

"When I left CBS what I really wanted to do was open my own company and do what I could do as an entrepreneur. My father was an entrepreneur, and I've always worked for other people. . . . I opened a company right next door to CBS, a little production company that had all the equipment I needed, and I had some funding, put my own money into it, hired some people, and the basic working plan was to start doing commercial work, videos for companies. . . . I had been a Pentagon correspondent, so I had a lot of contacts in that area. . . . And as it worked out, we did get our share of very big companies. . . . Along came the war in the Middle East, and I was hired by Kuwait to go there to help them rebuild their television industry, which was decimated . . . and during the war itself we acted as advisers to the Royal Saudi Government, training them in simple things like setting up a news conference. . . . Meanwhile, my health was not holding up very well. . . . I decided around the millennium to try and see if I could merge my company with another one, and I found one that was streaming, and we merged . . . and I acted as an adviser to them. . . . My income kept up pretty well, and by that time my children were grown and on their own and making their own living rather well. . . . And so that is the overview [of what] I did after I left CBS News. I did not stay in hard news, and I went on to become a businessman. I'm going to be 75 in April [2007]."[35] Ike Pappas died on August 31, 2008.[36]

OF THE FORTY network reporters interviewed, some had significant second careers, as when Marvin Kalb became the founding director of the Shorenstein Center at Harvard. Bernard Kalb and Carl Stern became spokesmen for the secretary of state and the Attorney General respectively, and Bob Abernethy created *Religion and Ethics Newsweekly* at PBS. But half of them had full careers at the networks, often the same network, measuring 30 or 40 years. Their jobs paid well. They didn't have to leave to pay their children's college tuition, nor were they pushed out by age-etched lines on their faces. Seven moved to cable, an option that did not exist in 1978, or to public television. Fewer than ten left television—an unexpected record of stability. Why? *"Well, all I can say,"* said Herb Kaplow, who had worked at NBC and ABC, *"is I loved it, and most of the people—other journalists I knew—loved it."*[37] To them it was the Golden Age or the Glory Days in network TV, although they couldn't agree on when that era started or stopped. Bruce Morton, an elegant essayist who had worked at CBS and CNN: *"You know, I think old guys always think the good old days were better. But the good old days were better."*[38]

IN THE RIGHT OR WRONG PLACE

LIFE WAS GOING to be very different if your employer in 1978 happened to be the *Washington Star* rather than the *Washington Post,* United Press International rather than the Associated Press. While it is possible to be in the right place at the right time, it is also possible to be in the wrong place at the wrong time.

The *Washington Star,* which was founded on December 16, 1852, was an afternoon newspaper and for many years the city's newspaper of record. It ceased publication on August 7, 1981. Roberta Hornig-Draper could never forget the day:

"Aside from my husband's death, the day the Washington Star *folded was the worst day of my life. I had no notice. My boss called at 6 a.m. to tell me so I wouldn't hear it on the radio. So I walked into the kitchen and made myself a Manhattan. I thought, 'How many times do you have a death in the family?' It was intense. I had been there since 1957. I started out as a copy boy. It was a wonderful place to work, even though it was conservative, because they gave reporters absolute free rein. No one ever told you what to do."*[1]

What took place next, according to John Fialka, was "a fire sale of reporters." Fialka, who had a law degree from Georgetown and a master's in journalism from Columbia, "wound up at the *Wall Street Journal.*" He, too, called the *Star* "a wonderful place to work," but the lesson that he took from the paper's demise was that *"journalists have to be kind of agile and not get too comfortable."* During Fialka's long career at the *Journal,* he was the paper's lead reporter in the 1991 Gulf War, after which he wrote a book about the battles between the press and the military. *"I'm happy with my career path. I never wanted to be any more than a reporter or writer."*[2]

As for Hornig-Draper: *"A friend from NBC called with a job offer. I became their Senate producer, which is a euphemism for off-camera. I did all the Tuesday lunches, all the interviews, all the press conferences, wrote memos, and told the reporters what to report. I stayed at NBC for nearly 20 years."*

The death of the *Star* should not have been a total surprise. Staffers themselves referred to the paper as "The Financially Troubled *Washington Star.*" Barbara Cochran, who joined the paper as a trainee on the copy desk and rose to managing editor, "finally decided it was time to move on" in 1979 and joined National Public Radio, where she was instrumental in creating *Morning Edition.* Her career continued as executive producer of NBC's *Meet the Press* and as Washington bureau chief of CBS; she then served 12 years as president of the Radio-Television News Directors Association.[3] Investigative reporter Ed Pound also left the *Star* in 1979, after 2 years, to spend 3 years at the *New York Times,* 11 years at the *Wall Street Journal,* 4 years at *U.S. News & World Report,* and 4 years at *USA Today;* he then went back to *U.S. News* and later to *National Journal* for 2 years. In 2009 he went to work for the federal government's Recovery Accountability and Transparency Board. In a sense, he said, he never changed jobs, only employers, moving *"[whenever] I wasn't getting the opportunity to do the investigative reporting that I wanted to do. It generally comes down to a feeling that you don't think you can accomplish what you want to accomplish at the place you're at."*[4]

Several reporters moved from the *Star* to on-camera jobs in TV. In a rare transition, Lisa Myers, the *Star*'s young White House correspondent, was hired by NBC and ultimately became its chief investigative correspondent.[5] Stephen Aug went to ABC News, *"where I covered business and the economy for them from 1981 until they had enough of me in 1995, and then I retired. Quite frankly, I was burned out. I was tired. After 30-some odd years of daily reporting with deadlines every day, I really just had it, and they decided not to renew my contract. I was not upset at all."*[6]

Specialists seem to have had a smoother path to reemployment. Lyle Denniston, the *Star*'s Supreme Court reporter, said, *"I went almost immediately to work for the* Baltimore Sun, *covering the Supreme Court.*

I stayed with the Sun *until February of 2001, when I was eligible for a buyout and for retirement. I took both and thereafter for three years was a freelancer for the* Boston Globe, *always covering the Court, of course.*"[7] He continues with a Supreme Court blog. *"I'm just having so much fun doing my kind of online journalism. I'm at the Court every day when the Court is in session."*

In 1978 newspapers like the *Baltimore Sun* and *Boston Globe* were a step down in political Washington's rankings of papers, and reporters accustomed to the *Star's* prominence would have to adjust to a lesser status. Lance Gay noted, *"I can tell you that it's the devil to get people to call you back when you work for something strange and anonymous like Scripps Howard News Service, even though we still have 21 newspapers and a wire service that goes to some 400 clients."*[8]

"The older editors were hardest hit and had to leave town," according to Hornig-Draper. One went to Florida, another to Connecticut. Dan Poole, the assistant managing editor for features, had been at the *Star* since 1957: *"I wanted to stay in journalism, and I did stay in journalism, although not in newspapers. . . . I found a job in New York. . . . I went to work for a trade organization called the Insurance Information Institute as vice president in charge of publications. . . . I was given the assignment to start a monthly magazine with a target audience of insurance agents. That, of course, is called a trade magazine. . . . I was in charge of various advertising campaigns, such as the initial Mothers Against Drunk Drivers. . . . I had a marvelous time. . . . Had the* Washington Star *not gone out of business, I would certainly, by choice, have stayed there."*[9]

Diplomatic correspondent Henry Bradsher was surprised by his subsequent career: *"I was actually approached by the CIA, and it had never occurred to me that I wanted to work for them, but they recruited me. It was a time, '81, when the CIA was expanding. Reagan had just put in Casey at the head, and they offered me a fairly senior position. It was a good offer, and I decided what the heck, I'd do it for awhile. So I spent 18 years with them."*[10]

Top prize in the "fire sale" was Mary McGrory, the eloquent liberal columnist, who had won a Pulitzer in 1975. She was lured to the rival *Post,* where she continued her commentary almost until her death in 2004. James Dickenson, the *Star's* last national editor, also moved to the *Post,* remaining as a political editor or reporter until 1989, when he joined Democratic Party activist Ted Van Dyk in a politics-and-media consulting business.[11]

IT WAS NOT preordained that the *Star* would fail and the *Post* would succeed, although the odds were stacked against a big-city evening newspaper as TV and suburban living changed Americans' preferences for getting the news. Yet media conglomerate Time Inc. did not buy the *Star* in 1978 as a loss leader. (*Time* sustained after-tax losses of $35 million when the paper was shut down in 1981.) The new owners failed to factor in the entrenched position of the *Post* in the post-Watergate years. Advertisers needed better reasons than the *Star* gave them to turn from the market's dominant newspaper. In the 1975–2000 period, remembered correspondent John Goshko, *"The Washington Post was a tremendously rich, profitable, powerful, and influential organization."*[12]

That did not mean that every *Post* reporter or editor would remain at the paper or stay in journalism. Still, Goshko, whose final assignment was covering the United Nations in New York, concluded, *"I got to do what I wanted to do, so you can't really ask for very much more than that."* What Helen Dewar wanted to do was chronicle the U.S. Senate, which she did for 25 years, after first becoming the paper's expert on Virginia politics. What Bill Claiborne wanted to do was get away from *"the newspaper's somewhat insular obsession with political power and process."*[13] When surveyed on April 10, 1978, he was preparing for his first overseas assignment. Six weeks later he left for Jerusalem. In 2001, when he and his wife retired to Melbourne, Australia, to be closer to their daughter and granddaughter, he had spent 32 years and 7 months with the *Post,* of which he calculated that 101 months (8.4 years) had been in Washington, most of that time at the beginning of his *Post* career in Washington on the Metro staff.[14] *"I believe I still hold the record at the* Washington Post *for the most bureau assignments—eight: New York, Jerusalem, New Delhi, Jerusalem again, Johannesburg, Toronto, Los Angeles, and Chicago. I sometimes wonder how I was able to maneuver myself into that kind of career path to fit my particular interests. I was very lucky."*

Don Oberdorfer also had an overseas assignment, Tokyo, but his primary beat for 17 years was as the paper's diplomatic correspondent in Washington. *"I never thought that I or anybody could cover a single beat for almost two decades and find it satisfying, but I did. The beat counted, particularly during the cold war. We owned the front page. All I had to do was say 'I have a front-page,' and automatically it went to the front page. . . . I covered a whole variety of secretaries of state, and it was a high-wire act, which meant that you had to really throw yourself into it. It was a six-days-a-week job, and you felt like you were doing something that made a contribution to the greater intelligence of Americans and others."*

From time to time Oberdorfer climbed down from the high wire. *"I had actually five leaves of absence. Two of them were to write books. But the other three times I was a professor at Princeton, my alma mater. I taught a course about journalism, a seminar. And each time I audited courses and went to the library and met faculty members, listened to them, and learned. It was a great help to me. A journalist situated as I was knows about a thousand trees. If you were to ask me then what's going on in Upper Volta, I could rattle it out and tell you in a few hours. But journalists situated as I was are not good at knowing the forest, the big picture. That's where a great university comes in."*[15]

What distinguished interviews with *Post* reporters from those in other large organizations—with the possible exception of the *Wall Street Journal* during this period—was the degree to which they claimed that management found ways to give them a chance to mold their careers to fit their interests or needs. T. R. Reid wanted to write about computers and relocate to Colorado:[16]

"In around 1980 or so I was in Washington covering Congress [when] the first personal computers came out. I got very, very interested in them and built a computer. . . . Don Graham, who was then the publisher, said, 'If my congressional reporter wants to go learn about computers, that's okay with me. . . . Maybe the Washington Post *will benefit somewhere along the line.'. . . And sure enough, I then wrote a column on computers for about 12 years that was syndicated nationally, so I guess they did.*

"Anyway, so we moved out to the mountains of Colorado while I wrote this book about microchips. My wife is a native Coloradan. Most Coloradans, I think, wherever they live, have a dream of getting back to Colorado, and so my wife kept working on me and I kept working on

the Washington Post, *and so in 1984 they opened a Denver bureau, or Rocky Mountain bureau. It's just a nice company, that's all I can say."*

Walter Pincus, whose "Fine Print" column examines the CIA and national security, has been with the *Post* off and on since 1966, with time out to lead an investigation of U.S. involvement in Vietnam for the Senate Foreign Relations Committee, to switch to the *New Republic* as executive editor, to take on part-time news consulting for NBC and CBS (until the *Post* bought up his TV contracts), and to earn a law degree at night from Georgetown when he was 68.[17]

Of the seventeen *Washington Post* reporters in our 1978 survey, three were still there in 2011: intelligence columnist Pincus, automobile columnist Warren Brown, and foreign affairs columnist Jim Hoagland. Another eleven had still been with the paper when they retired or died. Three left the *Post:* Hal Logan, a computer innovator, made his fortune in Silicon Valley; Bill Richards, for personal reasons, moved to Seattle and spent most of his years in journalism with the *Wall Street Journal;* Carole Shifrin, a specialist in transportation news, became bureau chief in Dallas and London for *Aviation Week.*[18] (Of the seventeen *New York Times* reporters surveyed, seven were still with the *Times* when they retired from journalism, and ten left the *Times* for other jobs, in or out of journalism.)

TWO GIANT AMERICAN wire services—Associated Press and United Press International—provided the structure for Washington news gathering in 1978. Their reporters kept track of basic events, constantly updating stories as new developments arose. Wire service employment was an anomaly in the pecking order: other Washington reporters gave the wires' product high ratings, but only a third said that they would want to work for the wires. While over time the wires would encourage more investigative reporting and interpretive writing, they were then largely engaged in nuts-and-bolts reporting. Their stories tended to appear without a byline in newspapers because editors were not motivated to give credit to reporters who were not on their staff. Nor were the wires high-paying operations, at least by the scale of other major organizations. Yet, perhaps as with firefighters, there were those who loved the work, and wire service reporters had their own set of traditions, myths, and heroes.

Reporters at UPI did not have to turn on the radio to hear that UPI had folded. The company went down more like a tire with a slow leak, and one morning the tire was flat. A merger of two private companies, UPI would never be able to compete on equal footing with the AP, a cooperative owned by its contributing newspapers and radio and television stations, which could assess members to cover its costs. But the challenge gave the "Unipressers," as they called themselves, a feistiness that also had characterized the *Washington Star.* Helen Thomas, who began covering the White House for UPI when Kennedy was president, recalled, "If we beat the AP by one minute, there was a big celebration, two minutes was nirvana."[19] In 1977 UPI still had 106 "bodies" in its Washington bureau, according to manager Grant Dillman, including 26 editors to process copy and 39 national reporters, including 3 at the White House, 2 at the Supreme Court, and 2 at the State Department.[20] But squeezed in part by the decline in afternoon newspapers, its major customers, UPI was to go through seven owners between 1992 and 2000. It went into Chapter 11 bankruptcy twice and eventually was acquired by the publisher of the *Washington Times.* Thomas resigned the day after the sale in 2000. *"It was a bridge I couldn't cross, a bridge too far, philosophically. The Reverend Moon outfit. They're very conservative. He's a Korean cleric, I think."*

We surveyed fifteen print and three radio Unipressers. All left before Thomas. Three retired, including radio correspondent Pye Chamberlayne, whose distinctive baritone was heard once an hour from the White House starting in 1962 and from the Senate from 1966 to 1999.[21] Four were hired by other wire services: Ed Shields and Mike Conlon went to Reuters, Mike Feinsilber to AP, and Jim Anderson to DPA, the German press agency. Anderson had been UPI's State Department reporter for 15 years: *"It was too depressing to see what was happening to a great organization. I had to leave."* In late 1990, he changed seats in the briefing room and became DPA's English language reporter. *"The State Department press corps is fairly small, and it doesn't make much difference whether I'm representing DPA or UPI. Basically I was covering the same territory I did for UPI, which was very handy for DPA because it gave DPA an entré into the inner circle of State Department reporters. [I had] a very pleasant 11 years with DPA."*[22]

Feinsilber's career was divided equally: he spent 21 years with UPI and 21 years with AP, moving from one to the other in 1980. "[At AP] *I became sort of a reporter at large, I think that was my title, and so I could pretty much do anything I wanted to do as long as no one else was doing it. I did essentially stories that illustrated the news—sidebars, profiles, think pieces, analyses, or color stories, a lot of color stories. . . . If I had to do it over again, I would have tried to join AP earlier. I guess I regret it took me twenty years to break loose from UPI."*[23]

There were interesting moves, but no distinct patterns characterized the careers of the other journalists who left UPI. Nicholas Daniloff had been hired in London while studying philosophy at Oxford. Although he worked for the wire service for 20 years, in Washington from 1966 to 1980, he did not see himself as a typical Unipresser: *"My senior colleagues were people who came out of the Depression. Very often they were people who did not have a college education, who had gone into journalism when they were 17, 18, 19, and made very good careers for themselves, and they were either jealous or intimidated or looked on that kind of education that I had in a negative way because their view was that their experience was more important than education, and therefore I always tried to hide from them the details of my education."* Daniloff switched to *U.S. News & World Report* and was sent to Moscow in 1981. *"At the last week of my assignment* [in 1986], *I was arrested because the FBI had arrested a Soviet spy in New York, and I was arrested essentially as a pawn or a hostage so that they could get their man back. I then returned to the United States, and then in the fall of 1989, Northeastern University in Boston hired me to teach journalism, which I did."*[24] Professor Daniloff wrote *Of Spies and Spokesmen: My Life as a Cold War Correspondent,* published in 2008.

Diplomatic correspondent John Barton went to the Voice of America and then to the U.S. Information Agency. *"I thought, 'Gee, I'm 52, I better get out before everyone else does.'"*[25] Ira Allen, a White House reporter, spent a year as a congressional press secretary—*"I wasn't terribly successful, as I would've liked"*—and eventually found a more satisfying position with the Center for the Advancement of Health. *"When you are between jobs and not working, it is worse than being dead in this town. People will not return your phone calls; they won't acknowledge that you exist. I thought I could hook up with something good in journalism because everyone knew who I was, but the downside is maybe they didn't like me. I don't know."*[26] Thomas Malia turned to niche publishing and became the executive editor of *Telecommunications Report.* Edward

DeLong founded a marketing and graphic design company before departing for Australia, where he became editor of the *Mudgee Guardian and Gulgong Advertiser.* John Milne moved to New Hampshire, where he became editor of a "semi-alternative" weekly called *New Hampshire Times,* covered northern New England for the *Boston Globe,* and wrote a column for the *Eagle Tribune* in Andover, Massachusetts.[27] Bob Kaylor worked for *U.S. News & World Report,* became a press spokesman in the Commerce Department, and then got a degree in architecture and became an architect.[28]

Gregory Gordon started with UPI in 1975 while still a student at the University of Minnesota, came to Washington in 1977, and ultimately ended his UPI career by co-authoring a book with Ronald Cohen, called *Down to the Wire,* about the financial collapse of UPI. *"The new owners of the company didn't want that kind of book to be coming out, so they demanded to see me. So in the spring of 1989, when I refused to let them see the manuscript, they fired me."* Gordon was out of work for two months before being hired by the *Detroit News.* In 2006 he became an investigative reporter in the McClatchy Washington bureau.[29]

IN THE AP's Washington bureau, the reporter profiles were decidedly different: George Gedda was the State Department correspondent for 38 years; Richard Carelli covered the Supreme Court for 24 years; Frank Cormier reported on five presidents as White House correspondent; Jerry Baulch spent a decade on the communications beat; and Howard Benedict was the AP's aerospace writer so long that he was known as the "dean of space reporting."

From the record, it's clear that most newly minted AP reporters appreciated the type of journalism that they would engage in. Of our twenty-two print reporters, fifteen became "lifers," even though some also had a post-AP career, such as Dale Nelson, who after 39 years with the AP moved to Wyoming and for over a decade was the Laramie reporter for the Casper *Star-Tribune.*[30] Walter Mears, who worked for the AP for over 45 years, left briefly in the mid-1970s for the *Detroit News* but soon realized that he was *"a wire service creature. I couldn't stand the pace. There were no deadlines and no pressure* [at the newspaper]. *I was lucky enough to have the AP take me back."*[31] James Adams switched to Reuters for what he saw as a better opportunity. *"It was a smaller organization. . . . With Reuters I could go straight to* [Capitol] *Hill chief. So I took that."*[32] A subset of AP reporters had sought wire service employment because it might lead to becoming a foreign correspondent. Bob Cullen, waiting for an overseas assignment on the AP foreign desk, was hired by *Newsweek* to replace its Moscow bureau chief, who had been thrown out of the country.[33]

But there were some for whom writing for the wires was an uncomfortable fit, as it was for Brian King. *"Write short and simple. They didn't like the way I was writing, and I didn't like the way they wanted me to write."*[34] Instead he found "a pretty good fit" at the nonprofit Appalachian Trail Conference in Harpers Ferry, West Virginia, where he became associate director of communications. Others became restless. Brooks Jackson had been in Washington since 1970. *"I pretty much covered every beat there was at the AP except the Pentagon. [In] '79 I was at the White House. I was there a year and a half, two years. I didn't like covering the White House. Just being spoon fed stuff from press secretaries. At the end of the day every reporter had the same damn story, pretty much. There wasn't enough scope for original reporting, certainly not enough to satisfy me. . . . The AP's a fine organization, but I wanted to take my reporting to another level, and I had the feeling that the AP was not the place to do that . . . because of the constraints of wire journalism."* Jackson joined the *Wall Street Journal* in 1980, spent ten years there writing prize-winning stories on money in politics, took his specialty to CNN in 1990, and was fired in 2003. *"The whole culture of CNN I think was kind of decayed from the top after the Time-Warner merger."* He then launched FactCheck.org, a project of the Annenberg Public Policy Center. *"I tell people this is actually too much fun and that this job has thwarted my plan to fade into an obscure semi-retirement."*[35]

Unlike the print reporters, however, none of the five radio reporters stayed with AP. Four of them were in their twenties when we interviewed them in 1978. Mark Knoller, 26, switched to CBS Radio in 1988 and became a fixture covering the White House: *"I miss it when I'm on vacation."*[36] The other radio reporters benefited from the needs of a newly created CNN. Walter Rogers, 38, who had been covering the White House in 1978, was able to move into television and had a long career as a foreign correspondent for ABC and CNN.[37] John Holliman, 29, covering agriculture for AP Radio, became part of media history as a member of the CNN team that reported live from Baghdad (along with Peter Arnett and Bernard Shaw) as U.S. bombs fell, starting the Gulf War. He died in an automobile accident in 1998. Bob Berkowitz, 28, whose beat was the Senate and political news, left AP Radio in 1980. After time at CNN and ABC, he said, *"I invented a beat for myself. I became the men's correspondent for the* Today Show *at NBC. This was in the '80s, and everybody was talking about all the changes women were going through. . . . But nobody was reporting on how men were reacting to these changes. . . . You know, what was going on with men while women seemingly were changing? And I carved out that niche for myself, and, as best as I could tell, I was the only reporter in the world that had an exclusive beat covering men for a major news outlet."*[38] Kirsten Lindquist, 24, also left for CNN, moving on to anchor local stations in St. Paul and Minneapolis. When her contract was not renewed, *"I became very involved in the apple business that my husband and his family founded. I spent ten years, just about, doing that. . . . Then I got a divorce. . . . I moved back to California. That was in 2000. My mother was a broker, and she convinced me that working in real estate would be a good way to get my feet back on the ground. It was not something that I had thought seriously about, but it turns out I love it."*[39]

LUCK OR CHANCE? It's often hard to figure out how much *chance* there was in what journalists said happened by chance, how much *luck* was involved when they said that they were lucky. Sometimes the answers are obvious. *"I didn't realize that John Hinckley was standing off my left shoulder with a gun,"* said Walter Rogers. *"I didn't realize I was squeezing right in front of Jack Ruby, who was waiting to shoot Oswald,"* said Ike Pappas.[40] Yet how much of Tom Fiedler's considerable success—he became executive editor of the *Miami Herald*—should be attributed to what he called "an odd twist of fate"?[41] Still, as Bill Richards said of the newspapers that he worked for and when he worked for them, "I was fortunate to be at the right place at the right time."[42] Some others, of course, had the misfortune to be in the wrong place at the wrong time.

EIGHT

IN THE NICHE

NICHE JOURNALISM IN Washington has been around at least since the federal income tax was enacted in 1913. But it owes its exponential growth to President Johnson's Great Society in the mid-1960s, when the eruption of new laws and regulations created markets for information that was not published in a form that could be easily accessed and understood. The cost of starting a niche publication was relatively modest, and there was a ready supply of entry-level reporters who were eager and able to work.

Moreover, the process was helped along by a growing gap between mainstream and niche publications. By the 1990s the mainstream press believed that the public had lost its appetite for the sort of Washington news that one reporter called "turn-of-the-screw daily developments." Newspaper reporting from Congress in 1978 had mirrored the classic textbook treatment of how a bill works its way through the legislative process, rightly giving special attention to the complicated hand-in-glove work in the committees. But by 1998 the emphasis overwhelmingly shifted to final up-or-down votes on the Senate or House floor. Committee stories dropped from 37 to 16 percent; floor action stories shot up from 35 to 60 percent.[1] The new focus might have been sufficient for the casual consumer, but it failed readers who needed to know the fine points of governing to do business.

Thus the congressional press galleries became populated with reporters from such pricey publications as *Endangered Species & Wetlands Report, Food Chemical News, Medical Devices Report, Heavy Duty Trucking, Waterways Journal, Mine Safety & Health News, Set-Aside Alert,*

Pharmaceutical Executive, General Aviation News, Inside Mortgage Finance, Public Utilities Fortnightly, Credit Union Journal, Oil & Gas Journal, Textile World, Radio Business Report, Broadcasting & Cable, Satellite Business News, Employee Benefit Advisor, Federal Computer Week, Public Lands News, Space News, Government Contractor, Health Market Survey, National Underwriter, and *Corporate Crime Reporter.*

The Newsletter Publishers Association was founded in 1976 by seventeen small companies that used a basic formula to spread their costs over an expanding line of niche products: find subjects with an expected market of 15,000 to 30,000 readers, shoot for 10 percent saturation, and locate subscribers able to pass on the high sticker price to their employers.[2] Most of these vest-pocket entrepreneurs would retire as millionaires after selling their companies to such international conglomerates as Reed Elsevier and McGraw-Hill. The only major player from the Washington area was the Bureau of National Affairs (BNA), whose more than 350 publications had almost four times as many reporters accredited to Congress by 2009 as *Time, Newsweek,* and *U.S. News & World Report* combined.

Kiplinger Washington Editors, a closely held family business, chose to buck the trend. Founded in 1923 as the *Kiplinger Letter,* its highly condensed telegraphic style was a pioneer in the newsletter industry. *"I do have some regrets that we overdid the staying small and personal,"* mused third-generation editor-in-chief Knight Kiplinger in 2007. *"Our company would be healthier today if we had diversified our product and our service line more broadly than we did. We should have said we needed more publications in different fields, especially more small, specialty periodicals that people are willing to pay higher subscription fees for."*[3] Being small also meant that survival depended on offering *"our subscribers something that they cannot obtain elsewhere,"* explained Robert Cazalas, who went from reporter to owner of a publication that covers the maritime industry.[4] But "elsewhere" would get harder to find in the new world of the Internet. In 1980 Edward Zuckerman left the Knight Ridder bureau in Washington to create a niche publication for those seeking information about PACs—political action committees—only to watch the Internet turn into "a two-edged sword" as the same information that was available to him became available to his subscribers. After 25 years, he gave his publication a "decent burial."[5]

WHAT WOULD HAVE been striking if a photographer had taken group portraits of the mainstream and niche reporters surveyed in 1978 is how many of those from the niche sector were young women. Of the fifty-eight women interviewed, thirty-five were niche journalists. Thirty-one women were in their twenties, and the niche sector accounted for sixteen of them; of the sixteen, only six stayed in journalism. Overall, niche reporters were far more likely to drop out by the ten-year mark than were reporters for mainstream publications, and they were far less likely to be journalists when they reached retirement age. In part that is a reflection of how niche reporters got to the niche business in the first place. There were basically three groups: those who arrived by accident, journalists who were sidetracked, and a smaller number of specialists.

The Accidental Journalist

"Accidental journalist" is what Nancy Aldrich called herself.[6] For college graduates without experience and in some cases without even an interest in journalism, here were low paying entry-level jobs in a desirable city. Martin Sibley, a philosophy major, *only took the job* [with an aviation magazine] *because I needed a job. I had no idea how to write a news story.*"[7] Nancy Koran, English major and high school teacher in Binghamton, New York, tried journalism when her husband got a job in Washington.[8] Janet Walker, an art history major, went to work as a copy editor and was then pressed into service to start a newsletter on federal programs for the handicapped.[9]

Koran worked for *Oil Daily* and *Oil Express,* reporting on issues of interest to petroleum distributors and later plaintiff attorneys, until the birth of her second child. She is now an artist. Walker found life "very stressful" in the niche sector and moved on to nonprofit publishing for organizations such as the National Trust for Historic Preservation and the Society for American Archaeology. She is now managing editor of the Brookings Institution Press. Aldrich started her career in 1973 with a small newsletter company *"as a reporter. I became an editor. I was an occasional managing editor. Then in 1984 they bought out the human resources publication of another company and I was given the opportunity to write about aging issues, which I agreed to do and has been my main topic ever since."* She remained with the company for 23 years. She now freelances. Sibley is the copy editor of one of McGraw-Hill's aviation publications.

The Sidetracked Journalist

Jack Robertson, who took a double major at Northwestern University in journalism and political science, got a job on the copy desk at the *Chicago Daily News.* But his wife recalled that "he hated the copy desk," so he answered an ad from Fairchild Publications for a "traveling editor," believing that it meant that he would be covering "exotic resorts and destinations." What Fairchild meant, however, was an "editor who could travel." Robertson's new job was to report on the retail industry for *Women's Wear Daily* until reassigned to a fledging weekly publication called *Electronic News.* His wife said, *"Jack avoided science classes* [in college] *like the plague, but he was a fast learner."* During nearly 30 years at the Pentagon, he wrote about multimillion-dollar systems and trade issues involving the semiconductor and electronic industries, winning business journalism awards along the way. Robertson died at 78 years of age in 2010.[10]

Karen Haas Smith was 27 years old in 1978, part of a two-person team putting out five monthly magazines for the construction industry. Her dream was to work on a daily paper in Washington. But how does someone with an M.A. in journalism from Syracuse University break into Washington reporting? She thought that if she found a job on a daily outside of Washington, she might eventually get a transfer. But she didn't land that job, and she went to work for a weekly instead. After several years she was making more money than an entry-level daily reporter and didn't want to take a pay cut. Although she was happy to have a writing-reporting job, she no longer felt that she would ever work for a daily in Washington.[11] She was right, according to another interview conducted 30 years later. Smith went from a niche publication to a trade association in the same field and on to a career *"largely working in the transportation industry, mostly for the Federal Highway Administration as a consultant doing tech writing,"* including a stint in Denmark. *"I think I would have been so good as a reporter."*[12]

Some remembered the gulf between niche and mainstream journalism in end-of-career interviews. Morris Ward recounted that *"in the early '70s, like most young reporters, I wanted to be the political writer for the* New York Times *or the* Washington Post. *But David Broder and R. W. Apple weren't retiring any time soon. So I ended up with BNA."*[13] Yet six of the niche reporters ultimately crossed over into the mainstream. Two of them used McGraw-Hill—the giant specialized publisher that also owned *Business Week,* the widely circulated consumer magazine—as their escape route. If niche reporters in the organization could break through to *Business Week,* they were almost there.

That was the history of Judith Dobrzynski and Anne Swardson, both of whom went directly from university journalism programs to training at McGraw-Hill. As Dobrzynski put it, *"Naturally, anyone who was good wanted to move out of the trade magazines and move over to* Business Week, *so that was what I did as fast as possible."* In 19 years at *Business Week* she did "pretty much every job there was," including the job of senior editor supervising the Washington bureau, and during her final year she was assistant managing editor. She relocated to the *New York Times* for eight years, then became executive editor of CNBC, and now writes about the arts for the *Wall Street Journal* and other publications.[14] Swardson traveled from *Business Week* to the *Dallas Morning News* to the *Washington Post,* taking assignments that included tours teamed with her husband as foreign correspondents in Canada and France. She has been in Paris for Bloomberg News since 2000.[15]

The Specialist

Richard Smolka, a professor of political science at American University, worried that "there was no vehicle to get information related to election administration out to election officials." So in 1971 he started *Election Administration Reports: "Journalism had nothing to do with my decision to start the newsletter. I don't operate by journalistic standards. I don't try to be the first to report anything. I only try to make sure that I have everything that happens in the newsletter. There were issues dating back to May that I haven't written about until now* [July]; *I assume most of my readers get the daily news from regular newspapers."* Smolka's publication *"comes out every two weeks. I like working from home. There's no commute. Most people thought a newsletter about election administration wasn't necessary when I started it. Now people spend hundreds of millions of dollars* [exploring election administration]."[16]

Jonathan Eberhart, "a burly, pony-tailed Harvard dropout [was] captivated by the nascent science of space," which he covered for *Science News* from 1964 until, hobbled by multiple sclerosis, he was forced to retire in 1991.[17] A folksinger, he took time off from reporting to perform on the sloop *Clearwater* with Pete Seeger and to write songs, including "Lament for a Red Planet," inspired by his coverage of NASA's Mars Explorer mission.[18] After Eberhart died in 2003 at 60 years of age, astronomers named an asteroid ("Joneberhart") to honor his contributions to science journalism. The "satisfaction level" for specialists in journalism is markedly higher than it is for generalists.[19]

WHILE SOME "ACCIDENTAL" and "sidetracked" reporters dropped out, others went on to long and successful careers. Paula Lazor Cruickshank remembers going to work at CCH (Commerce Clearing House), her first job after college, *"exactly thirty years ago* [in 1977], *and I started there through a personnel agency. After six months they asked me if I was interested in covering the White House as they had just gotten accreditation. . . . [It] was daunting because I was only 24 years old. We had never had anyone there before so there was no guidance. I could count the number of females in the White House press corps at the time: Helen Thomas, Lesley Stahl, Judy Woodruff, one other woman from Prentice-Hall, and me. I faded into the background for a few years. I was in awe of Helen Thomas. Plus, they were all working for mainstream publications, and I was working for a trade. . . . I've been at the White House ever since. . . . Two years ago I became Washington bureau chief."*[20] Vicky Mason also rose from entry level to editor-in-chief at *Telecommunications Report,* beginning in 1974 while she was a graduate student at American University. She retired in 2002; the next year she set up her own consulting business.[21]

Oliver Patton wanted to be a journalist and wanted to be in Washington, but it was a "total accident" that he ended up in niche publishing. *"This was about 30 years ago,"* he recalled in 2005. *"I was pretty fresh out of school, and I didn't have any money. I had two job offers. One was with the* Northern Virginia Sun *and the other was with a weird paper that I'd never heard of before called* Transport Topics. *The* Northern Virginia Sun *offers me $5,000 a year, and* Transport Topics *offered me $7,500 a year. So I went with the money. I figured I'd have a cup of coffee there and move on. But it turned out that for reasons I can't explain the subject matter turned out to be interesting to me. And I stayed there for a long time and eventually became the editor and director of their publications."* He then became correspondent for *Heavy Duty Trucking.* Reporting on the trucking industry involves *"a whole bunch of public policy issues—safety, the environment, taxation, highway policy, security—so there's a lot that goes on in Washington, up on the Hill and in the various bureaucratic agencies, that affects truckers."*[22]

WHEN INTERVIEWS TURNED to professional matters, responses from niche and mainstream journalists were profoundly different. Mary Bruce Batte, an editor at *Housing & Development Reporter* in 1977, recounted attending the funeral of an *"important Hill staffer. . . . There weren't more than ten people there—other than family—that I didn't know."* She noted with satisfaction, *"We know everyone in the housing network."*[23] Mainstream journalists connect at the political level of government, elected or appointed. But according to longtime niche journalist Charles Aldrich, *"The relationships you developed [were] with the career civil service, the mid-level people who were in charge of all the different kinds of programs and reports and sections, [who] put out the manuals and the regulations and all the different reports that we needed. . . . We were not in an adversarial relationship with our sources in the government. We were more like the exact opposite: we were more like compatriots or associates because they used our publications."*[24]

Mainstream reporters thought of bureaucrats as speaking a foreign language and tried not to see their sources as compatriots. They also had a different view of their readers, sometimes talking with disdain of what they considered irritating or irrelevant reader feedback on their stories. Niche reporters, on the other hand, took pride in their readers. Paula Cruickshank: *"Our readership doesn't have a lot of time, so they want accurate, concise information. Thankfully, we're in demand. They really value news."* Nancy Aldrich: *"It was really my newsletter subscribers that let me know if I was doing a good job or not."* Charles Raab, having worked at the *New York Post* and *New York Daily News* before moving to *Aerospace Daily & Defense Report,* summed it up from the niche perspective: *"Readers have a financial stake in what I write."*[25]

Our questions about "pack journalism," "political bias," "duplication of effort," "personality journalism," and "attribution of sources" were vigorously debated by mainstream journalists but were of little interest to niche journalists, some of whom had no opinions on those subjects. Here were two groups of Washington journalists, reporting on one government but living in separate worlds professionally. Niche journalists' focus was designed to be narrow; they took pride in their specialness.

No single pattern characterized niche reporters who dropped out of journalism. Bill Hickman thought that the work "was getting boring" and got a job managing the National Press Building.[26] Judy Haberek "hated the boss" and started a landscaping company on the Eastern Shore of Maryland: *"I'd rather be outside now. I just don't want to be in an office anymore."*[27] Many of the reasons sounded like those of younger people testing the parameters of journalism as an occupation. *"Being a journalist was fun and fascinating,"* recalled Lucy Knight, *"but I wasn't sure I wanted to do that for the rest of my life."* What Knight wanted to do was write a book about Jane Addams, founder of the Settlement House movement in America. She left Washington, writing grant proposals and doing other development-related work for universities and nonprofits. Finally, *"I decided that the only way I would finish the book was to work for myself part-time and sacrifice some money so that I could have the time to work on it. . . . I was trying to learn how to write narratively, and that was a real change. Journalism is sort of anti-narrative, and proposal writing is persuasive writing, which is a second kind of writing. So I was venturing into a third kind of writing."* Her book, *Jane Addams and the Struggle for Democracy,* was published by the University of Chicago Press in 2005.[28]

Richard Payne covered Washington for a newsletter directed at international business executives. *"The issue about journalism was that you are an observer all the time. You are a commentator, not a participant. . . . I'd rather participate and have a direct impact rather than an indirect impact."* Payne left journalism in 1981 to become a consultant on human resources and has since worked in Hong Kong, Australia, and San Francisco. For Phil Battey *"the decision to go from the* American Banker *to the American Bankers Association was entirely based on my salary. They doubled my salary."*[29] His career continued as speechwriter for the Comptroller of the Currency, public affairs director at the Federal Deposit Insurance Corporation, and vice president of Promontory Interfinancial Network, a financial services company.

Probably irrespective of gender differences, niche journalists used the language of "working conditions" (*family-friendly* and *autonomy* and *flexibility*), which was not prominent in interviews with mainstream journalists. Mort Paulson remarked that *"the Kiplinger organization had more in the way of benefits, medical insurance, pension plan, that sort of thing."*[30] BNA's website declared that it was on *Fortune* magazine's list of "100 Best Companies to Work For in America." Cynthia Bolbach went to work for BNA the week after she graduated from Georgetown Law School in 1972: *"I was interested in journalism and wanted some way to combine journalism and law."* In 1978 she was managing editor of *Media Law Reporter.* When interviewed again, in 2007, she was a vice president and corporate secretary, and her duties included overseeing the stock purchase operation. *"Once you're at BNA for a certain number of years you have the opportunity to buy stock in the company; you have the opportunity to sort of help figure out what direction the company is going to take. And it just seemed to me to be a pretty good place to spend a career."*[31]

For Deanne Neumann, who joined BNA in 1967, *"the stock holdings have proved to be a very good investment. And also during the time I've been here I've had the opportunity to move up the corporate ladder, change jobs, take on more responsibility. And I have found it to be continually interesting and challenging. . . . I've enjoyed the people that I work with at BNA. I think being an employee-owned company has a big influence on our culture. . . . The people who work here, they're my friends as well as my colleagues. For whatever reason, people stay here a long time. You're a newcomer if you've been here 10 years, and most people who are here such a long period of time become very expert in what they do, so I'm surrounded by people who know what they're writing about. They're respected within the Washington community for their knowledge and are good people to spend time with at the office."*[32]

A HYBRID FORM of niche publishing that focused a much wider lens on its subject first evolved at *Congressional Quarterly,* a mislabeled publication that comes out weekly. Created in 1945 by Nelson and Henrietta Poynter, the owners of the *St. Petersburg Times, CQ* conformed to the niche pattern of small-circulation, high-sticker-price publications available only through subscription. But rather than reporting on one law or regulation, its niche was all of Congress. Designed initially as a source of congressional news for local papers, the publication printed running tabulations of legislators' votes and committee actions that were cherished by scholars and librarians. "CQ *had always been a little bit of a schizophrenic organization,"* remembered Bob Merry, the company's president in 2007. *"It wasn't clear whether* CQ Weekly Report *was a news magazine or a kind of reference tool, and in various times it had tilted one way or the other way."*[33] That tilting was reflected in its personnel.

CQ journalists had subsequent careers so wildly dissimilar as to suggest that those doing the hiring either didn't know what they needed or weren't very good at identifying it. A 1979 interview with editor Wayne Kelley was mostly about "the boredom factor" among his reporters and his limited success in trying to retrain Ph.D.'s as journalists.[34] Christopher Buchanan, at *CQ* from 1977 to 1981, said that his *"career path [was] completely unplanned and patched together as I've gone along";* he later became a coordinator or location manager for movies by the Coen brothers and by Spike Lee. *"I get hired by different producers to work on different things, and whatever they hire me for is what I do."*[35] Irwin Arieff went in the other direction, from *CQ* to a wire service, Reuters, where he moved up the ranks, reporting from Paris and the United Nations, and retired after 25 years.[36] For Elizabeth Wehr, *"journalism got a little thin"* by 1989. *"I wanted to do something more substantive with my life at that point."* After getting a law degree, she concentrated on child health policy, first at George Washington University, then at the National Institutes of Health.[37]

Bob Rankin left *CQ* for a fellowship at the Columbia Journalism School, eventually working as "a middle-management editor" in the McClatchy Washington bureau, *"anonymous and invisible, though not without influence."*[38] Kathy Gest stayed at *CQ* for ten years, rising to managing editor before becoming Senator William Cohen's press secretary; that position was followed by executive positions at Powell

Tate Public Affairs and the National Democratic Institute. *"I'm not sure I ever really had a clear idea of where I wanted to go. . . . I was fine switching jobs. I just always wanted something that'd be challenging."*[39] Rhodes Cook was the one *CQ* alumnus who looked like he was molded for *CQ*. *"I did not go there because I was passionate about journalism. . . . Rather, I was interested in the subject of American politics and was trying to put it into historical context."* He retired from *CQ* in 1997 to write election-related books and a bimonthly political newsletter.[40]

Tom Schroth had become *CQ's* editor in 1955. *"In 1969, after a long-simmering dispute with Mr. Poynter over* Congressional Quarterly's *editorial direction, Mr. Schroth was fired. Almost immediately he announced a new publication, to cover the executive branch and general policymaking,* National Journal."[41] The magazine was similar to *CQ* in appearance and price. It defined its niche in terms of depth rather than subject area and covered all aspects, domestic and foreign, of the U.S. government. As Dom Bonafede, the White House correspondent, explained, *"We're not a magazine of record, like* CQ; NJ *goes in for long analytical pieces when the rest of the media is going in the other direction."*[42] Dick Kirschten, who covered energy and the environment, later remarked, *"You know,* National Journal *is famous for writing pieces that some would say were too long, but we enjoyed them."*[43]

Management knew where to look for writers who had the appropriate qualities and temperament, and by 1978 publisher John Fox Sullivan concluded that "the reporting staff was now very stable."[44] There were five *National Journal* reporters in our survey: Bonafede stayed for 15 years, leaving to become a professor at American University; Kirschten retired after 26 years; congressional correspondent Richard E. Cohen stayed for 32 years, switching to *Politico* in 2010; Rochelle Stanfield, whose beat was mainly social policy, remained for 23 years. "National Journal *was my kind of place,"* she said. *"The magazine was very substantive. You could be analytical. It was a weekly, but we had three weeks to a month to develop a story, and we had a fair amount of space to use."*[45]

THE HISTORY OF non-mainstream journalism in Washington unfolded as a complex tale of mergers, acquisitions, and "begets." *Congressional Quarterly* begat *CongressNow*, a daily, and an online legislative tracking service, *GalleryWatch*, as well as focused newsletters such as *CQ*

Homeland Security and *CQ HealthBeat.* The Economist Group bought CQ in 2009 and merged it with *Roll Call,* previously purchased, to become the CQ–Roll Call Group. *Roll Call* had started as a community newspaper for Capitol Hill that within a half-century grew into a popular source for congressional staffers to follow congressional maneuverings. The beauty of having a devoted audience was that those who wished to influence them could advertise for a great deal less in *Roll Call* than in the *Washington Post* or *New York Times.* That led Jerry Finkelstein, owner of the *New York Law Journal* and other New York publications, to hire Martin Tolchin of the *New York Times* to challenge *Roll Call* with a startup called *The Hill* in 1994. The *National Journal* was purchased in 1997 by David Bradley, owner of a company that did specialized research for corporations. Two years later he bought *The Atlantic,* moving the venerable magazine from Boston to Washington, and merged his two publications into the Atlantic Media Company. He also added *Congress Daily,* in direct competition with *CQ*'s *CongressNow,* and other specialized publications.

Politico was launched in 2007 by two reporters from the national desk of the *Washington Post,* John F. Harris and Jim VandeHei, and financed by the Allbritton family, which had once owned the *Washington Star.* On the publication's fifth birthday, Harris and VandHei recalled that *"there was an animating idea behind POLITICO, then and now. The idea was that the era of the traditional news organizations—the metropolitan dailies, weekly news magazines, and broadcast news networks—that produced general-interest content for a mass audience was fading, and that the future more likely belonged to sites that defined a special niche and then dominated that niche with manic intensity."*[46] While politics was its niche, by 2011 it was also offering subscribers what it called "human intelligence" on such topics as energy, technology, and health care.

In 2011 *Bloomberg News,* the major financial data provider, inaugurated *Bloomberg Government (BGOV),* a publication narrow-casting Washington information for various industry sectors, including health care, energy, and transportation. *BGOV* called itself "a customized resource for professionals who need to understand the business implications of government actions so they can work quickly, decisively, and effectively," a description that its competitors also could claim.

All of these enterprises were staffed at the top by deeply experienced Washington mainstream journalists and staffed at the lower levels by those who aspired to be their successors. On August 25, 2011, Bloomberg LP bought BNA, acquiring the employees' stock for about $990 million. Long-vetted workers could retire with $5 to $6 million or more. Within 24 hours Bloomberg executives informed those who wished to remain that "we do not anticipate any layoffs . . . in the short-term."[47] The media establishment was seeing unrealized beauty in niche journalism.

NINE

THE GRIDIRON CLUB

THE SOLE PURPOSE of the Gridiron Club, composed of current and former Washington journalists, is to throw a party.[1] Male guests at this annual spring affair are instructed to wear white tie and tails. Women are resplendently gowned. All are seated at a giant gridiron-shaped table, the evening's speakers at one end, the stage and orchestra at the other. Over the evening, four musical skits are performed by club members, some of whom can carry a tune, supplemented by ringers known as "limited members," who are of very good voice; they are accompanied by the Marine Band, whose first leader, John Philip Sousa, composed a march in honor of the club. Skits alternate with four speeches, starting with the "Speech in the Dark," delivered by the club's president, its most senior active member, who serves a one-year term. The opening speech is followed by speeches by individuals of Senate or Cabinet rank representing the Democrats and the Republicans, which are followed by a closing speech by the president of the United States. (Should the president not accept the invitation, the vice president usually fills in.) The evening is long and spiritually fortified.

To give a properly received speech, according to Andrew Glass, "Speakers take their perceived weakest traits and most venerable qualities and exaggerate them to the point of absurdity."[2] When George W. Bush was a no-show in 2007, Vice President Cheney began, "The president is really sorry he couldn't be here tonight, but he had another obligation [*pause*]: his book club is meeting [*audience laughs*]." When Barack Obama was a no-show in 2009, Vice President Biden began, "President Obama sends his greetings. He can't be here tonight because he's busy getting ready for Easter [*pause*]; he thinks it's all about him [*audience laughs*]." The skits rarely provoke much offense, in keeping with the club's motto that a gridiron "singes but never burns." For a dinner at which President Clinton was to be a guest in 1998, during the Monica Lewinsky scandal, club president Robert Novak said that he vetoed "a wickedly clever parody of 'Thank Heaven for Little Girls.'"[3]

The 600 Saturday night guests include senators, ambassadors, Cabinet members, Supreme Court judges, the military's joint chiefs of staff, and, most important to club members: their bosses. Frank Aukofer, the *Milwaukee Journal Sentinel*'s Washington bureau chief, recorded that his paper's chairman sat next to President Reagan at the 1985 Gridiron dinner and "reacted like a star-struck teenager."[4] The skits are repeated the next afternoon for a larger audience of members' sources and friends. This "air of palsy-walsyness between politicians and journalists" is what the club's critics find most objectionable.[5]

THE CLUB WAS founded by and for Washington print journalists. For most of its history, that meant white, male, mainstream newspaper and wire service reporters. Columnist Carl Rowan was the first black member, elected in 1972; Helen Thomas became the first female member three years later. Journalists from television, radio, and magazines were admitted in 2004. Each change was painful to some members. Arthur Krock, in actively opposing Rowan's election, recalled that "parodies in the Negro dialect were very popular and not subject to protest." The admission of women came only after a "Counter-Gridiron" party drew a larger crowd than the Gridiron dinner itself.[6] The print reporters who objected to letting in TV reporters dubbed them the "sparklies."

At the start of 2011 there were a dozen Pulitzer winners among the active or associated members.[7] The club is really about the specialness of practicing journalism in Washington. *"Sometimes I look out my window,"* said Andy Alexander, *"I see the U.S. Capitol, I think wow! There's nothing really better than this!"*[8] There are now sixty-five "active members." Those who leave Washington or leave journalism get transferred to a nonvoting "associated" category.

These are the type of reporters made famous in Timothy Crouse's classic account of a presidential campaign, *The Boys on the Bus,* or the type who asks questions at a president's news conference from the front row. Their beat is essentially politics, whether reporting on government or elections. But after winning his Pulitzer for covering a presidential campaign and heading the Washington bureau of Knight Ridder for 20 years, Bob Boyd switched to science reporting and never looked back: *"I've been to the South Pole, spent three weeks on a research ship in the North Pacific. . . ."*[9] (He retired in 2010).

To rise to the top in an organization requires getting back to head-quarters and attempting to plant your flag. Coming to Washington and then going back home is a standard practice for the ambitious in journalism, notably at the *New York Times,* but that pattern applies less often to the Gridiron people, who sometimes returned to Washington after leaving. Walter Mears was the AP bureau chief in Washington when he was elevated to executive editor in New York: *"I never enjoyed myself or felt I was as productive as when I was reporting and writing. I didn't like New York. . . . After covering a bit of the 1988 presidential campaign, I returned to Washington in 1989."* (He retired in 2001).[10] Chuck Bailey came back from Minneapolis to be Washington editor for National Public Radio. James McCartney went back to Chicago in 1966 to be city editor of his paper but returned to the Knight Ridder bureau in Washington after two years. (He retired in 1990).[11]

There are exceptions. Some do go home again. Some leave journalism. *"The problem with being a political correspondent after many years* [in Washington] *is that you find yourself meeting yourself around the curve, writing the same stories over and over again,'"* said Lee Bandy. *"After 30 years covering some of the same people year in and year out, I was ready for the change. That shift gave me a whole new world to explore."*[12] He returned to his paper in South Carolina, where he writes a column.

For Arthur Wiese, it was another kind of problem: *"I got to be* [Houston Post] *bureau chief at the age of 27, and I was elected president of the National Press Club when I was 32, and I was in the Gridiron Club when I was 35. I got to do a lot of things that ordinarily happen to somebody much later in their careers. So I sort of ran out of obvious rewards, things to look forward to."* Wiese became director of public relations at the American Petroleum Institute: *I've found communications work on the corporate side to be intellectually very stimulating. It's sort of journalism in reverse. . . . My old friends in journalism all ask, 'Don't you miss it?' I always reply, 'Never on payday.'"*[13]

Still, Gridiron members are likely to remain in journalism and remain in Washington.[14] Gridiron members also are more attentive to the maintenance of their profession. Only 9 percent of journalists belonged to the Society of Professional Journalists in 2002, while 30 percent of doctors belonged to the American Medical Association and 35 percent of lawyers to the American Bar Association.[15] But the resumes of Gridiron members are filled with professional activities: Allan Cromley, of the *Daily Oklahoman,* was one of many who also served as president of the National Press Club; George Condon, formerly of Copley Newspapers, was among those who headed the White House Correspondents Association; and Alan Emory, of the *Watertown* {N.Y.] *Daily Times,* and others were members of the Standing Committee of Correspondents of the Congressional Press Galleries.

AT THE ANNUAL Gridiron dinner of 1978, 40 percent of the active members worked for papers that probably were not household names outside of their own households, among them the *Indianapolis Star, Birmingham News, Kansas City Star, Des Moines Register, Milwaukee Journal, Daily Oklahoman, Richmond Times-Dispatch, Omaha World-Herald, Buffalo Evening News, New Orleans Times-Picayune, St. Louis Globe-Democrat.* Those bureaus typically had two to four reporters and required only modest managing; there was even a single-reporter bureau. Bureau chief Dick Dudman, of the *St. Louis Post-Dispatch,* confided in 1977, *"Administration bores the hell out of me."* From behind a desk piled high with books, magazines, letters, and old press releases, he announced, *"I have a fear of filing."*[16]

There were club members from the great cosmopolitan centers, of course—the *Washington Post* and *Washington Star* together had six seats at the table—and there were some syndicated columnists, such as Roscoe Drummond, Marquis Childs, and Joseph Kraft. Yet this was an establishment in which an organization's size and reach were not among the criteria for membership.

MEMBERS CREATED THEIR own sidebars: Jim Free, of the *Birmingham News,* wrote a history of the first 100 years of the Gridiron Club; Edgar Allen Poe, of the *New Orleans Times-Picayune,* retired at 88 years of age, still writing his column, "Washington Panorama" (he died four years later); Jerry terHorst, the *Detroit News* bureau chief, was President Ford's press secretary for a month, then promptly resigned when Ford pardoned Richard Nixon and returned to his paper as a columnist; conservative columnist James J. Kilpatrick married liberal columnist Marianne Means, both Gridiron members; Herblock, the great *Washington Post* cartoonist, surprised his fellow club members when he left an estate in the neighborhood of $90 million;[17] at the *Baltimore Sun,* Muriel Dobbin, ahead of her time in 1980, wrote a novel about vampires, while her colleague Pat Furgurson was to become a civil war historian who wrote multiple volumes on the subject.

OUR FOCUS ON the Gridiron Club, beyond its uniqueness as a Washington institution, was a way to unravel the twists and turns of the news business as seen through the lives of its members and the news organizations that they worked for. Had Rip Van Winkle been a charter member at the club's inception in 1885, ninety-three years later he would have awakened to the continued good fellowship of his colleagues—strangely dressed, otherwise quite recognizable—and the prosperity of the newspaper business. In short order, however, he would become disoriented by a riot of corporatization in which the bosses were frantically buying, selling, merging, and divesting themselves of newspapers. Assume that Van Winkle was the Washington bureau chief of the *Minneapolis Tribune* in 1978 and never changed jobs. In 1982, after the city's morning and afternoon papers merged, he would be working for the *Star Tribune;* in 1998 he would be working for a California company called McClatchy, known for papers named *Bee,* in places like Modesto; eight years later he would be working for a New York–based private equity firm that bought the *Star Tribune* for less than half of the $1.2 billion that McClatchy had paid the Gardner Cowles family for it. In 2009, the *Star Tribune* filed for bankruptcy.

Knight Ridder

Knight Newspapers and Ridder Publications became Knight Ridder in 1974. The new bureau had four club members. Knight's leading papers were in Philadelphia, Miami, Detroit, and Akron; Ridder's were in St. Paul and Duluth, Minnesota, and San Jose and Long Beach, California.

"It was not necessarily an easy changeover," recalled Ridder reporter Gil Bailey. *"Most of the Ridder management disappeared."*[18] The shuttered Ridder office had consisted of a bureau chief and four regional reporters.[19] The combined bureau, representing thirty-four papers and a 3.6 million circulation, had fifty reporters, including ten regional correspondents for the ten largest papers. Those papers were "not read in Washington," regretted Knight Ridder bureau chief Bob Boyd in an interview in 1977, but now they would "gain weight" since *"the bigger you are, the more power you have."* Bigness would allow the bureau to *"show the flag, so they will know we're there,"* to cover more breaking news, to be more visible asking questions at presidents' press conferences.[20]

Newhouse

Although Newhouse had thirty papers, its influence was unfelt in the corridors of power. According to bureau chief Dean Reed in 1977, each paper was "terribly autonomous": local editors picked their own regional reporters, and regional reporters worked for their local editors.[21] That began to change in 1990, when Deborah Howell, the dynamic editor of the *St. Paul Pioneer Press,* arrived in Washington determined to redesign the bureau: "Instead of covering buildings—the Capitol, White House, Pentagon, State Department," she announced that her reporters would focus on such topics as race, gender, sexuality, technology, and religion.[22] It was a valiant effort, but other organizations were not looking to New-house to set the pace. Howell retired from Newhouse in 2005 to join the *Washington Post* as ombudsman. (She died in a freak accident in New Zealand in 2010. She was 68.)[23]

Gannett

At Gannett, growth seemed to be written into the company's DNA. When I met John Curley in 1977, virtually his first words were "Management is my bag."[24] He was the only Washington journalist to make that claim. Curley was the bureau chief and general manager of the Gannett News Service. With headquarters in Rochester, New York, the company then owned fifty-five papers, soon to expand to seventy-three through acquisition. That would make it the largest group in number of papers, but it was behind Knight Ridder and Newhouse in circulation. Average circulation of a Gannett paper was around 40,000. Curley explained how the bureau was soon to be split into three regional wires and described in detail the budget, the responsibilities of the various levels of editors, and even how many file drawers there were per reporter (eight). He did the hiring. Unlike in other Washington bureaus, there was no pay differential between national and regional reporters. The regionals might go on to be managing editors of small papers in the chain, in which case three years of Washington experience was about right, Curley concluded. *"We develop people who will be editors."*

Armed with a graduate degree in journalism from Columbia, Curley went from the army to the AP. *"I really wanted to be an editor. I mean, you have to be a reporter, you should be a reporter; you shouldn't be an editor without being a reporter, in my view. But I really wanted to be editor of a newspaper. When I was 21 years old that was the goal to be when I was 35. That's why I went from the AP, which was a wonderful organization, to newspapers."*[25] Curley joined Gannett in 1969 at its flagship paper in Rochester and moved a year later when there was an opening for the top editor at a paper in Plainfield, New Jersey; he went on to Washington in 1974. He became publisher of the *Delaware News Journal* in 1980. *"All these things were considered promotions, and so I took the jobs."*

In January 1982, Curley returned to Washington, where the company's CEO, Al Neuharth, was creating *USA Today;* Curley would be the first editor. The paper, which was launched on September 15, 1982, had a difficult beginning. Nonetheless, *"there was really no doubt in the minds of the people who were doing it that we were going to be successful. I never thought about it much. Frankly, it doesn't work like that. Either you're doing it, working, and going on, or you're not there. We were all committed. Remember, I was at Gannett for a long time; it wasn't an in-and-out kind of deal."* Others on the staff were less sanguine, according to Peter Prichard in *The Making of McPaper.*[26]

By the end of 1983, *USA Today* was selling more than 1.3 million copies a day. Curley succeeded Neuharth as CEO in 1986, the same year that a poll of Wall Street analysts named Gannett the best-managed publishing company in the country, and the company decided to relocate its headquarters to Arlington, Virginia, in a building with a panoramic view of Washington. Curley retired from Gannett in January 2001, noting that the date "had more to do with getting into another tax year, really." (He is now a professor at Penn State, where the John Curley Center for Sports Journalism is located.) Like other news organizations, Gannett, including its Washington bureau, has been affected more recently by the decline of print journalism.

Cox

Cox Newspapers hired David Kraslow in 1974 to create a Washington bureau. The cash flow from the papers was an important source of income for family-owned Cox Enterprises Inc., which was expanding into fields outside publishing.[27] While papers in the chain had modest offices for their regional reporters, it was Kraslow's assignment to put them under one roof, hire a national staff for the first time, and answer the question "Who ever heard of Cox in this town?"

A special problem of the combined bureau was that the company owned fiercely competitive morning and evening papers in the same cities. Kraslow's solution was to seat the prestigious national reporters in an open bullpen in the center of the office, while giving the regional reporters their own offices around the perimeter, with doors to shut, physically placing competing reporters as far from each other as possible.

The "who ever heard" question was less pressing after former Georgia governor Jimmy Carter moved to Washington. Cox owned the Atlanta papers—the *Atlanta Constitution* in the morning, the *Atlanta Journal* in the afternoon—and Kraslow made sure that the president and first lady got free home delivery, even if home was the White House. Those who might wish to see what the president was reading could pay for their papers at coin-operated boxes installed on downtown street corners.[28] The new Georgia elite in government visited the Cox bureau to give their interviews. (On the day that I visited in 1977, the guest was to be Attorney General Griffin Bell.)

Kraslow, whom Bob Donovan had chosen to succeed himself as *Los Angeles Times* bureau chief, was subsequently an assistant managing editor at the *Washington Star,* but more important for his next assignment was the time he spent with the *Miami Herald*. The Cox-owned *Miami News* was having problems with a joint operating agreement with the more successful *Herald.* The company asked Kraslow to be the paper's publisher, and he returned to Miami in 1977.[29]

Kraslow's replacement in Washington, Andy Glass, also came from the world of national reporting, having worked at the *New York Herald Tribune, Washington Post,* and *National Journal. "My mantra was growth,"* Glass said, looking back on his 20 years as bureau chief (1977–97). As an example, he cited *"the opportunity to build a foreign staff, to go in many cases from stringers to super stringers to full-time correspondents to having a strong foreign editor in Washington, to resisting some internal pressures to break this up."*[30] Still, a chain of seventeen geographically dispersed papers comes with local agendas and "too many egos" that have to be serviced in order for a bureau chief to retain the support of the papers' editors: *"I spent lots of time on the road negotiating and ingratiating."* Large bureaus cover the day's breaking news first; small bureaus cover their readership's congressional delegation and community interests before covering other issues or events; medium-size bureaus, like Cox, must look for in-between opportunities, finding ways to infuse national news with a local angle and occasionally, in Glass's words, "coming up with real good stuff that nobody else had."[31] (After retiring from Cox, Glass spent a semester at Harvard's Shorenstein Center and subsequently became managing editor of *The Hill.* He is now a contributing editor at *Politico.*)

The third and final bureau chief, Andy Alexander, spent his entire career with Cox. He grew up in Ohio, went to Ohio University, and joined the Cox paper in Dayton in 1971 (*"It was nearby"*), which sent him to Washington in 1976 as its regional correspondent. *"I was young, and I was cheap, and I was single."* Eight years later he was elevated to the national staff and eventually to foreign editor, deputy bureau chief, and bureau chief in 1997. Whereas Glass claimed growth as his mantra, *"It is fair to say,"* said Alexander in February 2008, *"that my mantra is survival."*

He watched his papers "becoming more local in their focus." He wondered when "they" would ask whether a Washington bureau was giving the papers "what they need to survive."[32] Finally, he described the end:

"What happened was on August 13, [2008], this giant corporation decided essentially they were going to sell a lot of their newspapers. . . . The corporate leaders made a strategic decision . . . I think because they

*felt newspapers had reached their peak in terms of business enterprises.
. . . I got the word that this was going to happen the day before they
actually announced it. . . .* [I called] *a staff meeting because obviously I
had to explain what was going on. I remember telling people, 'If you are
asking me should you be looking for a job right now, the answer is yes.'
Now we didn't know that the bureau would close, but you didn't have to
be a genius to know that if you had far fewer papers paying the freight
for a Washington bureau, there would not be as much support for a large
bureau. . . . What subsequently happened was they just decided [that]
we're going to get so small we just can't afford it. Or that we don't want
to afford it—I think that is a better way [to put it]. So it was in November that I had a meeting with the people down at corporate* [in Atlanta],
*and they said we're going to close it. . . . I told the corporate leaders,
'Look, I've told these people you ought to be looking for work and the
problem that many of them have is that they have jobs that they can get
right now, but they're afraid if they leave Cox and take that job . . . they
will miss out on the buyout offer.' That buyout offer was very lucrative.
. . . They said, 'You can tell your people go ahead and take those jobs,
and we'll still pay you the money.' . . . In addition, the company gave a
huge lead time.* [The Washington bureau closed on April 1, 2009.] *What
struck me about this bureau was that we had really good journalists,
and they're all ending up getting good jobs, if not all in journalism. One
guy became a speechwriter for John Kerry."*[33] (Alexander moved to the
Washington Post as the paper's ombudsman, a job he said that he would
have taken even if the bureau had not closed.)

Minneapolis Tribune

With a tip of the hat to Rip Van Winkle, the real bureau chief of the
Minneapolis Tribune in 1978 was Finlay Lewis. When he had been a
young *Trib* reporter living at home, *"A friend, who was president of a
small bank, called to tell me about a robbery. I was not in. My father
took the message.* [His father was editor-in-chief of the rival paper.] *Next
morning I read about it in the* St. Paul Pioneer Press. *Father said, 'You
got a call. The story* [in the *Pioneer Press*] *is the message for you.'"*[34]
Years later, Lewis looked back on "the job of newspapering": *"Slowly
we learned how to construct a story and learned habits like fairness,*

accuracy, and impartiality."[35] In 1972, after six years of local learning, Lewis was sent to Washington, where the paper had a four-reporter bureau. Its major obligation was to cover Minnesota news, but the paper also had strong national tendencies fueled by a congressional delegation that included Hubert Humphrey, Walter Mondale, Eugene McCarthy, several prominent House members, a secretary of agriculture, and even two Supreme Court justices. *"If we* [had been] *from Nebraska, I don't know what we'd do."* That worked fine for Lewis until "there were some senior changes in the structure of the paper," and in 1987 he switched to Copley, a collection of California and Illinois papers.

Copley

"I wanted to refocus my energies on reporting and not be diverted by management or budgetary issues, and that fit in nicely for Copley," said Lewis. *"The bureau chief who hired me* [George Condon] *is a very good manager."* Moreover, Condon came from the group's flagship paper, the *San Diego Union,* which had a long-standing interest in national stories. Lewis eventually moved into economics reporting and wrote a weekly column covering fiscal and monetary policies and trade issues: *"It was a good challenge."*

There were ten reporters at Copley. Two were in the Gridiron Club, which was rare for such a small bureau, but Lewis had been invited to join while he was at the *Tribune.* Copley won its first-ever Pulitzer in 2006 for a series by Washington reporters Marcus Stern and Jerry Kammer that sent San Diego congressman Randy Cunningham to prison for accepting $2.4 million in bribes. Then, *"Copley unraveled with dizzying speed."*[36] Owner Helen Copley died, and her son sold the papers to pay inheritance taxes. The bureau, which had been in Washington for 64 years, was down to Condon and Lewis by Election Day 2008. *"I helped George with the melancholy task of closing the bureau."* The lights went out at the end of the year.

Lewis became a contributing writer at *CQ Weekly* in January 2009. It was a good arrangement, he said, in that "[I was not] *obliged to reinvent myself in order to function online. CQ offered an opportunity to continue print journalism, with the added bonus of more space and time to develop stories I care about and that are important to the magazine's audience.* "[37] For the younger Condon, *"When Copley folded, I went almost immediately over to* Congress Daily, *a sister publication of* National Journal, *as* White House *correspondent. Our readership is considerably smaller but far more influential—members of Congress, staff, lobbyists, other journalists. Interestingly, every member of the Copley bureau landed a job. But none at a newspaper."* [38] What of the two Pulitzer winners? Marcus Stern went to ProPublica, a nonprofit newsroom, doing investigative reporting supported by foundation funding. Jerry Kammer does research and writing for an advocacy think tank, the Center for Immigration Studies.

Des Moines Register

There was a time in the late 1960s when the entire Washington bureau of the *Des Moines Register*—three reporters—had won Pulitzer Prizes.[39] The paper was then a sister publication of the *Minneapolis Tribune,* and both were owned by the Cowles Media Company. James Risser, the bureau chief in 1978, already had one Pulitzer for a series disclosing large-scale corruption in the grain exporting industry and would soon win a second for reports on damage to the environment from farming. After his first Pulitzer, he turned down job offers from the *Washington Post* and *New York Times: "There's a tremendous amount of freedom working in a bureau like this. I'm not restricted to any beat. It's lots of fun."* [40]

The "flat rule" was that the paper's Washington reporters *"first have to have worked in Des Moines. They must know the paper and the state's political climate."* Risser guessed that each reporter spent a third of his time on Iowa-related news and otherwise sought *"national news stories we think are not well covered or that we're personally interested in."* Working in Washington was considered a permanent assignment; they would not be rotated back to Des Moines. *"More than 75 percent of the time editors in Des Moines don't know what we're working on until they see it."*

In 1985 the Cowles family sold the *Register* to Gannett. In the same year Risser became a professor at Stanford and director of the John S. Knight Fellowships for Professional Journalists. The *Register's* Washington bureau had dropped to two by 2002 and to one when Jane Norman, who had been in the bureau for ten years, was laid off in 2008. After being out of work for seven months, she was hired by *CQ*. James Risser retired from Stanford in 2000; looking back on his career, he said, *"I was lucky to work for a newspaper which was, at least at the time, interested in the coverage of government and public affairs."*[41]

St. Louis Post-Dispatch

Dick Dudman, the bureau chief with the "fear of filing," retired in 1981 at the age of 62. His last story was the assassination attempt on President Reagan. He and his wife Helen *"had our eye on the coast of Maine* [where] *she used our rather meager resources to buy a local radio station in Ellsworth,"* now under the management of their daughter. He said that he did a lot of sailing and had built a small wooden sailboat.[42] But eventually he drifted back into journalism and now writes two editorials a week for the *Bangor Daily News*. The *St. Louis Post-Dispatch* was a seven-person bureau when Dudman left Washington; it now has one reporter in the capital. The paper was founded by Joseph Pulitzer in 1878 and managed by family members until 1995. Today it is owned by Lee Enterprises, a chain of mostly small dailies based in Davenport, Iowa.

THE PROPORTION OF Gridiron active members working for individual newspapers had dropped from 40 percent in 1978 to 20 percent by 2011. Tabulating declines in circulation and advertising, the managing editor of the *American Journalism Review* watched the papers leave town, concluding that they see *"Washington bureaus as luxuries they simply cannot afford."*[43] Newspaper groups, once so optimistic about expanding their Washington coverage, were also pulling out or cutting back: Newhouse followed Copley, closing its bureau after the 2008 election; Media General, with papers in Richmond, Tampa, and Winston-Salem, followed Cox, closing its bureau in March 2009; Knight Ridder was sold to McClatchy in 2006 and slimmed down through attrition. Some changes were brought about by corporate blunder; others seemed almost evolutionary. United Press International (UPI), still a player in 1978, was replaced by Reuters as the second wire service.

These kaleidoscopic rearrangements often followed the shake-up that occurred when the heirs of a great media family lost energy and/or interest in journalism. The Chandlers' four-generation control of the *Los*

Angeles Times ended when Otis stepped down in 1995. The company was purchased in 2000 by the parent company of the *Chicago Tribune,* which was taken over in 2007 by billionaire Sam Zell, described by media critic David Carr as "a hard-charging real estate mogul with virtually no experience in the newspaper business." Less than a year later, the company filed for bankruptcy protection.[44] Besides the *Los Angeles Times* and the *Chicago Tribune,* the merged company also owned the *Baltimore Sun, Newsday, Hartford Courant,* and *Orlando Sentinel*—all newspapers that once had independent Washington bureaus. When the Tribune Company emerged from bankruptcy in 2012, its new owners were a group of bank and hedge funds: JPMorgan Chase; Angelo, Gordon, & Company; and Oaktree Capital Management.[45]

While the elders were retiring, usually secure in their pensions if not always in their stock options, often their younger colleagues were trapped in difficult transitions. Some took jobs for which they were "overqualified." There are good and bad times to be looking for work; jobs depend on the job market. The journalists' skills and contacts ensured that they would be employed somewhere, but that is cold comfort for those who love journalism and being journalists.

Yet at the same time, there was a powerful upside created by the emerging world of the Internet and new forms of technology. Most of the start-ups had trouble figuring out how to make a profit, but there was one stunning exception, Bloomberg News. For 35 years, starting in 1965, Albert Hunt had been with the *Wall Street Journal* in Washington: congressional and national political reporter, bureau chief, columnist, executive editor. The parent company, Dow Jones, put him on the board of its Ottaway Newspapers, and he served as president of the Dow Jones Newspaper Fund. *"By all conventional measurements,"* he said, *"I had a great job."*[46] Then in January 2005, Hunt left the *Wall Street Journal* to become Washington managing editor at Bloomberg News. He was 62 years old. *"I went to Bloomberg because I thought it was a great challenge. I thought it would be fun. I thought I had one more big challenge left in me."* The challenge was there because Michael Bloomberg, after being fired from Salomon Brothers in 1981, used his $10 million severance to create a financial data system so valuable that 300,000 executives felt the need to pay $20,000 a year to lease his desk-top terminals. With that massive revenue stream, Bloomberg could create a news organization that did not rely on advertisers. Twenty years later, Bloomberg News employed 2,300 journalists, including such major figures in Washington as Hunt, Clark Hoyt, and Michael Tackett, all Gridiron members.[47]

IN 2011 THE "Speech in the Dark" was given by Susan Page, the Gridiron's fifth woman president and, she noted, "the first member of the Baby Boom generation to serve as Gridiron president." Page was Washington bureau chief of *USA Today*. A third of the active members were now women, and a fifth of the members worked in television and radio.[48] Career patterns also were different. Three-fourths of all reporters in our 1978 survey had spent their entire Washington career working for one employer; if they did change jobs, they went from print to print or from broadcast to broadcast, rarely crossing the media tracks.[49] But rapid job change had become an American habit, relating to rising levels of education and mobility and changing notions of loyalty to employers and employees. Even in the modest sample that is the Gridiron Club, six members changed jobs between the annual dinners of 2010 and 2011. There was shuttling between different types of news organizations as well: Vickie Walton-James, from the *Chicago Tribune* to National Public Radio; Jan Crawford, *Chicago Tribune* to CBS News; Jeanne Cummings, *Wall Street Journal* to *Politico* to Bloomberg News; Chuck Todd, *Hotline* to NBC News; John King, AP to CNN; John Dickerson, *Time* to the online magazine *Slate* to CBS News political director; Annie Groer, *Washington Post* to *PoliticsDaily* to writing a book; James Angle, NPR to Fox News.

Other Gridiron members were finding ways to do journalism outside the mainstream: Jon Sawyer, former *St. Louis Post-Dispatch* bureau chief, now directed the Pulitzer Center on Crisis Reporting; Miles Benson, White House correspondent for Newhouse, became "earth focus correspondent" for Link TV; Sarah Fritz, *L.A. Times* investigative reporter, was publisher of an electronic news service, *Youth Today;* Sandy Johnson, former AP bureau chief, became managing editor for politics and government at the Center for Public Integrity.

The Gridiron added three new members in 2011. James Carroll of the *Louisville Courier-Journal* does the type of regional correspondence on which the club was founded and that remains an important strand of its composition. Candy Crowley, CNN's Sunday anchor, would have been beyond the ken of the club's founding gentlemen: *"My dad read a great comic strip called 'Brenda Starr.' Brenda was a reporter. He always used to say, 'Oh, you should be Brenda Starr, you could be Brenda Starr.'"*[50] David Corn is Washington bureau chief for *Mother Jones,* a magazine in the muckraking tradition. Introducing this trio at the annual dinner, Carl Leubsdorf, the club's secretary, explained, "They reflect the changing Washington press corps and the Gridiron Club's ability to keep up with that change."

THE CHALLENGE OF change veils the continuity of basic news gathering. Even as the "platforms" change, reporters are expected to ask the same questions and use the same tools of inquiry, adjusting to the demands and opportunities of new technologies: in the twentieth century, from print to radio (AM to FM) to television (broadcast to cable) and on to the Internet. When the Gridiron met in 1978, David S. Broder was an active member. He had left the *Pantagraph* of Bloomington, Illinois, to come to Washington in 1955 for a job at *Congressional Quarterly.* He covered his first presidential election, Kennedy versus Nixon, for the *Washington Star,* and at the *Washington Post* he never missed an even-numbered year of national campaigning from 1966 onward. The greatest political reporter of his generation, "Broder saw political reporting as a lifetime calling."[51] Along with the breaking news, there was a twice weekly syndicated column, a course on "politics and the press" as a tenured professor at the University of Maryland, and seven books (one with this writer). *"Reporting is for young people,"* Broder told my students in 2005. *"I think . . . having young people with a lot of energy and the willingness to work those hours is a great advantage."* "What do you do with old reporters?" he was asked. *"Shoot 'em,"* he replied.[52] David Broder wrote his last column on February 6, 2011. He died at the age of 81 on the Wednesday before the Saturday Gridiron dinner. In her "Speech in the Dark," Susan Page said, *"He loved the Gridiron Club, and we loved him. He embodied the values of thoughtful and civil engagement on the most critical issues we face as a nation."*

WHATEVER HAPPENED TO THE WASHINGTON REPORTERS?

"WHAT IS THE job [in journalism] that you would best like to have someday?" Asked of the Washington reporters interviewed by phone in 1978, the question offered them a brief and unexpected opportunity to look into their own future and dream grandly—it was merely talk and could do no harm. Yet the collective results are surprising, even shocking, in terms of what they say about how journalists then contemplated their careers.

A very small number were specific in their aspirations. Stanley Degler wanted to be president of BNA, the vast niche publisher. When he retired in 1990, after 33 years with the company, his title was senior vice president. "Yes, I am satisfied," he told us in 2007.[1] Vicky Mason, a 26-year-old editor at *Telecommunications Reports,* wanted to be—and became—the publication's editor-in-chief.[2] Todd Kiplinger looked forward to being "managing editor of *Kiplinger."* At his death in 2008, at 62 years of age, the *Washington Post* wrote, "He spent most of his 38 years [with his family's company] managing the firm's portfolio of financial assets and real estate."[3] Helen Dewar, on the labor beat for the *Washington Post* in 1978, aspired to "political reporting." The next year she was reassigned to the Senate, where she joyously reported on the politics of "hallway stakeouts and midnight votes" until her last story was published on January 20, 2005.[4] Hays Gorey, senior correspondent when he retired from *Time* in 1991, after a 27-year career with the magazine, imagined someday being managing editor.[5] Judith Dobrzynski, at 29 years of age, could see herself as a future editor-in-chief at

Business Week; by 1995 she had risen to assistant managing editor and left to work for the *New York Times.*[6] Karen Elliott House said she would "like to be David Broder," and Sam Donaldson said he would "like to be Mike Wallace."[7]

Yet in numbers almost equal to the number of all other answers combined, journalists answered *"What I'm doing"* or even *"Don't know."* These were workers so deeply involved in the moment—in the satisfactions and frustrations of the job at hand, in the deadlines and competition built into producing a solipsistic product that defines the world as starting anew each morning—that apparently they paid only glancing attention to the sort of career planning encoded in the DNA of members of other professions or occupations. They were ambitious, but their ambition seemed to radiate within a relatively small sphere. Jack Fuller remembered being a young reporter on the police beat in Chicago: *"How long do I have to cover dead bodies in bathtubs? I'm tired of it. . . . I really lobbied hard to be sent to Washington."*[8]

Looking back on their careers, reporters often credited chance, luck, or even fate for their promotions, assignments, and successes. Tom Fiedler, who rose to become executive editor of the *Miami Herald*, remembered getting his first job: *"I just walked in the door at the right time* [1971]. *. . . In a real odd twist of fate, an editor asked me if I would be interested in having assignments related to the presidential primary that year* [1972] *in Florida. . . . Then to get thrown into a presidential campaign primary* [1976], *almost by accident, again because nobody else wanted to cover George Wallace, and then to have Wallace become as big a story as it did, led to* [other] *opportunities."*[9]

The unplanned in journalism fits the journalist personality, reflected at one extreme in the fatalism that I saw when studying foreign correspondents working where the consequences could be deadly: *"What will be, will be."* At this point, Stanley Karnow, a famed foreign correspondent, would say, "Journalism is the only profession in which you can stay an adolescent all your life." As I wrote in *The Washington Reporters,* "The best reporters never lose this sense of excitement, often associated with youth." The ones I studied were intelligent people, above average in both quantity and quality of education. Although a majority of them did not major in journalism, at some point they decided to try journalism. Could their unusual absence of focus on their professional future result more from what they do than from who they are?

REGARDLESS OF HOW the journalists that we surveyed contemplated—or didn't contemplate—their own future in journalism, they did not hesitate to describe what "the prototypical career" was supposed to look like. The mantra was short: "You go 'til your legs go." Or, in long form:

Journalism is at best a semi-profession. A college degree in journalism is useful for learning skills before you apply for a job, but it is not necessary. A graduate degree in journalism from the right place—Columbia, Northwestern, Missouri—is useful in introducing you to alumni who can point you to available jobs. Thanks to the U.S. Constitution, journalists do not have to be certified; that helps make journalism easy to get into. All you need to be a journalist is a job in journalism.

Journalism is poorly paid. This is okay when you are young, especially if you are single, because doing journalism is a lot of fun. There will come a time when it makes a difference.

Journalism is high-energy work. The days can be long and schedules erratic. Expect to burn out. This is what the British call "a young workforce with high churn."[10] While some choose to switch from reporting to editing, a job that offers work hours that are more easily adjusted, becoming an editor does not fit every reporter. *"I never wanted to be any more than a reporter,"* said John Fialka. *"Other people do."*[11]

Journalism is a "bridge" semi-profession. The not-so-young-anymore journalist has acquired skills that are transferable and desired in other types of work and at the same time has made contacts who can open doors to jobs in public relations, lobbying (pro bono and for profit), government, and a widening universe in which the ability to write fast and accurately is in short supply. Journalism is easy to get out of.

That is the portrait that was painted for me by Washington reporters in 1978 and in subsequent interviews:

Jeff Lubar, the Washington news director at Susquehanna Broadcasting: *"If I had still been single at that point, I probably would have stayed in reporting. But I have no regrets. . . . My decision was really a function of facing the imminent threat of paying some college tuition."*[12]

Donald Bacon, most of whose career was with the *Wall Street Journal* and *U.S. News & World Report*: *"I had a good career as a reporter and loved it, but I always figured that reporting is a young person's game. I wanted to be off the street by the time I was 40.*"[13]

Greg Conderacci, who left journalism after eight years: *"The skills that make you a good journalist, especially the skills that go to asking good questions, can make you pretty good at most anything else. Journalism is a great preparation for almost any kind of business—nonprofit or for profit or government. Better than law school."*[14]

Cheryl Arvidson, who left journalism after 21 years: *"A lot of skills that I had as a reporter are simply called other things in other professions."*[15]

So that is the career pattern in journalism that I passed along without question to those who read *The Washington Reporters.* It matched that in the limited literature that has been produced by sociologists interested in the world of work.[16] But after adding up a generation of careers, one by one, I found that they did not conform to what practitioners, scholars, and I myself expected. The future did not look like the past. The traditional pattern had been turned upside down.

ALTHOUGH "THE PROTOTYPICAL career" model came with no numbers or percentages, presumably the pattern—easy in/easy out, with a bridge in the middle—starts during a short period when young people test the fit and feel of journalism, which is followed by a mid-life transition when they must face reality and then by steady attrition from journalism into second careers. Those who remain continue to climb the steep slopes of their organizations, while a precious few ascend to celebrity.

We assessed the journalism career of each individual surveyed, from first paid job (preceding Washington in most cases) to retirement or death. We did not count seven people who died well before they might have retired.[17] Then we created three categories: those who left journalism before 15 years ("dropouts"); those who were journalists for 15 to 29 years ("transitional journalists," or TJs); and those who remained in journalism from 30 years to more than 50 years ("lifers").

Of those that we were able to track down, 11 percent were dropouts, 20 percent were TJs, and 69 percent were lifers. If we include those that we could not locate—nearly 10 percent—we estimate, on the basis of their profiles, that 13 percent were dropouts, 23 percent were TJs, and 64 percent were lifers.[18]

The Dropouts

Some of the dropouts have already been introduced because of the special circumstances of their careers: Edward Alwood, a CNN reporter who would become a university professor; Richard Burt, who went from the *New York Times* to the State Department; Hal Logan, who left the *Washington Post* to go to Silicon Valley; Doug Lowenstein, who left Cox Newspapers and eventually founded the Entertainment Software Association; Kathy Patterson, a former reporter for the *Kansas City Star* who was elected to the Washington, D.C., city council.

That most of the dropouts didn't stay long in journalism often relates to what they were looking for in Washington. An adventure? A job? A test of their personal talent?

J. Peter Segall was 24, working for Plus Publications; he left journalism in 1980. A newly minted Princeton graduate, he talked the publisher of a stable of niche publications into starting a newsletter called *Lobbying Reports,* which he then edited for several years. *"I enjoyed the work immensely but never thought of journalism as a permanent career."*[19] Segall is now director of the Washington office of Edelman, an international public affairs company.

John McClung was 34, working for Miller Publishing Company; he left journalism in 1981. *"When I got out of graduate school I had a wife and new baby and no job and no money. And I went to work for Miller Publishing Company* [a publisher of agricultural magazines]. *I needed a job. . . . Right after Reagan was elected an old friend asked me to go with him into government, and I did. I was a political appointee in the Department of Agriculture."*[20] McClung later became president and CEO of the Texas Produce Association.

Susan Fogg Braaten was 31, working for Newhouse News Service; she left journalism in 1980. *"During that time it became clear to me that I was unhappy. . . . I went into journalism partly because my father was a reporter. Plus, it's a lot of fun. . . . In retrospect, I probably was not temperamentally suited to being a reporter in any of the ways I am absolutely suited to being a teacher. . . . When my son was in pre-school I realized how much I enjoyed spending time in his classroom. . . . I started subbing and got certified. . . . So I'm changing the world one group of kids at a time."*[21]

Yet a top-tier reporter also was a dropout. Lynne Olson had been a Moscow correspondent for AP and White House correspondent for the *Baltimore Sun;* she left journalism at age 32 in 1980. *"I was just tired of the daily grind. I was never really all that comfortable with the daily pressures of journalism, even though I worked for a wire service for seven years and then a newspaper for three years. I did pretty well at it, but I never liked not having time to think and to really get into a story. . . . What I really wanted to do was write books. I remember when I was a really young journalist reading that David Halberstam had quit the* New York Times *to write books and [I] thought, 'How could he do that! He's got the best job in the world as a reporter for the* New York Times.' *Well, ten years later I knew why he had left the* New York Times *to do it, and that's something I really wanted to do too."* [22] Four of Olson's five critically acclaimed books—all on history—have dealt in some way with London during World War II.

The Transitional Journalists

The transitional journalists had careers that reflect the prototypical bridge formulation: they made a mid-career move into a related occupation, often because of a dwindling bank balance or the sense that their future possibilities in journalism were limited.

Yet among those who fell short of becoming lifers were some of the most honored journalists in the survey, including James Risser, T. R. Reid, William Beecher, and Jo Thomas, suggesting that, as the late *Washington Post* editor Larry Stern was fond of saying, "When the history of the newspaper business is written, it will be about those who left it." [23] Some had second careers that were not an offshoot of having been a journalist, including Bettina Gregory (clinical psychology), Barbara Reynolds (prophetic ministry), Bob Kaylor (architecture), Kirsten Lindquist (real estate sales), Margaret Osmer McQuade (asset management), Frank Van Riper (commercial photography), and Sidney Sulkin (poetry and short stories).

Some moved away from Washington—to Austin, Baltimore, Boston, Los Angeles, New York. Cindy Parmenter, of the *Denver Post,* went back to Colorado to cover the legislature. *"Just for the lifestyle. I love Washington, but I really prefer to live here."* She then left journalism to become press secretary to a governor.[24] Doug Underwood, a Gannett regional correspondent, said that *"getting tired of being a little fish in a big pond really made me decide that I wanted to come back to the Northwest."* He became the *Seattle Times* chief political writer, and he is now a professor at the University of Washington.[25] But most TJs stayed in Washington, working on Capitol Hill or in the executive agencies or at places like the National Association of Realtors, Council of Insurance Agents and Brokers, American Textile Manufacturers Institute, Public Welfare Foundation, Leadership Conference on Civil Rights, Association of General Contractors, American Petroleum Institute, Tobacco Institute.

The transition was not always easy. Some called themselves "recovering journalists." Kathy Burns edited a niche publication, *Washington Drug and Device Letter,* in 1978: *"From the time I was a young kid I wanted to be a journalist. But it was often a convoluted path. I envy some of those who found a comfortable niche and stayed there for 30 years, but that wasn't the option I had. So I had to continually reinvent myself with each new twist in the road."* She taught journalism courses at Washington area schools, did some trade and freelance work, was a foreign correspondent when her husband had a job in Australia, and remained "an active member of the Society of Professional Journalists since they first allowed women to join."[26]

From time to time journalists took paths out of journalism that bore their own special signature. Ferrel Guillory returned to Raleigh, North Carolina, to be the editorial page editor at the *News and Observer* in 1988. *"I knew I was particularly interested in the South as a region. . . . I grew up in Louisiana in the '50s and '60s, when race relations and the civil rights movement were moving along. I had a particular interest in issues arising out of poverty and the development of cities in the South."*[27] He left journalism in 1997 to found the Program on Southern Politics, Media, and Public Life at the University of North Carolina–Chapel Hill.

John Wallach, the foreign editor of Hearst Newspapers, left journalism in 1995. He had been a journalist for 28 years. Wallach created an organization called Seeds of Peace, a summer camp in Maine that brought together children from opposing sides of conflicts around the world. He started by inviting Arab and Israeli teenagers. *"The only answer to me was to bring the next generation together before they had been poisoned by the climate of their region."* Wallach then opened his camp to Turks and Greeks from Cyprus; Serbs, Bosnians, and Croats from the Balkans; Indians and Pakistanis; children from the ethnic factions in Afghanistan. He died in 2002 at the age of 59.[28]

Why They Left

The most cited reason for leaving journalism or changing direction was personal problems: children's health or educational needs; all manner of illnesses; a troubled marriage or other relationships; concern over aging parents. The demands of practicing journalism can make it hard to accommodate family needs. *"I lost track of my family, and I have a feeling that's fairly common."*[29] *"I would have a bag packed all the time."*[30] *"I missed soccer games. I missed taking my kids to school. It was a big family hurt. It really was."*[31] *"I suppose, given the dark ages we were in when it comes to being gay, I don't know that it would have been any easier in any other field, maybe academia. . . . Had I not been so miserable about who I was personally maybe I would have blossomed more in my career in Washington."*[32]

After personal matters, most cited were matters specific to the reporter's organization, generally prompted by some staff rearrangement or personnel change, although the fallout from Sam Zell's management at the Tribune Company was more profound and widespread. As a frustrated editor at *Newsday* said, "I would die for the First Amendment, but I wouldn't die for the Tribune Company."[33]

Stan Benjamin, of the AP: *"The bureau chief decided for various reasons to shake up the staff and reassign about a third of the reporters to different beats. And I was one of them. So I was taken from the environment beat and put on the Supreme Court, which was a very respectable job and had a bit of prestige attached to it. But I didn't like it. They never asked if I wanted to do that. I was just told that's where I was going. So I gave it a try, didn't like it very much, and [that] just sort of precipitated a lot of other things. So I quit."* He became a freelance writer, which *"worked out pretty well. I was able to save more money and have myself a better time and that sort of thing."*[34]

Mary Kay Quinlan, of the *Omaha World Herald:* *"There had been a management change in the newsroom. The tradition had been very much promotion from within. But during the early '80s they hired a new managing editor who came from the outside. He moved very quickly to antagonize virtually everyone in the newsroom and made it very clear that he was frustrated that he did not have control over the Washington bureau. . . . He moved behind the bureau chief's back to replace me in the bureau. . . . It was rather insidious as I think back on it."* Quinlan then got a job at the Gannett News Service, became president of the National Press Club, and eventually returned home to teach at the University of Nebraska College of Journalism.[35]

For some, however, the act of leaving in mid-career simply reflected the fact that life in journalism was not working out as they might have hoped and there was still time to change direction.

Christopher Bonner was a regional reporter covering Alabama and Georgia in the Knight Ridder bureau. *"After five years the job was becoming so cyclical I could look at a calendar a year in advance and tell a person what I'd be doing, reaction stories to State of the Union addresses, going to the Federal Election Commission and combing through donations to see who was doing what, checking out which lobbyists were visiting which congressmen. The stories were pretty much the same, only the names changed. . . . I knew I wanted to leave."* Bonner went to work for trade associations and eventually started his own consulting company. *"What I liked about public relations was the idea of seeing issues from several dimensions and trying to help manage reputations."*[36]

Christopher Conte, of the *Wall Street Journal*, went from daily reporting to editing. *"It was a chance for consistent, relatively well-paying work, and it seemed like the clear transition to make at the time. . . . Well, the truth of it is that I was stuck in a position with limited chances for advancement. . . . My repeated attempts to get back into reporting didn't work. My boss told me that he could get good reporters easily, but that good editors were very hard to come by. He might have been just trying to shield me a little bit. . . . I eventually decided to leave."* Conte became a freelance writer, specializing in research and reports for nonprofit organizations and the World Bank. *"The bottom line is that the money in freelancing just isn't as good as it is working for an organization, but the freedom is great and it allows me to do the work that I want to do."*[37]

Conte's quandary—editing or reporting—was faced by many others at mid-career. Some were like Mary Leonard, who noted, "[I] sort of bounced between reporting and editing throughout my career."[38] But that was rare. Frank Greve observed, *"If you're an editor, you have to be an adult. You have to field off a whole lot of details and confusion."*[39] Noted Elaine Shannon, *"They sit at their desks, and I can't do that."*[40] Greve and Shannon chose reporting. Bill Choyke chose editing. *"I enjoy being a quarterback. I enjoy the choreography of being an editor. . . . You can kind of bring a philosophy to the job about how you want your newspaper, section, and your team to be."*[41] Norman Kempster, who started and finished his career as a reporter (1956–2001), concluded in retirement that had he switched to editing, he could have worked longer.[42]

Sometimes journalists were lured away by a special opportunity. Herman W. Nichols, after 23 years at *Time* and *Fortune,* became U.S. ambassador to South Africa. Marlene Cimons, when offered a buyout, left the *Los Angeles Times* to pursue a Ph.D. at the University of Maryland; her dissertation was entitled "The Medicalization of Menopause: Framing Media Messages in the Twentieth Century." Dr. Cimons is now an adjunct professor at Maryland and a senior writer at the National Science Foundation.[43] Some journalists who had an unusual assortment of jobs may simply have been restless. See, for example, the career notes in the appendix on Bob Berkowitz, Karen DeWitt, Berl Schwartz, and Alicia Shepard, who spent three years sailing the South Pacific writing "Letters from Paradise."

Ultimately they left journalism for the same reasons that other people in other occupations leave their jobs. What was startling, given journalism's reputation, was how few mentioned the need for greater income as a decisive factor in their move.[44]

THERE SHOULD BE an asterisk to denote those journalists who were young enough to pursue a second career after 30 years in journalism yet who could not be labeled "transitional." Richard Carelli, after 31 years in journalism, went to Georgetown Law School at night while covering the Supreme Court for the AP. *"Don't do it, Dick, it's going to ruin your writing style,"* he said he was warned by other Court reporters. *"I don't think it did. I think it helped me appreciate how lawyers and judges think a little bit more."* At the "not-too-old age of 54," he took a job as "a spokesman for the federal court system."[45] Stan Crock became "senior editorial director" at Accenture in 2006; he was 56 and had been a journalist for 33 years, 23 of them with *Business Week*. His new employer told him that the company's government contract proposals came from "really, really smart software engineers. . . . but writing was not their core competency." Crock created an office he called "Words R Us"; he noted that writing a business proposal is like telling a story, *"more similar to journalism than I had ever imagined."*[46]

The Lifers

After working in the field thirty years or more, a journalist has a reasonable claim to the title "lifer." Yet a quarter of those in our survey were journalists for over 40 years, including thirteen who had careers of more than 50 years and three who had careers of at least 60 years.[47] Sixty-two were still "working journalists"—as they used to call themselves—when we closed our accounts. Once retirement at 65 years of age was the norm; now Americans, including journalists, were living longer and staying in the workforce longer.[48]

Some of those intrepid journalists have had the same employer since we first met them: Bill Plante, CBS; Ann Compton, ABC, has been covering the White House since 1974; Robert Bazell, NBC, has been the network's chief science and health correspondent for over 30 years; Warren Brown, Jim Hoagland, and Walter Pincus, all of the *Washington Post,* are now columnists; Paula Cruickshank, CCH, is now bureau chief; Betty Mills became owner of Griffin-Larrabee, the small regional news service that she worked for; Clayton Jones has had a career at the *Christian Science Monitor* that has included many assignments, including chief editorial writer; Richard E. Cohen, congressional reporter, was with the *National Journal* until 2010, when he moved to *Politico* and then *CQ Weekly.*

Some stay on the same beat, letting their employers change: Lyle Denniston, who covered the Supreme Court, went from the *Washington Star* to the *Baltimore Sun* to the *Boston Globe;* Kim Masters, who covered the entertainment industry, went from NPR and other organizations to the *Hollywood Reporter.* Some invent new beats: consumer technology in the case of Jim Coates at the *Chicago Tribune* and Walter Mossberg at the *Wall Street Journal* and aging in the case of Saul Friedman at *Newsday*. Some go home to continue: Lee Bandy went back to South Carolina; Ellen Warren, to Chicago.[49] Some adjust as their options change: Finlay Lewis went from the *Minneapolis Tribune* to Copley News Service to the *Congressional Quarterly*. Some create new options: James O'Shea founded the *Chicago News Cooperative*. Some move as personal circumstances require: Eleanor Randolph went from Washington to Moscow to New York, employed in turn by the *Chicago Tribune,* the *Los Angeles Times,* the *Washington Post,* the *Los Angeles Times* (for a second stint), and the *New York Times*. Some buy newspapers to stay in journalism: Roy Bode bought four small newspapers in central Texas; Berl Schwartz became the owner, editor, and publisher of an alternative paper in East Lansing, Michigan. Bob Abernethy retired from NBC and created *Religion and Ethics Newsweekly* for PBS. Judy Woodruff returned to PBS to be an anchor on the *NewsHour*. Bill Keller, a regional reporter for the *Oregonian* in 1978, is now a columnist for the *New York Times*.

If there are shared characteristics among the lifers, a sense of optimism and an absence of cynicism would be high on the list, surprising perhaps to those who prefer the stereotype of the hard-boiled reporter and the crusty editor of the movies. Most journalists had little time for or interest in introspection. *"Never from the time that I first decided that I was going to be a journalist have I ever looked back and said, 'Oh, I made the wrong choice.'"*[50] When they were asked about their career "regrets," the items were usually marginal: not to have known a foreign language or not to have had an overseas assignment. Richard Ryan can be placed at the low end of the regret scale: *"I grew up in Detroit, went to school in Detroit. My family always took the* Detroit News; *I used to deliver the* Detroit News *when in school."* Ryan worked for the paper for almost 40 years and retired in 2006 as its Washington bureau chief. *"No, no regrets at all. . . . I just loved, loved it."*[51] In the middle would be the reporter who longed to be bureau chief but never made it and the reporter who longed to be hired by the *New York Times* but never got the call. Rare, at the other end of the scale, is the regret of Richard Roth, of CBS: *"I've achieved success but not fame. . . . I think that had I enjoyed similar success in print, I probably would have, by now, produced a book that I might still be proud to have on my shelf or a different sort of body of work."*[52]

Why They Stayed

Two of three reporters surveyed in 1978 spent a lifetime as journalists, during good and bad times. The answer to why they did is more complicated than "because they could afford to." But "because they could afford to" must be considered first.

In a group of 450 there were some for whom affordability was not a determining factor. Three were from publishing families. For the rest, journalism in Washington during this period was not as poorly paid as it once had been or was imagined to be. We did not ask specific questions about salary. But during wide-ranging, open-ended interviewing from 2005–11, reporters did very little complaining about money. The *Washington Post* is not a typical employer, but neither are its jobs hypothetical: according to the Washington-Baltimore Newspaper Guild, during 2008 negotiations there were 269 jobs at the *Post* listed for "reporter, bureau chief, or columnist." At the low end were seven jobs ranging from $40,000 through $49,999; in the middle were fifty-three jobs from $90,000 through $99,999. One hundred ten jobs ranged from $100,000 to a dollar shy of $150,000; twenty-one jobs continued up to $239,999.[53] TV network correspondents chose to volunteer that money was not a problem. Robert Pierpoint, commenting on his 40-year career at CBS: *"The company always treated me relatively well, and it was an outlet that paid well."*[54] Walter Rogers, after his years with ABC and CNN: *"The good thing about having worked in broadcasting all those years, almost 40 years, is you were paid well, and if you were provident, you put the money away. I don't need to work."*[55]

Moreover, what happens in the White House or on Capitol Hill—just as on Wall Street or in Hollywood—offers some reporters opportunities beyond their day jobs. More than one in four also freelanced—specifically, a third of those who covered the president or Congress and nearly half of the diplomatic correspondents. At the top, for instance, David Broder was a panelist on NBC's "Meet the Press" more than 400 times. With the rise of cable TV, by the '90s weekends were annexed by the political press corps. James Fallows castigated his colleagues for their speaking fees.[56]

There is, however, a more encompassing reason why journalists were marching into the upper middle class. Like other Americans, they were forming two-career families. The percentage of women participating in the workforce rose from 40.5 percent in 1970 to 61.4 percent in 2010, and the figures for college-educated women were higher. Because people usually marry within their own socioeconomic group, the spouses of journalists would have an undergraduate college degree or more, earning incomes commensurate with their education. At the same time, the number of women journalists in Washington doubled. Male and female journalists married other journalists or doctors, lawyers, professors, lobbyists, and high-level government workers. *"I think most anybody in any profession always wants to earn more,"* explained Richard Cohen, then with the *National Journal. "I think my wife, as a lawyer in a government agency, makes a little more than I do. The two of us together live comfortably, and the extra money that I've made from book writing helps. . . . I don't have huge complaints."*[57] The two-career-world that included Washington journalists came with its own boundary problems. When Andy Alexander's wife, a lawyer, registered as a lobbyist, they created *"a family rule that nobody from Capitol Hill, whether it's a staffer or a member of Congress, would come to our house for supper unless we knew them outside of that circle."*[58] Andy Glass discovered by accident that his wife, a psychiatrist, had patients from the White House who complained about him: *"You work it out."*[59]

Why individuals remained in journalism reflected their gender and race and where their birth date fell within the extended generation of those we interviewed. Jim Doyle had a vigorous career at the *Boston Globe* and *Newsweek,* retiring in 1998 as executive editor of Army Times Publishing Co. *"I was born in 1935, the middle of the Depression. There were fewer births that year than in the surrounding years. I came from a smaller cohort. It was a lot more explainable, first of all, that I would get into college, then that I would graduate from college and walk right into a job. . . . It's also true that I was a white male at a time when there was no competition from either minority males or from women. . . . Throughout my career that was true; only by the time I had sort of gotten to the top had women become a big competition and blacks as well. If the talent pool had been expanded by that, I would've had a much harder time getting those jobs."*[60]

"Why" also relates to the state of the economy and the state of the news industry. Previous chapters charted the ups and downs of the

Washington Star and the *Washington Post,* of UPI and AP; internal politics at the *New York Times;* competition at the TV networks and the coming of cable; new models in niche publishing that recast a growing segment of the Washington press corps; and the declining role of newspaper chains, illustrated through the careers of the members of the Gridiron Club. Such developments affect companies' personnel decisions, of course, but surprisingly few people were pushed out of journalism, although some had to relocate and some took early retirement. Since the 1979 energy crisis, the economy has been on a rollercoaster; relatively short recessions were followed by a long period of expansion until the collapse of the speculative dotcom bubble, the 9/11 attacks, and the subprime mortgage crisis. William Hickman, a reporter who got his first job in 1961, observed that *"I got to work during the golden era. I didn't have to worry about getting fired."*[61] Christopher Ogden, whose first job was in 1970, said that *"all the options were out there. . . . you know, head off to Chicago or Detroit; there were really good jobs."*[62] But those looking for work in the early '80s had a hard time, harder still at newspapers in the early '90s; on the other hand, those who came later did very well. The reporter who bought a home in 1978 in Georgetown, Bethesda, or Alexandria for $75,000 and stayed there, paid off the mortgage, and remodeled the kitchen now lives in a house with a sticker price of $1 to $2 million. A few can afford a mansion in McLean, looking down on the Potomac, and perhaps a ranch out West too.

Being able to pay the bills is a necessary but not sufficient reason to explain why some people were journalists for life. They had the talent and energy needed to earn as much in other lines of work. We turn now to the sufficient reason.

IF A GENERIC media employer had placed a generic advertisement in search of a generic Washington reporter of this era, it might have looked like this:

Seeking Washington reporter, potential for lifetime employment; college degree at good school expected but not required; adequate pay, although not bountiful, with possibilities for additional income; bureaucratic hassles modest compared with those in most office jobs; competitive yet congenial colleagues; challenging hours and schedules; foreign and domestic travel related to specific assignments; an upfront seat at key public events, including scandals. Must be able to disregard important people calling you by your first name. Preference given to those who desire to do good. Necessary to have mega-curiosity and writing, editing, or speaking skills.

"Plus, it's a lot of fun." In how many jobs do workers talk about having fun? Fun is what you do after work. Some of the jobs even come with the possibility of covering a once-in-a-lifetime event, one that will go down in history. Ike Pappas, reporting for CBS, was at Dallas police headquarters in 1963: *"I entered the basement of the Dallas police headquarters. . . . and I didn't know where I was going to stand to try to report this story of the departure of Oswald, so I found a little spot by the fender of the chase car of the armored truck and I squeezed in, and I didn't realize it, but I was squeezing in right in front of Jack Ruby. . . . and I saw this man jump in front of me with a black coat on, fedora hat, and suddenly there was a bang and a flash on Oswald's sweater and a moan, and he goes down, and here's 'My God what has happened now?' The things that cross your mind as a reporter: "Could this possibly be the assassin of the United States president now being killed?' Put that in words. And I just said what I saw."*[63]

David Garcia, reporting for ABC, was at the Supreme Court in 1974: *"Sitting in the courtroom listening to the White House tapes . . . and knowing full well that the president was in severe trouble. And that, in fact, his, our AG and staff people were being convicted. . . . I covered* United States *v.* Nixon. *From a payphone in the U.S. Supreme Court [I gave] the signal that I was coming out with the opinion in my hand. But you don't want to arrive at the camera site out of breath, and you need a couple of seconds to figure out what the Supreme Court said. And I managed to get it right, thank God for that."*[64]

Walter Rogers was covering a speech by President Reagan in 1981 for AP Radio: *"The president emerged from that speech at the Washington Hilton, and I didn't realize it, but John Hinckley was standing off my left shoulder with a gun, and the odd thing was he and I had a bit of an altercation at the time, verbal, mostly him. Then he started shooting at the president and others, and . . . I was very quick to file."*[65] Richard Roth, reporting for CBS, was in Beijing in 1989: *"I was sent to China to cover the pro-democracy movement in Tiananmen Square, and the only thing that became memorable about it was the fact that I was beaten up and arrested the night of the assault on Tiananmen Square, and I happened to be on the telephone live with New York at the time, so it was something that was quite dramatic."* But despite such extraordinary events, James Adams, of Reuters, observed: *"No matter what you do, no matter how exciting it is overall, it's not all exciting."* Adams had covered the "Black Hawk Down" story in Somalia and had been in the Pentagon media pool assigned to the Gulf War. *"In fact,"* he said, *"a lot of it is not exciting at all."*[66]

They were interesting times to be a reporter. But what times are not interesting to those who experience them? Yet these reporters were watching the center of the political world shift to the place where they were located—and attract a vast foreign press corps that proved the importance of reporting on and from Washington. Foreign correspondents accredited to the Congressional Press Galleries multiplied nearly eight times during these years.[67] Robert Rankin, a government and political editor at the McClatchy bureau: *"I've been able in some small way to be part of the history of the times. I had a seat at the table where Washington's business was done for most of the last quarter of a century, and it's been fascinating."*[68]

They were also interesting times because of changes in the business of journalism. Bill Zimmerman worked at ABC from 1971 to 1980: *"We sort of invented television news."*[69] Jed Duvall: *"I can't imagine anything better than working at* CBS News *at that great time. . . . I was there from '66 to '82; it was a gorgeous period to work."*[70] Eleanor Randolph: *"I was lucky enough to work in one of the great newspaper periods in American history."*[71] Watergate, a story that belonged to Washington reporters, turned some journalists into movie stars and their books into best sellers, and the press corps basked in reflected glory.

The one person who said "I went into journalism to save the world" didn't stay long. Still, there were well-meant references to journalism as a "calling," and most claimed a social utility for what they were doing. *"I believe we really can make a difference."*[72] *"It was hard, demanding work, but it was useful work."*[73] *"When things go right you feel that you are contributing to something that is worth doing, and that's a good feeling.*"[74] "*I think journalism is more than a career, it's life. I think it's a wonderful life.*"[75]

Others were content to be their communities' storytellers, gathering and passing along what they and their readers and viewers considered interesting; sometimes it was important, sometimes not. "*It's been a blast,*" concluded Judlyne Lilly. "*Such a blast.*"[76] For James Canan, "*If there is such a thing as reincarnation, I hope I come back in my present form. I mean professionally, not necessarily physically! I'd do it all over again. I just love journalism. I'm a news junkie, and I like to write. So there you are.*"[77] Edward Behr was 87 years old when we asked him if he was satisfied with his career. "*Yes, I am. Yes. I didn't get to be rich or famous, but other than that it was OK.*"[78]

WE LAID OUT the questions. What happened to the 450 Washington reporters that we surveyed in 1978? Some left. Why? Most stayed. Why? Now we have the answer. They stayed because they could afford to and because they loved being journalists. "*You know, the news is what drives you. It's sort of the unpredictability of it, not knowing what is coming next, reacting to it. I love it. I absolutely love it.*"[79] "*It was a wonderful way to make your living and get paid for it, and I would say I've been about as satisfied as any human being could be.*"[80] The answer is so simple that it may surprise those of us who are not journalists. It also means that there always will be journalists. Journalism changes, not human nature; new career paths will appear, shaped by changes in technology, refracted through the market economy.

We now have a massive store of information that we can use to compare or contrast the career patterns of the reporters that we surveyed with those of future generations of Washington reporters. What aspects of continuity and change will be revealed, what similarities and differences? That information is a legacy of these reporters, who were willing to tell their stories, to those who believe that those stories are worth listening to, that the study of journalism is a worthwhile pursuit.

THE REPORTERS OF 1978

This appendix covers the subsequent careers of the Washington reporters surveyed in 1978. It also indicates whether transcribed interviews exist; if so, they will be available in the future at the Manuscript Division, Library of Congress. Following each name, in parentheses, is the year that the person is believed to have begun his or her career in journalism; if no year is given, it is unknown. An asterisk following a name identifies individuals who left journalism. In some cases, years given for beginning and ending jobs or assignments are approximate. Enclosed in parentheses following year of death is the source of the obituary, if available.

Abernethy, Bob *(1952)*
1978: 50 years old, correspondent, NBC News.
1984: takes leave to attend Yale Divinity School.
1989: becomes Moscow correspondent for NBC; 1994, retires from NBC.
1997: creates and hosts *Religion and Ethics Newsweekly* (PBS).
Interview, 2007

Abramson, Rudy *(1958)*
1978: 40 years old, correspondent, *Los Angeles Times*.
1994: becomes executive director, Protect Historic America.
1995: becomes co-editor, *Encyclopedia of Appalachia*.
2008: died (*Los Angeles Times*, February 15, 2008).
Interview, 2007

Adams, James M. *(1976)*
1978: 23 years old, investigative reporter, WTTG-TV; in 1987, becomes anchor.
1993: heads Silver Screen Productions.
1995: becomes anchor at WRTV-TV, Indianapolis.
1997: joins NBC 4, Washington, D.C.; 2007, becomes anchor; 2008, leaves NBC 4.
Interview, 2007

Adams, James *(1965)*
1978: 41 years old, investigative reporter, Associated Press (AP).
1982: moves to Reuters as Capitol Hill chief; 1983, becomes State Department reporter; 1984, becomes editor; late 1980s, becomes Capitol Hill reporter; around 1990, becomes Pentagon reporter.
1997: retires.
Interview, 2007

Adams, Robert *(1966)*
1978: 37 years old, reporter, *St. Louis Post-Dispatch.*
1993: retires.

Albright, Joseph *(1953)*
1978: 41 years old, correspondent, Cox Newspapers; 1983, becomes Rome correspondent.
1986: takes fellowship in international relations at MIT.
1987: returns to Cox as Washington correspondent; 1990, becomes Middle East correspondent; 1991, returns to Washington as correspondent; 1993, becomes Moscow correspondent; 1998, becomes Beijing correspondent.
2000: retires to start recreational ranch in Wyoming.
Interviews, 1977, 2007

Aldrich, Charles *(1968)*
1978: 35 years old, manager, Commerce Clearing House (CCH).
1996: retires.
Interview, 2007

Aldrich, Nancy *(1973)*
1978: 27 years old, editor, *Water Resources Newsletter*, Business Publisher, Inc. (BPI); 1984, switches from covering the environment to covering aging.
2002: leaves BPI to freelance.
Interview, 2007

Alexander, Andrew *(1971)*
1978: 30 years old, regional reporter, *Dayton Journal Herald,* Cox Newspapers Washington bureau; around 1984, becomes national reporter; 1986, becomes foreign editor; 1992, becomes deputy bureau chief; 1997, becomes bureau chief.
2009–11, works as ombudsman, *Washington Post.*
2012: becomes Distinguished Visiting Professional at E. W. Scripps School of Journalism, Ohio University.
Interviews, 2006, 2008

Allen, Ira R. *(1970)**
1978: 30 years old, reporter, United Press International (UPI); 1988, becomes White House correspondent.
1989: leaves journalism and becomes congressional press secretary.
1990: joins Center for Advancement of Health to manage public affairs; 2007, becomes press officer, U.S. Food and Drug Administration, and public affairs specialist, National Institutes of Health.
Interview, 2006

Alwood, Edward *(1974)**
1978: 28 years old, reporter/anchor, WTTG-TV.
1981: becomes reporter, Financial News Television Network, New York.
1982: becomes freelance reporter for CNN, Washington; 1982, becomes reporter, WFTV-TV, Orlando, Florida.
1985: becomes correspondent, CNN, Washington.
1987: leaves journalism and becomes public relations manager, American Bankers Association. 1995–97: works as senior public affairs specialist, U.S. Treasury Department.
2000: obtains Ph.D. in journalism/mass communications, University of North Carolina; becomes assistant professor, Temple University.
2002: becomes tenure track professor, Quinnipiac University.
Interview, 2006

Anderson, James *(1960)*
1978: 49 years old, State Department reporter, UPI.
1990: English language reporter for Deutsche Presse Agentur.
2001: retires and continues to do some freelance work.
2011: died (*Washington Post*, February 13, 2011).
Interview, 2002

Antevil, Jeffrey H. *(1964)*
1978: 37 years old, diplomatic correspondent, *New York Daily News.*
1979: moves to Reuters as national security correspondent; 1984, becomes news editor, Washington bureau; 1987, becomes assistant world news editor, London; 1990, becomes Americas editor, New York; 1998, becomes world features editor.
2002: retires.
2005: becomes part-time desk editor, *New York Times.*
Interview, 2007

Arehart-Treichel, Joan *(1963)*
1978: 36 years old, writer, *Science News.*
1983: moves to Germany with family; freelances for *Journal of the American Medical Association.*
1999: becomes senior writer, *Psychiatric News* (American Psychological Association).
Interview, 2007

Arieff, Irwin *(1974)*
1978: 31 years old, reporter, *Congressional Quarterly (CQ).*
1982: Joins Reuters in Washington bureau; 1994, goes to Paris bureau; 1999, goes to New York bureau; 2000, becomes UN correspondent.
2007: retires, becomes freelance writer.
2008: becomes copy editor, *LifeWire.*
Interview, 2009

Arvidson, Cheryl *(1971)**
1978: 30 years old, reporter, UPI.
1980: becomes national correspondent, Cox Newspapers.
1985: becomesWashington bureau chief, *Dallas Times Herald.*
1992: leaves journalism, joins Blue Cross, Blue Shield Association as communications director.
1994: becomes media relations director and program director for the Freedom Forum.
2002: becomes assistant director of strategic communications, Council of Insurance Agents and Brokers.

2009: becomes assistant director of communications, Recovery Accountability and Transparency Board.
Interview, 2006

Aug, Stephen M. *(1956)*
1978: 42 years old, regulatory agencies reporter, *Washington Star.*
1981: becomes business and economy reporter, ABC News.
1995: retires; freelances and teaches journalism part-time at Towson University.
Interview, 2007

Averill, John H. *(1948)*
1978: 55 years old, Senate reporter, *Los Angeles Times*; 1980, switches to writing obituaries because of poor health.
1984: died (*Los Angeles Times,* January 11, 1984).

Bacon, Donald *(1957)*
1978: 43 years old, associate editor, *U.S. News & World Report;* 1979, becomes assistant managing editor and later editor of congressional coverage; 1987, leaves *U.S. News & World Report.*
1988: becomes co-editor, *Encyclopedia of Congress.*
1993: retires.
Interview, 2009

Bailey, Becky *(1971)**
1978: 27 years old, reporter/anchor, Mutual Broadcasting.
1998: leaves journalism, becomes press secretary for Representative Louise Slaughter (D-N.Y.).
2001: becomes communications director for Senator Barbara Mikulski (D-Md.).
2001: joins Consumer Product Safety Commission as deputy director of public affairs.
2003: becomes director of public affairs, U.S. Mint.
Interview, 2007

Bailey, Gil *(1955)*
1978: 44 years old, reporter, Knight Ridder Newspapers.
1978: moves to Seattle and becomes reporter, *Seattle Post-Intelligencer.*
1998: retires.
Interview, 2007

Bain, C. Jackson *(1973)**
1978: 34 years old, correspondent, NBC News.
1981: hosts *Prime Panorama*, WTTG-TV, Washington; 1982, becomes managing editor.
1985: leaves journalism, joins Gray and Company, a public relations firm; 1988, becomes senior vice president of Hill and Knowlton after merger with Gray and Company.
1991: starts Bain and Associates.
2007: becomes vice president, public affairs, for the National Association of Children's Hospitals and Related Institutions.
Interview, 2007

Bandy, Leland *(1961)*
1978: 43 years old, correspondent, *The State* (Columbia, S.C.); 1992, transfers to the home office in Columbia as chief political writer and columnist.
2008: retires.
Interviews, 1984, 2006

Barbieri, Anthony *(1970)*
1978: 30 years old, reporter, *Baltimore Sun;* 1978, goes to Moscow bureau; 1984, goes to Tokyo bureau; 1989, becomes city editor; 2000, becomes managing editor.
2004: retires.
2005: becomes journalism professor, University of Maryland.
2007: becomes Foster Professor of Writing and Editing, Penn State University.
Interview, 2007

Barnett, David *(1952)*
1978: 56 years old, columnist, *U.S. News & World Report;* 1987, retires as managing editor.
1995: died (*Times Union* [Albany, N.Y.], January 20, 1995).

Baron, Stephen *(1972)**
1978: 29 years old, reporter, *Providence Journal-Bulletin;* leaves journalism and works for Raytheon.
[incomplete information]

Barton, John F. *(1959)*
1978: 46 years old, diplomatic correspondent, UPI.
1984: joins U.S. Information Agency, then Voice of America.
1998: retires.
Interview, 2009

Bascom, Jon *(1970)*
1978: 33 years old, anchor, Mutual Broadcasting.
1982: becomes chief congressional correspondent for Satellite News Channel.
1984: joins ABC Radio as a general assignment reporter.
2006: becomes anchor, Bloomberg News.
Interview, 2007

Battey, Phil *(1978)**
1978: 25 years old, reporter, *American Banker.*
1982: leaves journalism, becomes director of editorial services, American Bankers Association. 1986–93: becomes speechwriter and director of public affairs, Office of the Comptroller of the Currency.
1993–2003, becomes special assistant and director of public affairs at the office of the chairman of the FDIC.
2003: becomes vice president, legislative and public affairs, Promontory Interfinancial Network.
Interview, 2007

Baulch, Jerry T. *(1939)*
1978: 64 years old, reporter, AP.
1978: retires.
1985: died (Associated Press, February 7, 1985).

Bazell, Robert *(1971)*
1978: 32 years old, chief science and health correspondent, NBC News; still employed in that capacity.
Interview, 2007

Beecher, William *(1955)**
1978: 44 years old, diplomatic correspondent, *Boston Globe.*
1981: leaves journalism, becomes acting assistant secretary of defense for public affairs.
1993: becomes director of public affairs, U.S. Nuclear Regulatory Commission.
2004: becomes principal, Dilenschneider Group, New York.
2009: becomes adjunct professor, University of Maryland.
Interviews, 2006, 2007

Behr, Edward A. *(1945)*
1978: 58 years old, feature editor, *Wall Street Journal.*
1985: retires.
2012: died (*Washington Post,* September 28, 2012).
Interview, 2007

Bell, Stephen *(1967)*
1978: 42 years old, correspondent, ABC News.
1986: becomes anchor, KYW-TV, Philadelphia.
1992: becomes professor of telecommunications, Ball State University.
2007: retires.

Benedict, Howard *(1953)*
1978: 50 years old, White House correspondent and aviation and transportation writer, AP; 1984, becomes correspondent covering the NASA space program, Cape Canaveral, Florida.

1990: retires and becomes executive director, Mercury 7 Foundation, later called Astronaut Scholarship Foundation.
2005: died (NASA, April 27, 2005).

Benjamin, Stan *(1957)*
1978: 46 years old, environment and energy reporter, AP.
1981: becomes correspondent, Newhouse News Service Washington bureau.
1982: becomes a freelance writer.
1993: retires.
Interview, 2007

Berkowitz, Bob *(1974)*
1978: 28 years old, correspondent, AP Radio.
1980: becomes Senate correspondent, then White House correspondent, CNN.
1982: moves to New York; becomes ABC News correspondent.
1985: joins NBC *Today Show* as "men's correspondent."
1988: becomes late-night talk show host, Financial News Network.
1990: hosts *Real Personal* on CNBC.
1995: becomes regular commentator on *The View.*
2002: hosts *Naked New York with Bob Berkowitz.*
2006: produces a forty-video series for iVillage.com entitled *What Men Won't Tell You, But Women Need to Know.*
2008: becomes principal, Dilenschneider Group.
Interview, 2007

Berlow, Alan *(1972)*
1978: 28 years old, reporter, *CQ.*
1979: becomes Southeast Asia correspondent, National Public Radio.
1989: becomes freelance journalist, writes frequently about criminal justice issues.

Bernstein, Jonathan *(1977)**
1978: 27 years old, correspondent, *National Enquirer*; 1979, becomes Florida correspondent; 1980, becomes Los Angeles correspondent.
1981: leaves journalism; becomes manager of public relations, Playboy Enterprises.
1982: becomes executive director, Redondo Beach Chamber of Commerce.
1985: becomes senior account executive, Grody-Tellem Communication.
1989: becomes vice president for crisis communications, Ruder Finn, Inc.
1994: starts Bernstein Communications, later Bernstein Crisis Management.
Interview, 2007

Bethell, Tom *(1970)*
1978: 37 years old, editor, *Harper's Magazine.*
1981: begins freelancing for the *American Spectator*, becomes a senior editor; freelances for other publications.
Interview, 2007

Betts, Roy *(1977)**
1978: 22 years old, reporter, *Ebony* and *Jet* magazines.
1980: becomes reporter, Plus Publications.
1983: leaves journalism to join the public affairs department, U.S. Department of Commerce.
1988: becomes public affairs official, U.S. Postal Service.
Interview, 2007

Blake, Jr., Michael H. *(1956)*
1978: 42 years old, managing editor, Bureau of National Affairs (BNA).
1986: retires; died later that year (*Washington Post*, September 29, 1986).

Blanchard, Allan E. *(1954)*
1978: 49 years old, bureau chief, *Detroit News.*
1978: died (*Washington Post*, September 18, 1978).

Blatt, Dan *(1968)*
1978: 42 years old, managing editor of corporate practice series and legal editor, BNA.
1978: becomes financial columnist *Miami Review* (until 1983).
1990s: becomes BNA managing editor in Sacramento.
1998: becomes publisher, *FUTURECASTS* online magazine.

Bode, Roy E. *(1970)*
1978: 29 years old, bureau chief, *Dallas Times Herald*; 1979, becomes state editor; 1981, becomes assistant managing editor for news; 1985, becomes associate editor.
1986: becomes editor, *North Jersey Herald.*
1988: becomes editor-in-chief, *Dallas Times Herald.*
1991: becomes vice president of public affairs, University of Texas Southwestern Medical School.
2006: becomes owner and editor, Bar 30 Media Publications.
Interviews, 1978, 2007

Bolbach, Cynthia *(1972)*
1978: 30 years old, managing editor, *Media Law Reporter*, BNA; 2007, vice president and corporate secretary.
2012: died (*Washington Post*, December 22, 2012).
Interview, 2007

Bonafede, Dom *(1955)*
1978: 45 years old, White House correspondent, *National Journal*; 1980, chief political correspondent.
1985: becomes associate professor of journalism, American University.
1998: died (*Washington Post*, January 16, 1998).
Interview, 1978

Bonner, Christopher *(1967)**
1978: 30 years old, regional reporter, Knight Ridder Newspapers.
1982: leaves journalism; works in public relations for the American Textile Manufacturers Institute and the National Organization of Life and Health Guaranty Associations.
1992: joins the Arnold and Truwitt consulting practice.
1994, becomes president, Bonner Consultants, Inc.
Interview, 2006

Boyce, Richard *(1955)*
1978: 59 years old, diplomatic reporter, Scripps Howard.
1984: retires.
2000: died (Scripps Howard, January 25, 2000).

Bradee, Richard *(1949)*
1978: 46 years old, bureau chief, *Milwaukee Sentinel*.
1992: retires.
Interview, 2009

Bradsher, Henry S. *(1955)*
1978: 47 years old, chief diplomatic correspondent, *Washington Star*.
1982: senior analyst, CIA.
2000: retires.
Interview, 2009

Braaten, Susan *(née Fogg)**
1978: 31 years old, reporter, Newhouse News Service.
1980: leaves journalism.
1987: earns master's in education at George Mason University; begins teaching.
Interview, 2007

Brazaitis, Thomas J. *(1964)*
1978: 37 years old, correspondent, *Cleveland Plain Dealer*; 1979, becomes bureau chief; 1998, becomes senior editor; 2002, retires but continues as columnist.
2005: died (*Washington Post*, March 31, 2005).

Brown, Warren *(1969)*
1978: 30 years old, reporter, *Washington Post*; 1982, becomes business reporter and later, automotive industry columnist.
2009: retires; continues to write column under contract.
Interviews, 2007, 2011

Buchanan, Christopher *(1977)**
1978: 26 years old, reporter, CQ.
1981: works on a documentary project, National Public Radio.
1981: becomes freelance documentarian.
1985: becomes producer, NPR.
1986: leaves journalism, becomes production office coordinator on film *Raising Arizona*.
1996: becomes assistant location manager on film *Get on the Bus*.
Interview, 2008

Burkhardt, Robert D. *(1948)*
1978: 60 years old, commercial aviation writer, *New York Journal of Commerce*.
1990: retires.
1999: died (*Jack O'Dwyer's Newsletter*, February 3, 1999).

Burns, Kathleen M. *(1968)*
1978: 33 years old, editor-reporter, Capitol Publications.
1979: becomes business and economics reporter, UPI.
1980–89, other years: works as freelance writer and teaches journalism at Washington-area schools.
1990–95: works as freelance reporter in Australia for BNA, *Washington Post*, CNN.
1999–2002: works as editor, trade journal for bedding industry.
2000–02: serves as vice chair, Alexandria (Virginia) Traffic and Parking Board.
Interview, 2011

Burns, Robert *(1968)*
1978: 40 years old, correspondent/ anchor, Mutual Broadcasting.
1986: Voice of America newscaster.
Interview, 2007

Burt, Richard *(1976)**
1978: 31 years old, national security correspondent, *New York Times.*
1981: leaves journalism, becomes director of politico-military affairs, U.S. Department of State. 1983: becomes assistant secretary of state for European and Canadian affairs.
1985: becomes U.S. ambassador to Federal Republic of Germany.
1989: becomes chief U.S. negotiator, START talks.
1991: becomes partner, McKinsey & Company.
2001: becomes chairman, Diligence, Inc., and later senior director, McLarty Associates.
Interview, 2007

Byrd, Lee *(1966)*
1978: 33 years old, reporter, AP.
1993: retires.
2004: died (*Cleartime* [AP], 2010).

Cameron, Juan M. *(1952)*
1978: 52 years old, Washington editor, *Fortune.*
1982: retires.
2009: died (*Washington Post,* July 6, 2009).

Campbell, Don *(1968)*
1978: 34 years old, White House correspondent, Gannett News Service; 1983, becomes Washington editor, *USA Today;* 1985, becomes managing editor, Gannett.
1988: becomes director, Paul Miller Washington Reporting Fellowships.
1989: becomes director, Washington Journalism Center.
1993: becomes executive director, Chicago Sun-Times Features Syndicate, Chicago.

1994: becomes professor of journalism, Medill School of Journalism, Northwestern University. 1996: teaches journalism at the University of Oregon; 1999, teaches at Arizona State University; 2001, teaches at Emory University.
Interview, 2007

Camper, Diane *(1968)*
1978: 30 years old, editorial assistant, *Newsweek*
1983: serves on editorial board, *New York Times.*
1997: becomes public affairs manager for the Annie E. Casey Foundation.
2003: becomes senior fellow, Annie E. Casey Foundation.
2004: becomes assistant editorial page editor, *Baltimore Sun.*
2008: becomes communications officer, Public Welfare Foundation.
Interview, 2009

Canan, James *(1955)*
1978: 48 years old, national security correspondent, *Business Week.*
1983: becomes senior editor, *Air Force Magazine.*
1994: retires, begins to work as freelancer.
1996: becomes contributing writer, *Aerospace America Magazine.*
Interview, 2007

Carelli, Richard *(1969)*
1978: 32 years old, Supreme Court reporter, AP.
2000: becomes public affairs specialist for the federal court system.
Interview, 2007

Cary, James *(1947)*
1978: 58 years old, chief correspondent, Copley News Service.
1981: retires.
1984: becomes visiting professor of journalism, Brigham Young University.
Interview, 2007

Cawthorne, David *(1977)*
1978: 29 years old, reporter, *Journal of Commerce*.
1990: becomes writer, *Traffic World* magazine.
1998: died (*Journal of Commerce*, January 21, 1998).

Cazalas, Robert P. *(1969)*
1978: 35 years old, president, *Daily Maritime Bulletin*, Congressional Information Bureau.
2010: died (*Washington Post*, September 22, 2010).
Interview, 2007

Chamberlayne, Pye *(1958)*
1978: 40 years old, reporter, UPI Audio.
1999: retires.
2006: died (*Washington Post*, November 7, 2006).

Choyke, Bill *(1972)*
1978: 28 years old, correspondent, *Fort Worth Star Tribune*.
1979: becomes reporter, Cox News.
1981: becomes defense reporter, *Dallas Morning News*; 1987, becomes deputy bureau chief.
1991: receives MBA, University of Virginia.
1993: becomes marketing services director, Gannett Newspapers, Iowa.
1995: becomes editor and later assistant managing editor, *The Tennessean*.
2003: becomes business editor, *Virginian-Pilot*; 2008, leaves *Virginian-Pilot*.
Interview, 2006

Cimons, Marlene *(1967)*
1978: 33 years old, features writer, *Los Angeles Times*; 1980, general assignment reporter; 1983, sports beat; 1985, switches to health policy.
2001: becomes freelancer.
2002: becomes adjunct professor, University of Maryland.
2008: receives Ph.D. in journalism from the University of Maryland.

2009: becomes senior writer, National Science Foundation.
Interviews, 2006, 2011

Claiborne, William L. *(1960)*
1978: 42 years old, national correspondent, *Washington Post*; 1978, Jerusalem correspondent; 1982, South Asia bureau chief; 1985, Jerusalem bureau chief; 1986, South Africa bureau chief; 1990, Canada bureau chief; 1992, national correspondent; 1994, West Coast bureau chief, Los Angeles; 1998, national correspondent; 1999, Midwest bureau chief, Chicago.
2001: retires.
2013: died (*Washington Post*, March 3, 2013).
Interviews, 2007, 2011

Clymer, Adam *(1960)*
1978: 40 years old, national political correspondent, *New York Times*; 1983, becomes polling editor, New York; 1988, becomes political editor; 1991, becomes chief congressional correspondent; 1997, becomes Washington editor; 1999, becomes Washington correspondent; 2003: retires from the *Times*.
2004: becomes visiting scholar, Annenberg Public Policy Center.
2006: becomes freelance journalist.
Interviews, 1977, 2006

Coates, James *(1967)*
1978: 35 years old, correspondent, *Chicago Tribune*; 1983, becomes Denver bureau chief and Western correspondent; 1993, becomes technology columnist, Chicago.
2007: retires.
Interview, 2007

Cohen, Richard E. *(1973)*
1978: 30 years old, staff correspondent, *National Journal*.
2010: becomes senior congressional reporter, *Politico*.
2011: becomes staff writer, *CQ Weekly*.
Interview, 2006

Cohn, Victor E. *(1941)*
1978: 58 years old, science editor,
    Washington Post.
1993: retires.
2000: died (*Minneapolis Star-Tribune,*
    February 15, 2000).

Cole, Benjamin R. *(1938)*
1978: 61 years old, bureau chief,
    Indianapolis Star.
1986: retires.
2002: died (*Indianapolis Star,*
    December 24, 2002).

Cole, Martha *(1946)*
1978: 61 years old, reporter, AP.
1978: retires.
1986: died (*Washington Post,* January
    14, 1986).

Comarow, Avery *(1970)*
1978: 33 years old, correspondent and
    bureau chief, *Money Magazine.*
1980: becomes Washington editor,
    Consumer Reports.
1982: begins working for *Science*
    magazine; 1984, becomes assistant
    managing editor.
1986: becomes assistant managing
    editor, *U.S. News & World Report;*
    1999, becomes senior writer.
Interview, 2009

Compton, Ann *(1970)*
1978: 31 years old, White House
    correspondent, ABC News; 2000,
    becomes chief White House
    correspondent, ABCNews.com; 2001,
    becomes White House correspondent,
    ABC Radio News.
Interview, 2006

Conderacci, Greg *(1973)**
1978: 29 years old, economics
    correspondent, *Wall Street Journal.*
1980: leaves journalism and works for
    Catholic Charities, Baltimore.
1990: becomes marketing director, Price
    Waterhouse.
1992: becomes vice president, marketing,
    Prudential Healthcare Plan.

1996: becomes chief marketing officer,
    Alex Brown.
2003: starts Good Ground Consulting.
Interview, 2007

Conlon, Mike *(1964)*
1978: 37 years old, correspondent, UPI.
1983: becomes Chicago correspondent,
    Reuters.
2009: retires.
Interview, 2007

Connell, Christopher *(1971)*
1978: 29 years old, health, education,
    and welfare correspondent, AP; 1983,
    becomes education correspondent;
    1989, becomes White House
    correspondent; 1992, becomes
    health correspondent; 1995, becomes
    assistant bureau chief.
1999: becomes freelance project writer
    for foundations and nonprofits.
Interview, 2006

Connolly, Michael J. *(1975)*
1978: 28 years old, regional
    correspondent, Gannett News
    Service; 1981–84, works as White
    House correspondent.
1984–86: director of information, Texas
    General Land Office, Austin.
[incomplete information]

Conte, Christopher *(1974)**
1978: 27 years old, correspondent, *CQ.*
1979: becomes correspondent, *Wall
    Street Journal*; 1986, becomes editor,
    copy desk.
1994: leaves journalism and freelances
    for foundations.
2007: becomes Knight International
    Press Fellow, Uganda.
Interview, 2007

Cook, Rhodes *(1977)*
1978: 30 years old, reporter, *CQ*; 1987,
    becomes senior writer.
1997: retires, starts a website and works
    as freelancer.
Interview, 2006

Cormier, Frank *(1951)*
1978: 50 years old, senior White House correspondent, AP.
1980: retires.
1994: died (*New York Times,* February 11, 1994).

Cowan, Edward *(1957)**
1978: 45 years old, economics reporter, *New York Times;* 1983, becomes assistant news editor.
1986: leaves journalism; 1986, does investment research with Ried, Thunberg & Co.
1999: becomes Knight International Press Fellow, Indonesia.
1999–2002: works as associate editor, American Enterprise Institute.
2004: founds "Report to DC Voters," e-mail service on D.C. affairs.
Interview, 2011

Cox, Merrilee *(1972)*
1978: 28 years old, correspondent, UPI Audio; 1981, becomes bureau manager.
1982: moves to New York, joins ABC Radio as contemporary news radio director and later becomes general manager of programming; 2000, becomes Washington bureau chief of ABC Radio.
2005: retires.
2008: enters Ph.D. program in journalism, University of Maryland.
Interview, 2009

Crawford-Mason, Clare *(1958)*
1978: 41 years old, Washington bureau chief, *People* magazine; senior producer, *Weekend,* NBC News; 1980, leaves NBC.
1981: becomes president, CC-M Productions, Inc.
1982: leaves *People.*
Interview, 2007

Crock, Stan *(1973)*
1978: 28 years old, reporter, *Wall Street Journal.*
1983: becomes editor, McGraw-Hill World News.

1986: becomes news editor, *Business Week;* 1995, becomes chief diplomatic correspondent.
2006: becomes senior editorial director, Accenture (global management consulting company).
Interview, 2009

Crowley, Mary E. *(1978)*
1978: 21 years old, congressional and White House reporter, Thomson Newspapers.
1983: becomes assistant managing editor, *Communications Daily;* becomes editor, other newsletters.
2002: starts consulting firm, teaches journalism part-time, University of Maryland, George Washington University, University of Phoenix.
Interview, 2007

Cruickshank, Paula *(née Lazor) (1977)*
1978: 23 years old, White House reporter, Commerce Clearing House (CCH); 2005, becomes bureau chief.
Interview, 2007

Cullen, Robert C. *(1970)*
1978: 29 years old, diplomatic correspondent, AP.
1980: receives Knight Fellowship, Stanford.
1981: returns to foreign desk at AP.
1982: becomes Moscow bureau chief, *Newsweek;* 1985, becomes New York general editor.
1989: becomes freelance journalist and novelist.
2006: becomes English teacher, Prince George's County (Maryland) Public Schools.
Interview, 2007

Cunningham, Robert *(1971)*
1978: 29 years old, Washington correspondent, *The Record* (Bergen County, N.J.); 1983, moves to desk production/editing and later becomes page one editor, managing editor for copy desk, and managing editor for production.
2005: retires.
Interview, 2007

Curley, John *(1963)*
1978: 39 years old, Washington bureau chief, Gannett News Service.
1980: becomes publisher, *News Journal* (Delaware).
1982: becomes editor, *USA Today*; 1984, becomes president, Gannett News Division; 1986–97, serves as president and CEO; 1989–2001, serves as chairman.
2001: retires; is now a professor of journalism at Penn State University.
Interviews, 1977, 2009

Dalecki, Kenneth B. *(1971)*
1978: 35 years old, reporter, Thomson Newspapers.
1980: becomes editor, *Congressional Quarterly*.
1985: becomes reporter, Kiplinger Publications and later editor and deputy managing editor for special projects.
2004: retires; becomes contributing magazine writer, League of United Latin American Citizens.
Interview, 2007

Dancy, John *(1959)*
1978: 41 years old, Washington reporter, NBC News; 1994, goes to Moscow bureau; 1996, retires.
1997: becomes part-time professor, Duke University.
2002: becomes Shapiro Fellow, School of Media and Public Affairs, George Washington University.
Interview, 2007

Daniloff, Nicholas *(1959)*
1978: 43 years old, Washington correspondent, UPI.
1980: Washington correspondent, *U.S. News & World Report*; 1981, becomes Moscow bureau chief; 1986, arrested by Soviet Union and accused of espionage, released.
1989: becomes professor of journalism, Northeastern University.
Interview, 2007

Davey, Charles H. *(1945)*
1978: 62 years old, economics editor and columnist, *U.S. News & World Report*.
1979: retires.
1992: died (*Sacramento Bee*, May 26, 1992).

Dawson, Russell *(1976)**
1978: 29 years old, editor, Business Publishers, Inc.
1982: leaves journalism and becomes director of public affairs, National Criminal Justice Association.
1983: becomes assistant for communications to the administrator, Environmental Protection Agency.
1990: becomes senior vice president, Potomac Communications Group.
Interview, 2007

Dear, David R.
1978: 50 years old, owner, Dear Publications.
1986: sells Dear Publications, retires.
Interview, 2007

Degler, Stanley *(1964)*
1978: 48 years old, associate editor, BNA; 1980s, becomes division head, later executive editor; 1989, becomes senior vice president.
1990: retires.
Interview, 2007

Delaney, William *(1964)**
1978: 38 years old, politics and education reporter, *Washington Star*.
1978: leaves journalism.
1991: died (*Washington Post*, August 24, 1991).

Delong, Edward
1978: 35 years old, reporter/editor, UPI; leaves UPI to found marketing and graphic design company.
2001: moves to Australia; becomes editor, *Mudgee Guardian and Gulgong Advertiser*.

Denniston, Lyle *(1948)*
1978: 47 years old, Supreme Court reporter, *Washington Star.*
1981: becomes Supreme Court reporter, *Baltimore Sun.*
2001–04: becomes Supreme Court reporter, *Boston Globe.*
2005: becomes Supreme Court blogger, SCOTUSblog, and adviser on constitutional literacy, National Constitution Center.
Interview, 2007

Devroy, Ann *(1970)*
1978: 29 years old, regional and national politics reporter, Gannett Newspapers.
1985: becomes political editor, *Washington Post*; 1989, begins covering White House.
1997: died (*New York Times*, October 24, 1997).

Dewar, Helen *(1959)*
1978: 41 years old, reporter, *Washington Post*; 1979, becomes Senate reporter.
2004: retires.
2006: died (*Washington Post*, November 5, 2006).

DeWitt, Karen *(1972)*
1978: 34 years old, feature writer, *New York Times.*
1981–82: host of "Karen's Kitchen," WETA-BETA cooking show.
1982: joins *USA Today*, becomes assistant national editor, White House correspondent, and foreign correspondent.
1990: returns to *New York Times* as a Washington correspondent.
2001: becomes senior producer for *Nightline*, ABC.
2001–04: works as media consultant.
2004: becomes director of public affairs, D.C. Water and Sewage Authority.
2006: becomes Washington editor and columnist for the *Examiner;* subsequently becomes director of communications for the Leadership Conference on Civil Rights.
Interview, 2006

Dickenson, James *(1959)*
1978: 46 years old, national political reporter, *Washington Star*; 1979, becomes national editor.
1980: becomes political editor, *Washington Post.*
1989: becomes media consultant.
1999: works on contract basis, Library of Congress.
2005: works on contract basis, U.S. Department of State.
Interview, 2007

Dininny, Paulette *(1976)*
1978: 33 years old, associate editor, *Kiplinger Letters*, and reporter, other independent publishing companies.
1991: becomes writer/editor for a professional association.
1996: begins writing newspaper and magazine articles as a freelancer.
Interview, 2007

Dobrzynski, Judith *(1973)*
1978: 29 years old, Washington correspondent, *Business Week*; 1979, becomes London correspondent; 1983, becomes department editor; 1986, becomes associate editor; 1987, becomes senior writer; 1991, becomes senior editor.
1995: becomes business reporter, *New York Times*; 1997, becomes culture reporter; 2000, becomes Sunday business editor.
2003: becomes managing editor, CNBC; 2005, becomes executive editor.
2005: leaves CNBC, becomes freelance writer.
2006: joins faculty, Columbia University Graduate School of Journalism, specializing in arts and lifestyle reporting.
Interview, 2007

Dombrowski, Cathy *(1970)*
1978: 30 years old, reporter and editor, BPI.
1988: starts newsletter on hazardous waste treatment technology.
2006: becomes writer, *Pink Sheet*, covering the FDA and pharmaceuticals.
Interview, 2006

Donaldson, Sam *(1960)*
1978: 44 years old, White House correspondent, ABC News; 1981, becomes panelist, *This Week* with David Brinkley; 1996, co-hosts *This Week* with Cokie Roberts; 1998, becomes anchor, *20/20;* 2002, steps down as *This Week* host, continues as panelist; 2010, becomes contributor and analyst, ABC News.

Doyle, James *(1960)*
1978: 42 years old, chief political correspondent and deputy bureau chief, *Newsweek*; 1983, becomes contributing editor.
1983: becomes assistant editorial director, Army Times Publishing Company;1984, becomes vice president and executive editor.
1998: retires.
Interview, 2009

Duke, Robert *(1958)*
1978: 45 years old, correspondent, Scripps Howard; subsequently financial writer for American Banker–Bond Buyer and housing editor for CD Publications, Maryland.
2001: died.

Dunsmore, Barrie *(1957)*
1978: 39 years old, diplomatic correspondent, ABC News; 1984, becomes senior foreign correspondent; 1992, becomes Washington diplomatic correspondent; 1995, retires from ABC.
1996: becomes fellow, Shorenstein Center on Press, Politics, and Public Policy, Harvard.
1996: moves to Vermont, writes column for two Vermont newspapers and becomes commentator, Vermont public radio.
Interview, 2007

Duvall, Jed *(1961)*
1978: 41 years old, correspondent, CBS News.
1982: becomes reporter, *Nightline*, ABC; 1984, becomes *Weekend News* reporter; 1989, hosts *Good Morning America*.
1990: becomes freelance writer.
1993–1994: becomes London and Mogadishu correspondent, NBC News.
1994–95: works as freelancer, CNN.
1996–97: works as freelancer, Fox News.
Interview, 2008

Eagle, Jacqueline E.
1978: 49 years old, editor and writer, *Telecommunications Reports.*
1995: retires.
2011: died (*Washington Post,* February 8, 2011).

Eastham, Tom *(1945)*
1978: 54 years old, correspondent, Hearst Newspapers.
1982: becomes director of public information, City of San Francisco, and later press secretary for Mayor Dianne Feinstein.
1987: becomes vice president and Western director, Hearst Foundations.
2005: retires.
2013: died

Eaton, William *(1954)*
1978: 47 years old, reporter, *Los Angeles Times*; 1984, becomes Moscow bureau chief; 1988, becomes Washington reporter.
1994: retires.
2005: died (*Washington Post,* August 26, 2005).

Eberhart, Jonathan *(1960)*
1978: 35 years old, space sciences editor, *Science News.*
1991: retires.
2003: died (*Washington Post,* February 26, 2003).

Eberle, Jim *(1974)**
1978: 34 years old, reporter, Scripps Howard.
1978: leaves journalism, becomes vice president for communications, National Savings and Loan League, which merges with U.S. League of Savings Institutions, which merges into America's Community Bankers.
Interview, 2007

Egerstrom, Lee *(1968)*
1978: 36 years old, regional correspondent, *St. Paul Pioneer Press* (Knight Ridder Newspapers); 1980, returns to St. Paul, becomes agriculture and rural economics writer; 2005, becomes website writer.
2007: joins St. Paul-based think tank Minnesota 2020.
Interview, 2007

Elsasser, Glen *(1958)*
1978: 42 years old, editor and Supreme Court reporter, *Chicago Tribune.*
2002: retires, continues writing occasionally for *Chicago Tribune.*
2011: died (*Washington Post,* August 18, 2011).
Interview, 2007

Emory, Alan S. *(1947)*
1978: 56 years old, correspondent, *Watertown* (N.Y.) *Daily Times.*
2000: died (Associated Press, November 27, 2000).
Interview, 1977

Epstein, Aaron *(1957)*
1978: 46 years old, regional correspondent, *Philadelphia Inquirer,* Knight Ridder; 1980, becomes national correspondent, legal affairs; 1999, retires.
2000: does pro bono legal work; helps elementary school fifth and sixth graders put out a newspaper with the motto "Thou Shall Not Bore the Reader."
Interview 2011

Eskey, Ken *(1961)*
1978: 47 years old, business and economics reporter, Scripps Howard.
1995: retires and takes a six-month public relations position, American Federation of Teachers.
1997: becomes chairman, National Press Club Speakers Committee.
Interview, 2006

Everett, Glenn David *(1944)*
1978: 56 years old, correspondent, several Ohio newspapers; owner, Potomac Color Printer.
1996: died (*Washington Post,* August 19, 1996).

Falk, Carol *(1956)**
1978: 36 years old, Supreme Court/legal affairs reporter, *Wall Street Journal.*
1979: leaves journalism, becomes "full-time mother."
Interview, 2007

Fanning, Patricia *(1963)*
1978: 30 years old, reporter, *Wall Street Journal.*
1980: becomes editor, *Washington Star.*
1981: becomes editor, Time Life Books.
1982: teaches journalism at Northwestern University's Medill School of Journalism in Washington.
1985: becomes business editor, *Baltimore Evening Sun;* 1991, becomes regional editor; 1992, becomes state and environment editor; 1998, becomes assistant sports editor; 2005, becomes deputy projects editor.
2009: becomes media relations special-ist, University of Maryland, Baltimore.
Interview, 2007

Farmer, Don *(1960)*
1978: 39 years old, correspondent, ABC News.
1980: becomes anchor, CNN.
1988: joins WSB-TV, Atlanta.
1997: retires; writes column for *Naples* (Florida) *Daily News.*
Interview, 2006

Farney, Dennis *(1965)*
1978: 37 years old, congressional correspondent, *Wall Street Journal*; 1985, becomes "Heartland" correspondent/Washington correspondent.
2001: retires, becomes freelance writer and writing coach.
Interview, 2007

Fattibene, James *(1971)*
1978: 30 years old, newsletter writer, Prentice-Hall.
1990: becomes acquisitions manager, BNA Books.
Interview, 2006

Feinsilber, Mike *(1956)*
1978: 44 years old, reporter, UPI.
1980: becomes reporter at large, AP; later news editor, then assistant bureau chief.
2001: retires, works part-time as a writing coach for AP.
Interview, 2007

Fentress, Simmons *(1945)*
1978: 53 years old, general assignment reporter covering CIA, *Time*.
1981: died (*New York Times*, August 12, 1981).

Fialka, John J. *(1965)*
1978: 39 years old, investigative reporter, *Washington Star*; 1979, becomes Pentagon reporter.
1981: becomes special projects reporter, *Wall Street Journal*.
2008: becomes editor, *ClimateWire*, Environment & Energy Publishing.
Interview, 2008

Fiedler, Tom *(1971)*
1978: 32 years old, reporter, *Miami Herald* (Knight Ridder newspaper); 1979, becomes White House correspondent.
1982: becomes urban affairs editor, *Miami Herald*; 1984, becomes political editor; 1999, becomes

editorial page editor; 2001, becomes executive editor.
2007: becomes Goldsmith Fellow, Shorenstein Center on Press, Politics, and Public Policy, Harvard.
2008: becomes dean, Boston University College of Communication.
Interview, 2007

Fogarty, John *(1971)*
1978: 34 years old, bureau chief, *San Francisco Chronicle*.
1986: becomes editor, Kiplinger's *California Report*.
1999: becomes senior consultant, John Adams Associates.
2002: becomes publisher of *White House Bulletin*.
2010: retires.
Interview, 2010

Foty, Tom *(1971)*
1978: 32 years old, reporter, UPI Audio; later becomes bureau manager, then executive editor, UPI Radio; Washington correspondent, NBC Radio News; news manager, Unistar; co-founder, AudioCenter Productions.
1997: becomes reporter, WTOP Radio.

Fox, Larry R. *(1964)*
1978: 33 years old, night city editor, *Washington Post*; 1987, becomes Weekend section writer.
2002: retires.
2013: died (*Washington Post*, January 6, 2013).
Interview, 2007

Free, James *(1935)*
1978: 69 years old, correspondent, *Birmingham News*.
1979: retires.
1996: died (*Washington Times*, April 5, 1996).

Friedman, Saul *(1953)*
1978: 49 years old, White House correspondent, Knight Ridder Newspapers.
1985: moves to New York, teaches journalism at Columbia University, joins staff of *Newsday*.

1995: begins writing column, "Gray Matters," for *Newsday*.
2011: died (*Washington Post*, January 11, 2011).
Interview, 2008

Fuller, Jack *(1962)*
1978: 31 years old, correspondent, *Chicago Tribune*; 1978, becomes editorial writer; 1981, becomes editorial page editor; 1989, becomes vice president and editor; 1993, becomes president and CEO.
1997: becomes president, Tribune Publishing Company; 2001, joins board of directors.
2004: retires.
Interview, 2009

Garcia, David *(1964)*
1978: 34 years old, White House correspondent, ABC News; 1979, becomes South America bureau chief, Miami; 1981, becomes reporter, Chicago.
1983: becomes anchor/feature reporter, KCBS News, Los Angeles; 1991, becomes environmental anchor.
2001: starts J. David Productions.
Interview, 2007

Gay, Lance *(1965)*
1978: 33 years old, labor reporter, *Washington Star*.
1981: becomes Pentagon/congressional reporter, Scripps Howard News Service; 1989, becomes European correspondent; 1995, becomes senior reporter.
2006: retires.
Interview, 2006

Gedda, George
1978: 31 years old, State Department correspondent, AP.
2007: retires.

Gerstenzang, James *(1970)*
1978: 30 years old, White House reporter, AP.

1984: becomes White House reporter, *Los Angeles Times;*
2008: leaves *L.A. Times*, begins freelancing.
2009: becomes editorial director, Safe Climate Campaign, Center for Auto Safety.
Interview, 2009

Gest, Kathryn *(1977)**
1978: 31 years old, reporter and editor, *CQ*.
1987: leaves journalism, becomes chief spokesperson for Senator William Cohen (R-Me.).
1997: joins Powell Tate Weber Shandwick as executive vice president.
2007: becomes director of public affairs, National Democratic Institute.
Interview, 2008

Gest, Ted *(1970)*
1978: 31 years old, associate editor, *U.S. News & World Report*; around 1981, becomes chief legal affairs writer; 1996, becomes national news editor.
1998: becomes president, Criminal Justice Journalists.
2000: leaves *U.S. News & World Report*.
2000: becomes senior fellow, Jerry Lee Center of Criminology, University of Pennsylvania.
Interview, 2008

Gettlin, Robert *(1977)*
1978: 26 years old, reporter, *States News*.
1980: becomes reporter, *Washington Star*.
1981: becomes reporter, *Hartford Courant*.
1982: joins Washington bureau of Newhouse Newspapers.
1988: goes on sabbatical to write book.
1991: becomes freelance reporter.
1995: becomes Washington bureau chief for A.M. Best Publications.
1998: becomes director of communications, Council of Insurance Agency Brokers.
2001: becomes managing editor, *National Journal*.
Interview, 2006

Gill, Kathleen D.
1978: 31 years old, managing editor,
   BNA; 1987, becomes associate editor
   of business and human resources
   services; 1993, becomes vice
   president and executive editor; 1997,
   becomes editor-in-chief.
1999: retires.

Gilmore, Daniel F. *(1941)*
1978: 56 years old, national security
   reporter, UPI.
1987: becomes senior correspondent,
   Maturity News.
1988: died (*Washington Post,* August 9,
   1988).

Glass, Andrew J. *(1960)*
1978: 42 years old, bureau chief, Cox
   Newspapers; 1998, becomes senior
   correspondent/columnist.
2001: becomes fellow, Shorenstein
   Center on Press, Politics, and Public
   Policy, Harvard.
2001: becomes president of the Gridiron
   Club.
2003: becomes managing editor, *The
   Hill.*
2004: becomes adjunct professor,
   University of Maryland, and
   columnist, *The Hill.*
2006: becomes contributing editor,
   Politico.
Interviews, 2006, 2008

Goldenberg, Gene *(1968)**
1978: 33 years old, legal affairs reporter,
   Scripps Howard.
1985: becomes director of new product
   development, Kiplinger Washington
   Editors.
1995: leaves journalism, becomes vice
   president for e-solutions, H&R Block.
2002: becomes vice president, Braun
   Media Services.
2004: becomes vice president for
   marketing, CCH Small Firm Services.

Gordon, Gregory L. *(1975)*
1978: 27 years old, reporter, UPI.
1990: leaves UPI after co-authoring a
   book on its financial collapse; joins
   Detroit News.
1994: becomes Washington
   correspondent, *Minneapolis Star
   Tribune.*
2006: joins McClatchy national staff as
   investigative reporter.
Interview, 2005

Gorey, Hays *(1950)*
1978: 54 years old, correspondent,
   Time.
1992: retires.
2011: died (*Washington Post,* April 14,
   2011).
Interview with son, 2009

Goshko, John *(1959)*
1978: 44 years old, reporter,
   Washington Post; 1995, becomes UN
   correspondent, New York.
1999: retires.
Interview, 2009

Graham, Fred *(1965)*
1978: 46 years old, legal correspondent,
   CBS News.
1988: becomes anchor, WKRN-TV,
   Nashville, Tennessee.
1990: becomes managing editor,
   Court TV.
2007: becomes senior editor, In Session
   (truTV).
Interview, 2008

Greenberger, Robert *(1974)*
1978: 36 years old, economics reporter,
   Wall Street Journal; 1983, becomes
   foreign policy reporter; 1999,
   becomes Supreme Court reporter.
2006: retires, does some freelance
   writing.
Interview, 2007

Gregory, Bettina *(1974)*
1978: 31 years old, correspondent, ABC News; 1995, becomes chief anchor for special events, ABC Radio.
2001: retires from ABC; hosts *The American Family*, Goodlife Network; becomes adjunct professor, Robert H. Smith School of Business, University of Maryland; becomes resident psychologist, Capitol Hill Center for Family and Individual Therapy.

Greve, Frank *(1972)*
1978: 32 years old, correspondent, Knight Ridder; 2001, becomes assistant national editor; 2004, becomes national correspondent.
2009: retires.
Interview, 2006

Guillory, Ferrel *(1975)*
1978: 31 years old, correspondent, the *News and Observer* (Raleigh, N.C.); 1979, becomes associate editor and Pentagon reporter; 1988, returns to Raleigh as government affairs editor and columnist.
1996: resigns to teach at the University of North Carolina–Chapel Hill, and becomes a senior fellow at MDC, a North Carolina foundation.
Interview, 2006

Gwertzman, Bernard *(1961)*
1978: 43 years old, foreign affairs reporter, *New York Times*; 1987, moves to New York, becomes deputy foreign editor; 1989, becomes foreign editor; 1996, becomes website editor.
2002: retires, becomes online consulting editor, Council on Foreign Relations.
Interview, 2006

Haberek, Judy*
1978: 30 years old, editor/writer, BPI.
1986: becomes editor/writer, Capitol Publications.
1987: becomes editor/writer, United Communications Group.

1990: leaves journalism, starts landscaping company.
1997: becomes editor, Federal Document Clearinghouse.
2003: moves to Eastern Shore of Maryland; works for Park Service.
Interview, 2007

Hall, Wilson *(1950)*
1978: 55 years old, foreign correspondent, NBC News.
1978: becomes anchor, WNYT-TV, Albany, N.Y.
1984: becomes professor of journalism, University of Tennessee.
1991: died (*New York Times*, January 12, 1991).

Halloran, Richard *(1957)*
1978: 48 years old, energy correspondent, *New York Times*; 1979, becomes defense correspondent; 1985, becomes military correspondent in the field.
1990: becomes director of communications and journalism program, East-West Center, Hawaii.
1994: becomes a freelance writer.
2001: becomes editorial director, *Honolulu Star-Bulletin*; 2002, writes weekly column on U.S.-Asian relations.
Interview, 2007

Hannifin, Jerry *(1940)*
1978: 60 years old, chief aerospace correspondent, *Time*.
1982: retires.
2008: died (*Washington Post*, October 3, 2008).

Hartge, John *(1969)*
1978: 29 years old, correspondent, Mutual Broadcasting
1992: does freelance work for radio and television in Washington.
1998: becomes CBS News Radio Network correspondent.
Interview, 2008

Hedges, Roger *(1945)*
1978: 47 years old, correspondent,
Gannett; 1982, helps launch *USA
Today* and later becomes a regional
editor for Gannett.
1995: retires.
Interview, 2007

Heinl, Robert D. *(1963)*
1978: 61 years old, military analyst,
Detroit News.
1979: died (*Washington Post*, May 7,
1979).

Heller, Jean *(1964)*
1978: 35 years old, correspondent,
Newsday.
1978: reports for Booth Newspapers
(Grand Rapids, Michigan).
1982: leaves Washington and
journalism.
1988: returns to Washington, becomes
correspondent for the *St. Petersburg
Times*; 1991, joins management in
Florida; 1993, becomes editorial
editor; 1995, becomes reporter.
2007: becomes public relations copy
writer.
Interview, 2007

Henck, Fred W. *(1941)*
1978: 56 years old, owner,
Telecommunications Reports; 1981,
sells *Telecommunications Reports;*
1984, retires as editor, serves as
consulting editor.
1988: died (*Communications Daily,*
October 12, 1988).

Herman, George *(1942)*
1978, 58 years old, "Face the Nation"
host, CBS News, until 1983.
1987: retires.
2005: died (CBS News, February 8,
2005).

Herzog, James
1978: 34 years old, White House
correspondent, Scripps Howard.
1982: died (UPI, August 10, 1982).

Hess, David *(1971)*
1978: 44 years old, reporter, *Akron
Beacon Journal* (Knight Ridder
Newspapers); 1978, becomes
Washington correspondent, Knight
Ridder; 1980, becomes assistant
news editor; 1985, becomes White
House correspondent; 1988, becomes
congressional reporter.
2001: writes for NationalJournal.com
and *Congress Daily.*
Interview, 2006

Hickman, William D. *(1961)**
1978: 38 years old, correspondent,
McGraw-Hill.
1981: leaves journalism and becomes
president and CEO, National Press
Building Corporation.
1991: does public relations for the
Association of General Contractors,
later for the American Petroleum
Institute.
2005: becomes newsletter editor,
Common Ground Alliance.
Interview, 2008

Hiner Jr., Louis C. *(1947)*
1978: 59 years old, bureau chief,
Indianapolis News.
1987: died (Associated Press, February
8, 1987).

Hoagland, Jim *(1966)*
1978: 38 years old, national reporter,
Washington Post; 1979, becomes
foreign editor; 1986, becomes
columnist and senior foreign
correspondent.

Holliman, John *(1969)*
1978: 29 years old, agriculture editor,
AP Radio Network.
1980: becomes daytime Washington
anchor, CNN; 1991, reports from
Baghdad, Iraq, during Operation
Desert Storm.
1998: died (*New York Times*, September
13, 1998).

Holmes, Peter *(1978)**

1978: 27 years old, reporter, *Columbus Dispatch.*

1981: becomes senior editor, *Nations Business Magazine.*

1985: becomes cofounder and editor, *Fed Fortnightly.*

1986: becomes assistant managing editor, *Washington Times.*

1990: leaves journalism, becomes executive director of urban development corporation in Cleveland.

1995: becomes vice president of executive search firm.

1999: does media consulting.

2000: starts social networking company.

Interview, 2007

Hornig-Draper, Roberta *(1958)*

1978: 40 years old, reporter, *Washington Star.*

1982: becomes Senate producer, NBC News.

2003: retires.

Interview, 2007

House, Karen Elliott *(1970)*

1978: 30 years old, diplomatic correspondent, *Wall Street Journal*; 1984, moves to New York, becomes assistant foreign editor; 1989, becomes vice president of Dow Jones international operations; 1995, becomes president of international operations; 2002, becomes publisher of the *Wall Street Journal.*

2006: retires; continues writing.

Interview, 2009

Houston, Paul *(1963)*

1978: 36 years old, reporter, *Los Angeles Times.*

1994: died (*Los Angeles Times*, May 31, 1994).

Howard, Lucy *(1963)*

1978: 37 years old, reporter, *Newsweek;* around 1983, returns to New York, continues reporting; 1985, edits Periscope section; 1994, becomes senior writer.

2002: retires.

Interview, 2009

Hume, Brit *(1965)*

1978: 35 years old, congressional correspondent, ABC News; 1985, becomes White House correspondent.

1997: becomes senior political analyst, Fox News; 1998, hosts *Special Report*; 2008, leaves *Special Report* but remains at Fox.

Interview 2007

Humphries, Harrison

1978: 62 years old, regional supervisor, AP.

1994: died (Associated Press, October 21, 1994).

[incomplete information]

Hunt, Albert R. *(1965)*

1978: 35 years old, political correspondent, *Wall Street Journal*; subsequently bureau chief, columnist, and Washington executive editor.

2004: becomes president of the Gridiron Club.

2005: becomes managing editor for government reporting, Bloomberg News, and host, *Political Capital.*

Interview, 2005

Hunter, Marjorie *(1942)*

1978: 56 years old, reporter, *New York Times.*

1986: retires.

2001: died (*New York Times*, April 11, 2001).

Hyde, John *(1973)*

1978: 33 years old, reporter, *Des Moines Register.*

1979: becomes reporter, *Detroit Free Press.*

1980: returns to Washington as reporter, *Des Moines Register*; 1988, leaves to write book.

2000: becomes executive director, Fund for Investigative Journalism.

2007: opens "Crossroads," a farmers' market for immigrants, Washington.

2009: died (*Washington Post*, March 14, 2009).

Interview, 2007

Irving, Macculloch (Cully) *(1978)**
1978: 23 years old, reporter, *Hartford Courant.*
1979: leaves journalism, becomes campaign press secretary and legislative aide to Representative Stewart McKinney (R-Conn.).
1981: moves to New York, attends Brooklyn Law School.
1985, admitted to New York Bar and begins general law practice.
Interview, 2009

Irwin, Don *(1941)*
1978: 61 years old, correspondent, *Los Angeles Times.*
1984: retires.
1991: died (*Los Angeles Times,* March 5, 1991).

Jackson, Brooks *(1968)*
1978: 36 years old, White House correspondent, AP.
1980: becomes reporter, *Wall Street Journal.*
1990: becomes correspondent, CNN.
2003: becomes director of Factcheck.org.
Interview, 2007

Jackson, Robert *(1956)*
1978: 43 years old, investigative reporter, *Los Angeles Times.*
2002: retires
Interview, 2011

Jaroslovsky, Rich *(1975)*
1978: 24 years old, energy reporter, *Wall Street Journal;* 1981, becomes White House correspondent; 1985, becomes national political editor; 1994, becomes managing editor, *Wall Street Journal Online;* 2000, becomes executive director, Dow Jones Interactive Publishing; 2001, becomes senior editor, *Wall Street Journal.*
2002: becomes research director, Ziff Brothers Investments.
2004: becomes managing editor, Bloomberg News; 2005, becomes executive editor.

2010: becomes columnist, *Business Week.*
Interview, 2008

Johnson, Mal *(1969)*
1978: 52 years old, senior radio and TV correspondent and corporate director for community affairs, Cox Broadcasting.
2000: retires from Cox, founds Medialinx International, a media consulting firm.
2007: died (National Association of Black Journalists, October 31, 2007).

Jones, Clayton *(1973)*
1978: 27 years old, correspondent, *Christian Science Monitor;* 1978, becomes New England bureau chief; 1983, becomes deputy foreign editor; 1985, becomes Southeast Asia bureau chief; 1989, becomes Northeast Asia bureau chief; 1994, becomes foreign editor, Boston; 1999, becomes chief editorial writer and commentary editor.
Interview, 2007

Jones, Philip *(1959)*
1978: 41 years old, correspondent, CBS News; around 1978, becomes Capitol Hill correspondent; 1990, becomes correspondent, "48 Hours"; 1995, becomes Washington correspondent; retires.
2001: becomes contributing correspondent, *Religion and Ethics Newsweekly,* PBS.

Kahn, Helen *(1952)*
1978: 55 years old, bureau chief, *Automotive News* (Crain Automotive Group).
1988: retires, continues writing stories as a senior correspondent.
1993: died (*Automotive News,* July 12, 1993).

Kalb, Bernard *(1946)*
1978: 56 years old, diplomatic
correspondent, CBS News.
1980: becomes diplomatic
correspondent, NBC News.
1984: becomes assistant secretary of
state for public affairs; 1986, resigns
from State Department.
1988: hosts *Reliable Sources*, CNN.
1991: becomes senior fellow, Freedom
Forum Media Studies Center,
Columbia University.
2001: ends hosting *Reliable Sources*;
travels as lecturer.
Interviews, 1978, 2006

Kalb, Marvin *(1957)*
1978: 47 years old, diplomatic
correspondent, CBS News.
1980: becomes diplomatic
correspondent, NBC News; 1980s,
becomes moderator, *Meet the Press*.
1987: becomes professor and director,
Shorenstein Center for Press, Politics,
and Public Policy, Harvard; 1999,
becomes professor emeritus.
1994: starts hosting *The Kalb Report*,
George Washington University.
Interview, 2006

Kaplow, Herb *(1951)*
1978: 51 years old, reporter, ABC.
1994: retires.
Interview, 2008

Karmin, Monroe *(1954)*
1978: 48 years old, correspondent,
Chicago Sun-Times; later becomes
senior editor, *U.S. News & World
Report;* becomes editor-at-large,
Bloomberg News.
1995: becomes president, National
Press Club.
1999: died (*New York Times*, January
19, 1999).

Kaylor, Bob *(1962)**
1978: 39 years old, Pentagon reporter,
UPI; 1979, moves to Paris for UPI.

1982: moves to Singapore and begins
working for *U.S. News & World
Report*; eventually returns to the
United States and continues working
for *U.S. News*.
1989: leaves journalism and becomes
press spokesman, U.S. Commerce
Department.
1992: completes architecture school and
becomes architect.
Interview, 2007

Keller, Bill *(1970)*
1978: 29 years old, reporter, *The
Oregonian*.
1980: becomes reporter, *CQ*.
1982: becomes reporter, *Dallas Times
Herald*.
1984: becomes domestic correspondent,
New York Times, Washington; 1986,
becomes Moscow correspondent;
1992, becomes Johannesburg bureau
chief; 1995, becomes foreign editor,
New York; 1997, becomes managing
editor; 2001, becomes columnist
and senior writer; 2003, becomes
executive editor; 2011, becomes
columnist.

Kelly, Orr *(1949)*
1978: 54 years old, reporter, *U.S. News
& World Report*.
1986: retires, writes books on military
history and novels.
Interview, 2008

Kelso Jr., David *(1955)*
1978: 55 years old, managing editor,
Labor Relations Reporter, BNA.
1985: retires.
1992: died (*Washington Post*, October
19, 1992).

Kempster, Norman *(1956)*
1978: 42 years old, reporter, *Los
Angeles Times*.
2001: retires.
Interview, 2011

Kiker, Douglas *(1955)*
1978: 48 years old, political correspondent, NBC News.
1991: died (*Atlanta Journal and Constitution,* August 15, 1991).

King, Brian *(1968)**
1978: 31 years old, reporter, AP.
1979: leaves journalism and works for Agriculture Department.
1981: works for agricultural nonprofit association.
1987: becomes associate director of communication, Appalachian Trail Conservancy.
Interview, 2008

King, Seth *(1944)*
1978: 57 years old, agriculture reporter, *New York Times.*
1985: retires, becomes a professor at Boston University; remains *New York Times* stringer until 2006.
Interview, 2007

Kiplinger, Todd *(1975)*
1978: 32 years old, reporter, Kiplinger Washington Editors; later becomes vice chairman of the board and vice president for investments, Kiplinger.
2008: died (*Washington Post,* October 8, 2008).

Kirkman, Donald *(1958)*
1978: 49 years old, chief science writer, Scripps Howard.
1995: retires.
2001: died (*Washington Post,* November 1, 2001).

Kirschten, Joseph (Dick) *(1961)*
1978: 42 years old, energy and environment reporter, *National Journal;* 1979, becomes White House correspondent; 1989, covers immigration issues; 1993, covers foreign policy; 1997, becomes contributing editor.
1990s–2001: writes column, *Government Executive* magazine.

2001: retires.
Interview, 2009

Klurfeld, James *(1968)*
1978: 37 years old, reporter, *Newsday;* 1981, becomes bureau chief; 1986, becomes editorial page editor.
2007: becomes professor of journalism, Stony Brook University.
Interview, 2007

Knight, Louise (Lucy) *(1975)**
1978: 29 years old, editor and writer, *Education Funding Research News.*
1978: leaves journalism, moves to North Carolina, becomes director of research support, Duke University, and begins writing book on Jane Addams.
1986: becomes development officer at Wheaton College, Massachusetts.
1990: becomes development director for a settlement house in Boston.
1993: moves to Chicago, does development consulting and teaches.
2005: publishes book, continues consulting.
Interview, 2007

Knoller, Mark *(1973)*
1978: 26 years old, correspondent/ anchor, Mutual Radio.
1988: becomes assignment editor, CBS News; 1992, is assigned to White House as both television producer and radio reporter; now works principally for radio.
Interview, 2007

Kole, John William (Jack) *(1956)*
1978: 44 years old, bureau chief, *Milwaukee Journal.*
1989: becomes press secretary for Representative David R. Obey (D-Wis.); does press work for House Appropriations Committee.
1997: retires.
2007: died (*Milwaukee Journal Sentinel,* September 16, 2007).

Koppel, Ted *(1962)*
1978: 38 years old, State Department
reporter, ABC News; 1980, becomes
anchor, *Nightline.*
2005: becomes managing editor,
Discovery Channel.
2008: becomes senior news analyst,
NPR and BBC.
2011: becomes correspondent, "Rock
Center with Brian Williams," NBC.

Koran, Nancy *(1976)**
1978: 27 years old, reporter on energy
legislation and regulation, *Oil Daily.*
1978: becomes reporter for *Oil Express.*
1983: begins writing *Telephone Angles*
newsletter for United Publishing
Company.
1985: does freelance and public
relations work.
1988: writes for legal newsletter aimed
at assisting plaintiff-side attorneys.
1993: leaves journalism, does public
relations for the Maryland Housing
Authority of Montgomery County.
1998: becomes artist.
Interview, 2007

Krause, Axel *(1958)*
1978: 44 years old, correspondent,
Business Week.
1979: moves to Paris, becomes
economics correspondent,
International Herald Tribune;
subsequently becomes corporate
editor, author, and freelance writer.
Interview, 2007

Kuckro, Rod *(1977)*
1978: 23 years old, congressional
reporter, *Cincinnati Enquirer* and
Oakland Tribune.
1979–85: works as congressional staffer.
1986: becomes reporter, McGraw-Hill
News Service.
1990: becomes reporter, *Financial Times.*
1992: becomes freelance reporter.
1993: becomes editor-in-chief, *FCC Week.*
1998: becomes editor, McGraw-Hill.
2002: becomes editor, *Oil Daily.*

2004: becomes chief editor, *Platts*
(McGraw-Hill).
Interview, 2006

Lanouette, William J. *(1963)**
1978: 37 years old, correspondent,
National Journal.
1983: becomes communications
director, World Resources Institute.
1988: becomes fellow at the Kennedy
School of Government, Harvard.
1989: becomes Washington
correspondent, *Bulletin of Atomic
Scientists.*
1991–2006: leaves journalism and
becomes senior analyst, GAO.
2006: Retires from GAO; does freelance
work and writes books
Interview, 2006

Lehner, Urban C. *(1969)*
1978: 30 years old, labor reporter,
Wall Street Journal; 1980, becomes
Tokyo bureau chief; 1983, becomes
Detroit bureau chief; 1985, becomes
managing editor, Europe; 1988,
becomes Tokyo bureau chief; 1992,
becomes editor-in-chief, *Wall Street
Journal Asia;* 2001, becomes vice
president for business development.
2003: becomes editor-in-chief, DTN
Smarter Decisions.
Interview, 2007

Leonard, Mary *(1971)*
1978: 30 years old, correspondent,
Detroit Free Press.
1985: becomes bureau chief, *Detroit
News.*
1988: becomes deputy bureau chief,
Newsday.
1994: becomes deputy bureau chief,
Boston Globe; 1997, becomes
correspondent.
2004: moves to Pittsburgh, becomes
assistant managing editor of the
Business section, *Pittsburgh Post-
Gazette;* 2005, becomes deputy
managing editor.
Interview, 2007

Leubsdorf, Carl *(1960)*
1978: 40 years old, correspondent,
   Baltimore Sun.
1981: becomes bureau chief, *Dallas
   Morning News*; 2008, becomes
   editorial columnist.
2008: becomes president of the Gridiron
   Club.
Interviews, 2005, 2006

Lewis, Finlay *(1964)*
1978: 39 years old, bureau chief,
   Minneapolis Star Tribune.
1987: becomes national political
   correspondent, Copley News Service;
   1992, becomes economics and trade
   correspondent; 1998, becomes
   national political correspondent.
1999: becomes president of the Gridiron
   Club.
2008: leaves Copley, joins *Congressional
   Quarterly.*
Interviews, 1977, 2006

Lewis, Robert *(1956)*
1978: 46 years old, correspondent,
   Booth Newspapers (owned by
   Newhouse); 1985, joins Newhouse
   national staff.
1990: retires and writes for *AARP
   Bulletin.*
Interview, 2007

Lilly, Judlyne *(1975)*
1978: 26 years old, anchor, WTTG-TV.
1983: becomes freelance journalist.
1985: becomes reporter, WTOP Radio.
1996: becomes producer, FOX.
2000: becomes part-time legislative
   reporter, Texas State Radio Network,
   Austin.
2007: starts a website, TalkingTV.tv.
Interview, 2008

Lindquist, Kirsten *(1975)**
1978: 24 years old, general assignment
   reporter, AP Radio.
1980: becomes anchor/reporter, CNN;
   moves to Los Angeles, working for
   CNN.

1985: becomes anchor, KARE-TV, St.
   Paul/Minneapolis.
1988: becomes anchor, KSTP-TV, St.
   Paul/Minneapolis.
1990: leaves journalism.
2001: becomes real estate agent in
   California.
Interview, 2009

Lindsay, John J. *(1946)*
1978: 55 years old, Senate reporter,
   Newsweek.
1988: died (*Washington Post,* November
   4, 1988).

Logan, Harold J. *(1973)**
1978: 27 years old, reporter,
   Washington Post.
1978: goes to Stanford Business School.
1980: becomes assistant to publisher,
   Washington Post; 1981, heads
   electronic publishing.
1984: joins Electronic Publishing and
   News Retrieval department, Dow
   Jones.
1988: leaves journalism; helps design
   Pacific Bell Directory, California;
   1995, Vicinity, Inc.; 1999, Manheim,
   Inc.
2008: becomes CEO, BuyBook
   Technologies, Inc.
Interview, 2007

Lord, Mary *(1976)*
1978: 24 years old, reporter, *Newsweek.*
1983: moves to Japan, joins Mori
   Company as a writer for a start-up
   magazine.
1986: becomes business correspondent
   for Asia for *U.S. News & World
   Report*; 1987, returns to Washington
   to become business editor; 1990,
   becomes news reporter.
2002: leaves *U.S. News* to freelance.
2008: begins serving on the D.C. School
   Board of Education.
Interview, 2009

Lowenstein, Douglas *(1973)**

1978: 27 years old, Washington correspondent, Cox Newspapers.

1982: leaves journalism and becomes legislative director to Senator Howard Metzenbaum (D-Ohio).

1986: becomes partner in National Strategists.

1992: becomes partner in Robinson Lake Sawyer, a communications firm.

1994: becomes executive director, Entertainment Software Association.

2007–11: serves as president, Private Equity Council.

Interview, 2007

Lubar, Jeffery *(1969)**

1978: 31 years old, news director, Susquehanna Radio Broadcasting.

1986: leaves journalism and becomes vice president of public affairs at the National Association of Realtors.

1999: moves to California to start an Internet-based company.

2000: moves back to Washington and becomes communications director at Mortgage Insurance Companies of America, Inc.

2010: died (*Washington Post,* July 19, 2010)

Interview, 2006

Lynch, Bill *(1975)*

1978: 32 years old, White House correspondent, NBC News.

1981: becomes Pentagon correspondent, CBS News; 1985, becomes writer/anchor of *World News Roundup,* CBS Radio, New York.

2000: retires.

Interview, 2007

Lynch, David *(1965)*

1978: 35 years old, correspondent, *Buffalo Courier-Express.*

1982: creates Lynch News Service, providing news to clients including the *Cedar Rapids Gazette* and the *Lincoln* (Nebraska) *Journal.*

1995: retires.

1998: died (*Omaha World Herald,* January 4, 1999).

Interview, 1984

Maclean, John *(1965)*

1978: 35 years old, diplomatic correspondent, *Chicago Tribune;* 1987, becomes foreign editor, Chicago; 1989, becomes financial desk editor; 1990, becomes financial desk writer.

1995: resigns and returns to Washington to write book, *Fire on the Mountain.*

Interview, 2008

Maitlin, Robert *(1968)**

1978: 35 years old, bureau chief, Newhouse Newspapers.

1979: leaves journalism and becomes press secretary to Representative Robert A. Roe (D-N.J.).

1987: becomes executive assistant to chairman, House Science, Space, and Technology Committee.

1991: becomes executive assistant to chairman, House Public Works and Transportation Committee.

1992: becomes a lobbyist.

Interview, 2008

Malia, Thomas *(1943)*

1978: 57 years old, reporter, UPI.

1980s: becomes executive editor, *Telecommunications Report.*

1982: retires.

1999: died (*Communications Daily,* March 11, 1999).

Maloy, Richard *(1947)*

1978: 53 years old, bureau chief, Thomson Newspapers.

1993: retires and continues to run a small newsletter, *Hints for the City Desk.*

Interviews, 1977, 2006

Margolis, Jon *(1973)*
1978: 37 years old, correspondent, *Chicago Tribune;* 1988, becomes sports columnist; 1990, becomes columnist and Washington correspondent-at-large; 1994, becomes political editor and writer.
1996: retires, becomes freelance writer and adjunct professor, University of Vermont.
2008: Begins blog, vermontnewsguy. com.
Interview, 2007

Marion, Larry *(1975)*
1978: 28 years old, correspondent, *Business Week.*
1980: becomes staff writer, *Forbes.*
1983: becomes writer, *Datamation.*
1987: becomes senior editor, *Institutional Investor.*
1991: becomes editor, *Reed Business Information.*
1994: founds Triangle Publishing.
Interview, 2008

Marro, Anthony *(1971)*
1978: 36 years old, correspondent, *New York Times*
1979: becomes Washington bureau chief, *Newsday;* 1981, becomes managing editor; 1985, becomes executive editor; 1986, becomes editor.
2003: retires.
Interview, 2007

Mason, Vicky *(1974)*
1978: 26 years old, senior editor, *Telecommunications Report;* 1989, becomes editor in chief.
2002: retires.
2003: starts private consulting business.
Interview, 2007

Masters, Kim *(1978)*
1978: 23 years old, reporter, Capitol Publications.
1979: begins writing for the *Daily Labor Report* at BNA.

1980: becomes reporter, *Legal Times.*
1986: moves to Los Angeles and becomes Hollywood business correspondent for N.Y. *Daily News* and later Hollywood business reporter for *Premier Magazine.*
1990: returns to Washington, becomes style reporter for the *Washington Post.*
1993, becomes, in addition to *Post* job, a contributing reporter, *Vanity Fair.*
1996: returns to Los Angeles, becomes contributing editor for *Time* and *Vanity Fair.*
2000: becomes columnist for *Esquire* and eventually becomes a correspondent for NPR.
2006: becomes columnist for Slate.com.
2010: becomes editor-at-large, *Hollywood Reporter.*
Interview, 2007

Mathis, Sue *(1973)**
1978: 29 years old, television correspondent, Cox Broadcasting.
1985: leaves journalism and becomes director of media relations, White House.
1980s: becomes public relations manager, Walt Disney World.
1988: becomes Florida communications director, George H. W. Bush presidential campaign. 1990: becomes deputy associate director for communications, NASA.
2002: died.

McCartney, James H. *(1952)*
1978: 52 years old, correspondent, Knight Ridder; 1985, becomes columnist and writes column until 1995.
1990: retires, teaches at Georgetown University.
2003: moves to Florida, becomes monthly columnist for *Bradenton Herald.*
2011: died (*Washington Post,* May 7, 2011).
Interview, 2007

McClung, John *(1969)**
1978: 34 years old, bureau chief, Miller Publishing Company.
1981: leaves journalism and becomes director of information, USDA Food and Safety Service Program.
1987: becomes vice president of governmental relations, United Fresh Fruit and Vegetable Association.
2000: becomes president and CEO, Texas Produce Association.
Interview, 2007

McConagha, Alan *(1956)*
1978: 45 years old, reporter, *Minneapolis Tribune.*
1983: becomes State Department correspondent, *Washington Times*; later becomes foreign desk, features, and national desk editor.
1997: retires.
Interview, 2011

McDowell, Charles *(1949)*
1978: 52 years old, correspondent and columnist, *Richmond Times-Dispatch.*
1978–96: becomes panelist, *Washington Week in Review*, PBS.
1983: becomes president of the Gridiron Club.
1998: retires.
2010: died (*Washington Post*, November 6, 2010).

McFeatters, Dale *(1968)*
1978: 36 years old, national and labor reporter, Scripps Howard; 1996, becomes columnist and chief editorial writer.
Interview, 2008

McMillion, Rhonda *(1976)*
1978: 24 years old, Federal Election Law reporter, Plus Publications.
1979: shifts focus to education and begins reporting for *Win Plus.*

1983: becomes editor and later assistant director of the Information Services Office of the American Bar Association.
Interview, 2006

McQuade, Margaret *(née Osmer)* *(1963)**
1978: 40 years old, reporter, ABC News.
1979: leaves journalism and becomes director of *World in Focus*, Council on Foreign Relations. 1993: founds Qualitas International, a media consulting firm; founds Riverside Capital International, an asset management company.
Interview, 2007

McWethy, John *(1970)*
1978: 31 years old, chief White House correspondent, *U.S. News & World Report.*
1979: becomes chief Pentagon correspondent, ABC News; 1984, becomes national security correspondent.
2003: retires, continues to file special reports with ABC News.
2008: died (*Washington Post*, February 8, 2008).

Mears, Walter *(1955)*
1978: 43 years old, bureau chief, AP; 1984, becomes executive editor; 1989, becomes columnist in Washington bureau.
2001: retires, writes books.
2004: becomes adjunct professor, University of North Carolina–Chapel Hill.
Interview, 2008
Membrino, John (1973) 1978: 27 years old, correspondent, States News Service; 1980, becomes managing editor.
1983: becomes assistant news editor and regional editor, Newhouse News Service; 2000, becomes news editor.
2009: becomes editor, AOL.

Methvin, Eugene H. *(1958)*
1978: 43 years old, editor, *Reader's Digest.*
1996: retires from *Reader's Digest* as a senior editor, continues as roving editor until 2002.
2012: died (*Washington Post,* February 8, 2012).
Interview, 2007

Miller, Judith *(1972)*
1978: 30 years old, correspondent, *New York Times*; 1983, becomes Cairo bureau chief; 1986, becomes Paris correspondent; 1987, becomes Washington news editor and deputy bureau chief; 1989, becomes co-coordinator of media coverage unit; 1990, becomes special Persian Gulf correspondent and Sunday magazine special correspondent.
2005: imprisoned for 85 days for refusal to testify to a grand jury about the identity of her sources related to the Valerie Plame affair; retires from *New York Times.*
2007: becomes adjunct fellow and contributing editor of *City Journal,* Manhattan Institute.
2008: becomes commentator, Fox News.

Miller, Loye *(1955)**
1978: 48 years old, general assignment and political reporter, Gannett.
1980: becomes White House correspondent, Newhouse.
1985: leaves journalism and becomes press secretary to the secretary of education.
1988: becomes head of public affairs, U.S. Department of Justice.
1989: becomes public affairs spokesperson, Northrop Corporation.
1994: retires.
Interview, 2008

Miller, Theodore J. *(1968)*
1978: 33 years old, assistant managing editor, *Changing Times*; 1990–2005, author and editor of Kiplinger books (1990–2003).

2005: retires as senior vice president and editorial director, Kiplinger Washington Editors.

Mills, Betty *(1972)*
1978: 28 years old, Griffin-Larrabee News Bureau; later becomes bureau chief and then owner.
[incomplete information]

Milne, John *(1967)*
1978: 32 years old, editor, UPI.
1979: moves to Miami, becomes editorial writer for the *Miami Herald.*
1982: moves to New Hampshire, becomes editor, *New Hampshire Times.*
1984: moves to Boston, becomes political reporter, *Boston Globe.*
1996: starts Business Today website.
2000: becomes anchor, New Hampshire public radio.
2004: becomes columnist, *Andover* (Massachusetts) *Eagle Tribune.*
Interview, 2008

Mintz, Morton *(1946)*
1978: 56 years old, reporter, *Washington Post*; around 1981, becomes investigative and financial reporter focusing on the tobacco industry.
1988: leaves the *Post* and becomes a freelancer.
1990–93: serves as chairman, Fund for Investigative Journalism.
Interview, 2006

Mochel, Patricia *(1973)*
1978: 26 years old, morning news anchor and reporter, Metromedia Radio News.
1980: joins WBAL-TV in Baltimore as a weathergirl, reporter, and substitute anchor.
1984: begins working for WBAL-Radio; becomes press secretary for congressional candidate Kathleen Townsend; teaches script writing at Goucher College.

1986: becomes news director for
  WMIX-FM.
1987: founds Pat Mochel Productions;
  begins freelancing for WMIX and
  WLIF radio.
1994: helps direct the Partnership for
  Drug-Free Maryland.
2004: becomes communications director
  for the Governor's Office of Crime
  Control and Prevention.
Interview, 2009

Morison, Robert *(1949)*
1978: 54 years old, reporter, *Journal of
  Commerce.*
1987: retires.
Interview, 2007

Morse, Robert *(1976)*
1978: 30 years old, economic unit
  contributor, *U.S. News & World
  Report*; 1987, begins working on
  college rankings for *U.S. News* and
  later becomes the director of data
  research for college rankings.
Interview, 2008

Morton, Bruce *(1963)*
1978: 47 years old, reporter, CBS News.
1993: becomes reporter at CNN.
2006: retires.
Interview, 2005

Mossberg, Walter S. *(1973)*
1978: 31 years old, energy and
  environment correspondent, *Wall
  Street Journal*; 1980, becomes
  chief foreign correspondent; 1983,
  becomes deputy Washington bureau
  chief; 1987, becomes international
  economics correspondent;
  1988, becomes national security
  correspondent; 1991, becomes
  consumer technology columnist.
Interview, 2007

Moulton, Charlotte *(1944)*
1978: 65 years old, Supreme Court
  reporter, UPI.
1978: retires.

2004: died (UPI, May 7, 2004).
*Interview, 1991 (with Washington Press
  Club Foundation)*

Myers, Lisa *(1974)*
1978: 26 years old, correspondent,
  Chicago Sun-Times.
1979: becomes White House
  correspondent, *Washington Star.*
1981: joins NBC and later becomes
  chief congressional correspondent;
  2002, becomes chief investigative
  correspondent.
Interview, 2009

Nease, Jack *(1954)*
1978: 44 years old, reporter, *Tampa
  Tribune.*
1988: moves back to Florida, becomes
  reporter for *Palm Beach Post.*
1990: becomes business columnist for
  South Florida Sun-Sentinel.
1997: retires, files unsuccessful age-
  discrimination lawsuit against
  Sun-Sentinel.
Interview, 2007

Nelson, W. Dale *(1949)*
1978: 51 years old, Washington
  correspondent, AP.
1992: retires and moves to Laramie,
  Wyoming.
1993: becomes Laramie reporter, *Casper*
  (Wyoming) *Star Tribune.*
2006: retires.
Interview, 2007

Neumann, Deanne *(1967)*
1978: 32 years old, managing editor,
  International Trade Reporter, BNA;
  1981, becomes assistant to the
  associate editor and later executive
  editor at BNA.
Interview, 2009

Nichols, Herman W. *(1958)*
1978: 49 years old, board of editors,
  Fortune.
1982–86: U.S. ambassador to South
  Africa.
[incomplete information]

Nordlinger, Stephen *(1958)*
1978: 48 years old, correspondent, *Baltimore Sun.*
1991: leaves *Baltimore Sun* to study art.
1992: becomes speechwriter and issues coordinator for the Clinton presidential campaign.
2002: joins Foundry Gallery, Washington, as an artist; also works as speechwriter and issues coordinator for the Chris Van Hollen (D-Md.) congressional campaign.
Interview, 2007

Norman, Lloyd *(1936)*
1978: 64 years old, Pentagon correspondent, *Newsweek.*
1978: retires.
1987: died (*Washington Post,* November 14, 1987).

Oberdorfer, Don *(1955)*
1978: 46 years old, diplomatic correspondent, *Washington Post.*
1993: retires.
1996: becomes journalist in residence, Foreign Policy Institute, Johns Hopkins University School of Advanced International Studies (SAIS).
2006: becomes chairman of U.S.-Korea Institute, SAIS.
Interviews, 1978, 2006

O'Brien, T. A. (Tim) *(1966)*
1978: 34 years old, Supreme Court correspondent, ABC News.
1999: becomes distinguished visiting professor of Law, Nova Southeastern University School of Law, Ft. Lauderdale (repeated in 2002, 2004, and 2008).
2000: becomes visiting professor of law, Hofstra University School of Law, New York.
2001: becomes Washington correspondent, *Moneyline,* CNN; becomes visiting professor of law, St. Thomas University School of Law, Miami.

2001: becomes contributing correspondent, *Religion and Ethics Newsweekly,* PBS.
2004: leaves CNN.
2005: becomes visiting professor of law, Loyola University School of Law, New Orleans.
Interview, 2010

Ogden, Christopher *(1970)*
1978: 33 years old, State Department correspondent, *Time;* 1979, becomes White House correspondent; 1981, moves to Chicago, becomes Midwest bureau chief; 1985, becomes London bureau chief; 1989, returns to Washington, becomes chief diplomatic correspondent; 1991, becomes foreign affairs columnist.
2001: retires from *Time* to become an author.
Interview, 2007

Olofson, Darwin R. *(1949)*
1978: 56 years old, bureau chief, *Omaha World-Herald;* 1985, retires.
1985: becomes associate director, National Press Foundation; 1988, retires.
2002: died (*Washington Post,* October 22, 2002).

Olson, Lynne *(1970)*
1978: 30 years old, reporter, *Baltimore Sun.*
1980: moves to Los Angeles, begins freelancing, and becomes author of numerous books with a focus on World War II.
Interview, 2008

Ordovensky, Pat *(1954)*
1978: 44 years old, reporter, *News Journal* (Wilmington, Delware).
1983: becomes education reporter, Gannett News Service and *USA Today.*
1992: retires, continues to do special projects for *USA Today.*
1999: died (*News Journal,* February 4, 1999).

O'Rourke, Lawrence *(1964)*
1978: 40 years old, bureau chief, *Philadelphia Bulletin.*
1980: becomes deputy assistant secretary of education for policy and planning.
1981: becomes White House correspondent, *St. Louis Post-Dispatch*
1991: becomes chief congressional correspondent, McClatchy Newspapers.
2005: begins Washington law practice representing abused, neglected, and abandoned children.

O'Shea, James E. *(1971)*
1978: 34 years old, Washington correspondent, *Des Moines Register.*
1979: becomes reporter, *Chicago Tribune*; 1982, becomes budget and national security reporter, Washington; 1990, becomes associate managing editor for foreign and national news; 1995, becomes deputy managing editor for news; 2001, becomes managing editor.
2006: becomes editor and executive vice president, *Los Angeles Times;* resigns in 2008.
2009: becomes fellow, Shorenstein Center on Press, Politics, and Public Policy, Harvard.
2010: becomes editor of *Chicago News Cooperative.*
Interview, 2011

Ostroff, Jim *(1976)*
1978: 27 years old, correspondent, Fairchild Publications.
2000: becomes associate editor, Kiplinger.
Interview, 2008

Ostrow, Ronald *(1955)*
1978: 46 years old, reporter, *Los Angeles Times*; in addition, in 1996 becomes consultant and teaches at Scripps School of Journalism, Ohio University.
1998: leaves *Los Angeles Times.*
Interview, 2007

Pagano, Penny *(née Girard) (1970)**
1978: 33 years old, reporter, *Los Angeles Times.*
1988: becomes assistant managing editor, *Broadcasting Magazine.*
1989: becomes freelance writer.
2001: leaves journalism and becomes chief of staff for Kathy Patterson, D.C. City Council; 2008: becomes director of Community and Local Government Relations, American University.
Interview, 2007

Pappas, Ike *(1957)*
1978: 45 years old, Pentagon reporter, CBS News.
1987: ceates Ike Pappas Network; becomes a freelance writer and lecturer.
2008: died (CBS News, September 2, 2008).
Interview, 2007

Parkhurst, Steven *(1977)**
1978: 26 years old, reporter, Newhouse.
1979: leaves journalism.
1981: becomes teacher at U.S. Army base in Italy.
1995: gets M.A. in education, University of Washington.
1997: becomes teacher, Department of Defense schools, Italy.
1998: becomes administrator of Child and Youth Services, Camp Darby, Italy.
Interview, 2007

Parmenter, Cindy *(1968)**
1978: 37 years old, reporter, *Denver Post.*
1979: returns to Colorado, covers local politics.
1985: leaves journalism and joins Roy Romer's campaign for governor; 1986, becomes press secretary to Governor Romer.
1995: becomes director of communications, Colorado Department of Health.
2006: retires.
Interviews, 1978, 2007

Patterson, Kathleen (Kathy) *(1971)**
1978: 29 years old, correspondent,
   Kansas City Star.
1984: leaves journalism
1986: becomes communications
   director, American Public Welfare
   Association.
1994–2006: serves as member on D.C.
   City Council.
2006: becomes federal policy director at
   Pre-K Now.
2009: becomes senior officer,
   government relations, Pew Center on
   the States.
Interviews, 2007

Paulson, Morton C. *(1950)*
1978: 54 years old, associate editor,
   Changing Times (Kiplinger).
1990: retires from *Changing Times*
   (renamed *Kiplinger's Personal
   Finance*).
Interview, 2008

Payne, Richard *(1976)**
1978: 26 years old, Washington
   representative, Business International;
   1981, becomes Hong Kong editor,
   Business Asia.
1985: leaves journalism and becomes
   vice president for Western Region,
   Business International.
1987: becomes general manager, human
   resources company.
1990: moves to Singapore; becomes
   manager for Corporate Resources
   Group.
2002: heads global corporate website,
   Mercer Human Resources, San
   Francisco.
2006: heads marketing development,
   IWNC, Tokyo.
Interview, 2007

Peterson, Bill
1978: 35 years old, political
   correspondent, *Washington Post.*
1990: died (*Washington Post,* July 19,
   1990).

Peterson, Roger *(1959)*
1978: 41 years old, ABC News.
1988: starts video production company,
   anchors medical program on the
   Discovery channel.
2004: died (*Washington Post,* April 24,
   2004).

Pianin, Eric *(1970)*
1978: 31 years old, reporter,
   Minneapolis Tribune.
1981: Metro desk reporter, *Washington
   Post*; 1993, becomes congressional
   reporter; 2007, becomes senior editor,
   washingtonpost.com.
2009: becomes Washington editor for
   the online publication *Fiscal Times.*
Interview, 2007

Pierpoint, Robert C. *(1950)*
1978: 52 years old, White House
   correspondent, CBS News; 1980,
   becomes diplomatic correspondent;
   1984, joins *Sunday Morning* program.
1990: retires.
2011: died (*Washington Post,* October
   24, 2011).
Interviews, 1977, 2008

Pincus, Walter *(1957)*
1978: 45 years old, reporter,
   Washington Post; editorial consultant,
   NBC News.
1982: leaves television; remains at the
   Post, covering intelligence, CIA, and
   national security.
Interview, 2006

Plante, Bill *(1960)*
1978: 40 years old, reporter, CBS News;
   1981, becomes White House and
   State Department correspondent.
Interview, 2006

Poe, Edgar Allen *(1930)*
1978: 72 years old, correspondent, *New
   Orleans Times-Picayune.*
1994: retires.
1998: died (*Washington Post,* August
   17, 1998).

Poole, Dan *(1957)**
1978: 45 years old, features editor, *Washington Star.*
1981: leaves journalism and becomes vice president for publications, Insurance Information Institute; starts a magazine for insurance agents.
1993: retires.
Interview, 2007

Pound, Edward T. *(1953)*
1978: 34 years old, investigative reporter, *Washington Star.*
1979: becomes investigative reporter, *New York Times,* Washington bureau.
1982: becomes investigative reporter, *Wall Street Journal,* Washington bureau.
1983: becomes chief investigative correspondent, *U.S. News & World Report.*
1997: becomes reporter, *USA Today.*
2001: becomes managing editor for investigations, *U.S. News & World Report.*
2007: becomes staff correspondent for investigations, *National Journal.*
2009: becomes communications director, Recovery Accountability and Transparency Board.
2013: becomes chief of investigative unit, Al Jazeera America.
Interview, 2007

Putzel, Michael *(1963)**
1978: 35 years old, reporter, AP; 1979, becomes White House correspondent; 1987, becomes Moscow bureau chief.
1991: becomes Washington correspondent, *Boston Globe.*
1999: leaves journalism, launches dotcom company; around 2003, becomes freelance book editor.
Interview, 2007

Quinlan, Mary Kay *(1974)*
1978: 27 years old, correspondent, *Omaha World Herald.*
1985: becomes regional correspondent, Gannett News Service.
1986: becomes president of the National Press Club.

1989: teaches part-time at University of Maryland College of Journalism.
1997: returns home to Lincoln, Nebraska; becomes professor at the University of Nebraska.
Interviews, 1978, 2007

Quinn, Charles *(1944)**
1978: 47 years old, reporter, NBC News.
1980: leaves journalism and does public relations for the American Petroleum Institute.
1990: retires.
Interview, 2007

Raab, Charles *(1962)*
1978: 44 years old, correspondent, *Aerospace Daily.*
2003: retires.
2008: died (*Aerospace Daily,* July 28, 2008).

Raeke, Carolyn *(1967)*
1978: 34 years old, reporter, *Dallas Morning News.*
1978: moves to Buffalo, begins working for an architectural research firm.
1981: returns to journalism doing rewrites, *Buffalo Courier Express.*
1982: moves to *Buffalo News* when the *Express* folds; 1991, becomes city editor; 2000, becomes editor-at-large.
Interview, 2009

Ramsey, McClain *(1971)*
1978: 26 years old, noon anchor, Metromedia TV.
1986: becomes vice president for corporate affairs, NBC.
1997: becomes chief spokesperson, Nike.
[incomplete information]

Randal, Judith *(1967)*
1978: 48 years old, science reporter, *New York Daily News.*
1980: becomes congressional fellow, Office of Technology Assessment; continues freelancing. 1981: returns to *New York Daily News.*
1985: becomes part-time writer for *Newsday;* continues freelancing.
Interview, 2008

Randolph, Eleanor R. *(1972)*
1978: 35 years old, reporter, *Chicago Tribune*.
1980: becomes national and environmental reporter, *Los Angeles Times*.
1984: becomes media reporter, *Washington Post*; 1990, becomes part-time Moscow correspondent; 1993, becomes New York correspondent.
1995: becomes New York correspondent, *Los Angeles Times*.
1998: becomes member of the editorial board, *New York Times*.
Interview, 2007

Rankin, Robert A. *(1972)*
1978: 28 years old, reporter on energy, *CQ*.
1979: enters fellowship program, Columbia University, studying economics journalism.
1980: becomes editorial writer, *Miami Herald*.
1985: becomes editorial writer, *Philadelphia Inquirer*.
1987: returns to Washington; becomes economics reporter, Knight Ridder; 2000, becomes government and politics editor.
Interview, 2006

Reichmann, Jean *(1956)*
1978: 57 years old, BNA.
1983: retires.
1998: died.

Reid, Thomas (T. R.) *(1977)*
1978: 33 years old, staff writer, *Washington Post;* 1983, becomes congressional reporter; 1984, opens Denver bureau; 1990, becomes Tokyo correspondent; 1995, becomes Denver correspondent; 1998, becomes London correspondent; becomes involved in documentary filmmaking; later returns to Denver.
Interview, 2007

Reinhold, Robert *(1964)*
1978: 36 years old, science reporter, *New York Times*; around 1985, becomes Houston bureau chief; around 1989, becomes Los Angeles bureau chief.
1994: becomes editorial writer, *Los Angeles Times*.
1996: died *(New York Times*, August 30, 1996).

Reynolds, Barbara *(1968)**
1978: 35 years old, correspondent, *Chicago Tribune*.
1983: becomes editor of the op-ed page and columnist, *USA Today*.
1992: leaves journalism and attends Howard University School of Divinity.
1998: receives Ph.D., United Theological Seminary.
2000: becomes communications director for Representative Eddie Bernice Johnson (D-Texas).
2005: becomes professor, Howard University School of Divinity; writes column on religion for the *National News Publishers Association*.
Interviews, 1978, 2009

Richards, Bill *(1970)*
1978: 36 years old, staff reporter, *Washington Post*.
1980: becomes writer, *National Geographic*.
1982: becomes Chicago correspondent, *Wall Street Journal*; 1990, becomes contract writer, Seattle; becomes 1995 deputy bureau chief, San Francisco; 1997, becomes senior writer; 1998, becomes contract writer, Seattle.
2002: becomes contract writer, *Seattle Post-Intelligencer*.
2006: becomes contract writer, Washington News Council, and writer/developer, crosscut.com.
Interview, 2007

Richards, Carol R. *(1966)*
1978: 33 years old, reporter, Gannett;
1982, becomes member of editorial
board, *USA Today*.
1987: becomes deputy editorial page
editor, *Newsday*, New York.
2006: becomes adjunct professor,
Hofstra University.
Interview, 2007

Risser, James V. *(1964)*
1978: 39 years old, bureau chief, *Des
Moines Register*.
1985: becomes professor, Stanford
University, and director, John S.
Knight Journalism Fellowships.
2000: retires; does freelance writing.
Interview, 2007

Roberts, Steven V. *(1964)*
1978: 35 years old, political reporter,
New York Times; 1980, congressional
reporter; 1986, White House reporter.
1989: becomes senior writer, *U.S. News
& World Report*.
1990: becomes adjunct professor of
journalism, George Washington
University.
1996: leaves *U.S. News & World Report*.
1997: becomes professor of journalism,
George Washington University.
Interview, 2007

Robinson, Marilyn *(1969)*
1978: 31 years old, NBC Radio reporter.
1978: produces *Labor News and Views*,
syndicated radio program.
1991: died (*Washington Post*, June 27,
1991).

Rogers, Walter *(1966)*
1978: 38 years old, White House
correspondent, AP Radio.
1981: becomes reporter, ABC News;
1984, becomes Moscow bureau chief;
1989, becomes Justice Department
correspondent.
1993: becomes Berlin correspondent,
CNN; 1995, becomes Jerusalem
bureau chief; 2000, becomes London
correspondent.

2005: retires; becomes visiting professor,
James Madison University.
Interview, 2007

Roper, James *(1937)*
1978: 63 years old, reporter, tax court
decisions, Newhouse newspapers.
1997: retires.
1998: died (*Washington Post*, November
13, 1998).

Rose, Julia *(1974)**
1978: 27 years old, reporter, *CQ*.
1979: leaves journalism and becomes
commercial officer, U.S. Embassy,
Paris.
1982, becomes member of the
Legislative Budget Board, Texas state
legislature.
1986: becomes freelance writer.
Interview, 2009

Rosenstein, Jay
1978: 23 years old, reporter, *American
Banker*.
1989: leaves journalism and becomes
senior writer/editor, Federal Deposit
Insurance Corporation.
Interview, 2010.

Rosenwasser, Marc *(1975)*
1978: 25 years old, regional reporter,
AP; 1979, editor on foreign desk,
New York; 1980, becomes Moscow
correspondent.
1982: becomes assistant editor, foreign
desk, ABC News, New York.
1990: becomes producer, NBC, New
York.
2006: becomes senior producer, *CBS
Evening News*, New York.
2007: becomes part-time professor,
William Penn University.
2008–2010: works as executive
producer, *Worldfocus*, an
international affairs program.
2011: becomes executive producer, *Need
to Know*, PBS.
Interview, 2007

Roth, Richard *(1972)*
1978: 29 years old, regulatory agencies correspondent, CBS; 1980, becomes presidential campaign reporter; 1981, becomes Vatican correspondent; 1986, becomes New York correspondent; 1990, becomes entertainment correspondent, Los Angeles.
1994: Becomes London correspondent, NBC.
1998: Becomes London correspondent, CBS.
Interview, 2007

Rowe, James C. *(1976)*
1978: 26 years old, Mutual Black Network.
1980: moves to Chicago; becomes news and public affairs director, WGCI and WVON Radio.
1985: becomes reporter/anchor, WBBM-AM NewsRadio 78.
1994: moves to Boston; becomes assistant news director, WBZ NewsRadio 1030.
1996: works for Avid Technology, Inc., Tewksbury, Massachusetts, in pre-sales support.
2009: starts Rowe and Co., broadcast news consultancy.

Rowe Jr., James L. *(1971)*
1978: 30 years old, staff writer, *Washington Post*; 1979–81, becomes economics affairs writer; 1982–87, becomes senior night national editor; 1987–88; 1989, becomes weekend national editor; 2006, becomes early Sunday editor.

Rutter, Judy *(née Gardner) (1967)*
1978: 32 years old, associate editor, *U.S. News & World Report.*
1983: becomes copy editor, *Washington Post;* moves to California and purchases radio station with spouse.
2003: sells radio station; returns to copy editing part-time for San Luis Obispo newspaper.
Interview, 2007

Ryan, Richard *(1962)*
1978: 40 years old, reporter, *Detroit News.*
2001: becomes president, National Press Club.
2005: becomes president, Gridiron Club.
2006: retires.
Interview, 2007

Salditch, Martin *(1952)*
1978: 49 years old, bureau chief, *Riverside Press-Enterprise.*
1993: retires.
1999: died (*Riverside Press-Enterprise,* June 18, 1999).

Sanders, Donald *(1939)*
1978: 62 years old, visual and performing arts writer, AP.
1979: died (Associated Press, November 23, 1979).

Sanoff, Alvin P. *(1968)*
1978: 36 years old, associate editor, *U.S. News & World Report;* 1992, becomes managing editor, "America's Best Colleges" and "America's Best Graduate Schools."
1998: becomes senior vice president for communications, Maguire Associates, a higher education consulting firm; later becomes project manager, Education Schools Project, Columbia University.
2007: died (*Chronicle of Higher Education,* May 21, 2007).

Scanlan, Dan *(1964)*
1978: 38 years old, reporter, Mutual Broadcasting System.
1985: becomes automotive reviewer, NBC-TV, Jacksonville, Florida.
1990: becomes reporter and automotive writer, *Florida Times-Union.*

Schakne, Robert *(1955)*
1978: 51 years old, investigative correspondent, CBS.

1988: retires.
1989: died (*Washington Times*,
September 1, 1989).

Schwartz, Berl *(1969)*
1978: 31 years old, reporter, *Louisville
Times*.
1979: becomes congressional reporter,
Scripps Howard; 1980, becomes
night editor; 1982, becomes assistant
managing editor.
1985: becomes managing editor,
Knoxville (Tennessee) *News Sentinel*.
1989: becomes executive editor, *York*
(Pennsylvania) *Daily Record*.
1990: becomes Washington bureau
chief, UPI.
1991: becomes publisher, *Oklahoma
Today*.
1994: becomes general manager, *State
News*, Michigan State University.
2000: becomes owner/editor, *City Pulse*
(East Lansing, Michigan).
Interview, 2007

Scott, Ivan *(1958)*
1978: 48 years old, correspondent,
Mutual Broadcasting System.
1980s: works as correspondent, CBS
News.
1990: becomes stringer at various news
stations.
2006: becomes public affairs liaison,
U.S. Department of Defense.
2008: died (*Washington Post*, March
22, 2008).
Interview, 2005

Segall, J. Peter *(1978)**
1978: 24 years old, editor, *Lobbying
Reports*, Plus Publications.
1980: leaves journalism; works for
Council of Energy Resource Tribes;
subsequently becomes vice president
of public affairs, Health Insurance
Association of America, and director
of Washington office, Edelman.
Interview, 2011

Shabecoff, Philip *(1960)*
1978: 44 years old, environmental
reporter, *New York Times*.
1991: founds *Greenwire*, an online daily
environmental news report.
1996: becomes environmental author.
Interview, 2008

Shannon, Don *(1947)*
1978: 55 years old, correspondent, *Los
Angeles Times*.
1992: retires; founds local paper,
Georgetown and Country.
Interview, 2007

Shannon, Elaine *(1968)*
1978: 31 years old, correspondent,
Newsweek.
1988: becomes correspondent,
Time, covering law enforcement;
2006, becomes State Department
correspondent.
2007: becomes communications officer,
Public Welfare Foundation.
2009: becomes editor-in-chief,
Environmental Working Group.
Interviews, 1978, 2008

Shepard, Alicia *(1978)*
1978: 25 years old, reporter, Scripps
News League.
1982: becomes reporter, *San Jose
Mercury News;* 1987, sails the South
Pacific writing column "Letters from
Paradise"; 1992, returns to *San Jose
Mercury News* as features writer.
1993: returns to Washington; becomes
writer, *American Journalism Review*.
2005–06: teaches journalism, University
of Texas.
2007: teaches journalism, American
University.
2007–10: teaches journalism,
Georgetown University.
2007–11: is ombudsman, NPR.
2012: becomes guest professor,
University of Nevada–Las Vegas.
Interview, 2007

Shields, Edward J. *(1949)*
1978: 54 years old, editor and audio
  service reporter, UPI.
1981: becomes editor, Reuters,
  Washington.
1989: retires.
1993: died (*Washington Post*, July 2,
  1993).

Shifrin, Carole *(1965)*
1978: 37 years old, business and finance
  writer, *Washington Post.*
1983: becomes transport writer for
  Aviation Week; 1985, becomes
  Dallas bureau chief; 1989, becomes
  London bureau chief; 1995, returns
  to Washington and becomes senior
  transport editor.
1999: works as freelancer.
Interview, 2007

Sibley, Martin *(1977)*
1978: 26 years old, reporter, *Aviation
  Daily*; later becomes copy editor;
  around 2006, leaves publication.
[incomplete information]

Siddon, Arthur *(1968)**
1978: 41 years old, correspondent,
  Chicago Tribune.
1985: leaves journalism and becomes
  senior public information officer,
  Treasury Department; 1989, becomes
  director of public affairs.
1990: becomes vice president for public
  affairs, Oversight Board for the
  Resolution Trust Corporation.

Sidey, Hugh S. *(1955)*
1978: 50 years old, White House
  correspondent, *Time.*
1996: retires and becomes contributing
  editor.
2005: died (*New York Times,*November
  23, 2005).

Simpson, Carole *(1965)*
1978: 37 years old, correspondent,
  NBC.

1982: switches to ABC; anchors Sunday
  edition of *World News Tonight*
  (1988–2003).
2007: becomes Leader in Residence,
  Emerson College, Boston.
*Interview, 1992 (with Washington Press
  Club Foundation)*

Sloyan, Patrick *(1960)*
1978: 41 years old, correspondent,
  Newsday; 1980, becomes Europe and
  Middle East correspondent, London;
  1986, becomes Washington bureau
  chief; 1988, becomes national security
  and Pentagon correspondent.
2001: retires.
Interview, 2007

Smith, A. Robert *(1950)*
1978: 53 years old, reporter, *Oregonian.*
1978: becomes editorial writer,
  Virginian Pilot.
1984: becomes editor, *Venture Inward*
  magazine.
2002: retires and writes books.
Interview, 2007

Smith, Hedrick *(1959)*
1978: 44 years old, bureau chief, *New
  York Times*; 1979, becomes chief
  Washington correspondent.
1989: becomes documentary producer,
  PBS.
1990: becomes owner, Hedrick Smith
  Productions.
Interviews, 1977, 2007

Smith, Karen Haas *(1975)**
1978: 28 years old, reporter, Cahners
  Publications.
1979: becomes freelance writer.
1983: becomes editor, *Architectural
  Technology*, Institute of Architects.
1984: becomes freelance writer.
1987: leaves journalism and becomes
  director of communications, Strategic
  Highway Research Program, National
  Research Council.

1992: becomes consultant to Danish Road Directorate

1993: becomes public relations specialist, Metropolitan Washington Council of Governments. 1996: opens communications and outreach consultancy.

Interview, 2009

Smith, Sam *(1975)*

1978: 30 years old, reporter, States News Service.

1979: becomes political writer, *Chicago Tribune*; 1983, becomes sports writer and later basketball columnist.

2008: retires from the *Tribune*; writes for Bulls.com.

Interview, 2007

Smolka, Richard G. *(1971)*

1978: 45 years old, editor, *Election Administration Reports*, Plus Publications; professor, American University.

1993: retires from teaching; continues publishing *Election Administration Reports*.

Interview, 2006

Spencer, Susan *(1969)*

1978: 31 years old, correspondent, CBS News; 1986, becomes medical correspondent; 1988, becomes Sunday anchor, *CBS Evening News*; 1989, becomes national correspondent; 1992, becomes White House correspondent; 1993, becomes correspondent, *48 Hours*.

Interview, 2009

Stanfield, Rochelle

1978: 37 years old, correspondent, *National Journal*; 1984, covers energy and environment; 1988, covers foreign policy; 1990, covers social policy.

1998: becomes freelance writer.

2006: retires.

Interview, 2006

Steif, William *(1946)*

1978: 55 years old, columnist, Scripps Howard.

1982: becomes columnist and reporter, *Virgin Islands Daily News*, St. Croix.

1998: becomes part-time reporter, *The State* (Columbia, S.C.)

Interviews, 1978, 2007

Stern, Carl *(1959)*

1978: 40 years old, Supreme Court and Justice Department correspondent, NBC News.

1993: becomes public affairs director, U.S. Department of Justice.

1996: becomes professor of media and public affairs, George Washington University.

Interview, 2007

Stertz, Marc *(1977)*

1978: 32 years old, associate editor, *Kiplinger's Washington Letter;* 1985, becomes editor, *Kiplinger's Florida Letter.*

1988: becomes editor-in-chief and publisher, *Automotive Executive Magazine.*

Interview, 2006

Strout, Richard *(1919)*

1978: 80 years old, reporter, *Christian Science Monitor*; "TRB" columnist, *New Republic.*

1984: retires.

1990: died (*Washington Post,* August 21, 1990).

Stuart, Peter C. *(1964)**

1978: 37 years old, *Christian Science Monitor.*

1981: leaves journalism; becomes writer in Information Office, Asian Development Bank; becomes author.

2011: died (*Battle Creek Enquirer,* February 15, 2011).

Sulkin, Sidney *(1955)**
1978: 60 years old, editor, *Changing Times*, Kiplinger.
1981: leaves journalism; writes poetry.
1995: died (*New York Times*, July 13, 1995).

Sullam, Brian *(1975)**
1978: 28 years old, reporter, *Journal of Commerce.*
1979: becomes business reporter, *Baltimore Sun*; 1989, becomes City Hall reporter;
1991, becomes court reporter; 1992, becomes editorial writer.
2000: leaves journalism; becomes editorial manager of T. Rowe Price.
Interview, 2006

Sullivan, Scott *(1963)*
1978: 40 years old, chief diplomatic correspondent, *Newsweek;* 1978, moves to Paris and becomes the European regional editor; 1997, retires from *Newsweek.*
1997–2001: becomes public affairs adviser, International Energy Agency, Paris.
Interview, 2011

Sutherland, John P. (Jack) *(1957)*
1978: 58 years old, correspondent, *U.S. News & World Report;* in 1980s, becomes associate editor.
1985: retires.
1988: died (*Washington Post*, March 18, 1988).

Swardson, Anne *(1976)*
1978: 25 years old, correspondent, *Business Week.*
1981: becomes correspondent, *Dallas Morning News.*
1985: becomes congressional reporter, *Washington Post*; 1989, becomes assignment editor; 1990, becomes business and economics reporter; 1992, becomes Toronto correspondent; 1996, becomes European economic correspondent, Paris.

2000: becomes European features editor, Bloomberg News, Paris; takes other assignments.
Interview, 1978

Thomas, Gary *(1973)*
1978: 28 years old, reporter, Griffin-Larrabee News Service.
1983: becomes writer, Voice of America; 1989, becomes foreign correspondent; 2001, becomes senior news analyst.
Interview, 2007

Thomas, Jo *(1966)*
1978: 34 years old, reporter, *New York Times*; 1979, becomes Miami bureau chief; 1981, becomes Justice Department reporter; 1981, becomes London correspondent; later returns to New York.
1986: becomes visiting professor of journalism, University of Illinois.
1994: becomes writer/assignment editor, *New York Times.*
2002: becomes associate chancellor, Syracuse University.
Interview, 2007

Thomsen, Dietrick *(1960)*
1978: 41 years old, senior editor, *Science News.*
1988: died (*Science News*, August 6, 1988).

Thornton, Lee *(1972)*
1978: 35 years old, White House correspondent, CBS News.
1981: becomes news anchor in Detroit.
1981: becomes anchor of *All Things Considered*, NPR.
1983: becomes business news reporter, ESPN.
1983: becomes professor of journalism, Howard University.
1998: becomes first Richard Eaton chair in broadcast news, University of Maryland.
Interview, 2007

Toedtman, James *(1967)*
1978: 36 years old, bureau chief, *Newsday.*
1982: becomes editor, *Baltimore News American.*
1987: returns to *Newsday* as managing editor.
2005: becomes editor, *AARP Bulletin.*
Interview, 2007

Tolchin, Martin *(1954)*
1978: 50 years old, congressional/White House correspondent, *New York Times.*
1994: becomes publisher and editor, *The Hill.*
2005: becomes senior publisher and editor, *Politico.*
2011: becomes senior scholar, Woodrow Wilson Inernational Center for Scholars
Interviews, 1978, 2007

Uliano, Richard *(1972)*
1978: 26 years old, anchor/reporter, Metromedia Radio News.
1980: becomes news director for WMZQ Radio, Washington.
1983: becomes reporter and space shuttle launch correspondent, AP Broadcast.
1999: becomes Washington correspondent, CNN Radio.
Interview, 2007

Underwood, Doug *(1974)*
1978: 30 years old, congressional correspondent and environmental reporter, Gannett.
1981: becomes Olympia bureau chief, *Seattle Times*; 1984, becomes chief political writer.
1987: becomes assistant professor of communication, University of Washington; now professor of communication and author of four books, including *Journalism and the Novel.*
Interview, 2007

Van Riper, Frank *(1967)*
1978: 65 years old, reporter, *New York Daily News.*
1987: becomes publisher of photography books.
1992: becomes photography columnist, *Washington Post.*
Interview, 2009

Volz, Joseph *(1970)*
1978: 43 years old, Pentagon reporter, *New York Daily News.*
1987–97: reports for Maturity News Service.
1997–2000: writes for *Monitor* (American Psychological Association).
2000–08: writes column on aging, Copley News Service.
2009: becomes weekly columnist, *Frederick* (Maryland) *News Post.*
Interview, 2009

Waggoner, Glenn *(1971)**
1978: 29 years old, correspondent, *Columbus Dispatch.*
1979: leaves journalism and earns law degree, George Washington University; becomes congressional aide.
1981: practices law in Cleveland.

Wagy, Norman O. *(1950)*
1978: 48 years old, bureau chief, Storer Broadcasting Company.
1988: retires.
Interview, 2007

Walczak, Lee *(1969)*
1978: 32 years old, White House Correspondent, *McGraw-Hill World News.*
1986: becomes bureau chief and later senior editor, *Business Week.*
2006: becomes political news editor, Bloomberg News.
2008: died (*Washington Post*, April 3, 2008).
Interview, 1978

Waldman, Myron *(1963)*
1978: 45 years old, White House correspondent, *Newsday*.
1993: died (Associated Press, July 20, 1993).

Walker, Janet *(1976)**
1978: 29 years old, editor, Plus Publications.
1980: becomes writer, *Current* (National Association of Educational Broadcasters).
1981: leaves journalism; becomes publications coordinator, chief editor, and production manager for art exhibitions, International Exhibitions Foundation.
1983: becomes general publications editor, National Trust for Historic Preservation; 1987, moves to Preservation Press department.
1994: becomes publications manager, Society for American Archaeology.
1998: becomes managing editor, Brookings Institution Press.
Interview, 2006

Wallach, John *(1968)*
1978: 35 years old, foreign editor, Hearst Newspapers.
1993: organizes Seeds of Peace summer camp for children from opposing sides of world conflicts.
1995: becomes executive director, Elie Wiesel Foundation for Humanity.
1996: becomes full-time head, Seeds of Peace.
1997: becomes senior fellow, U.S. Institute of Peace.
2002: died (*New York Times,* July 12, 2002).

Walters, Phil *(1964)*
1978: 36 years old, correspondent, CBS News.
1979: becomes reporter, WBBM-TV 2, Chicago.
1986: becomes general assignment reporter, WMAQ-TV 5, Chicago.

1999: died (*Chicago Tribune,* September 13, 1999).

Ward, Morris A. *(1972)**
1978: 32 years old, managing editor, BNA.
1979: leaves journalism; joins staff, National Commission on Air Quality.
1981: becomes editor, *Environmental Forum.*
1984: becomes environmental representative, American Electronics Association.
1988: becomes director, Environmental Health Center.
2002: provides education on environment and natural resources to media clients.
Interview, 2007

Warren, Ellen *(1970)*
1978: 30 years old, reporter, *Chicago Sun-Times.*
1984: becomes reporter, Knight Ridder newspapers.
1993: moves to Chicago and becomes metro reporter, *Chicago Tribune,* and later metro columnist, features columnist, and senior correspondent; 2004, becomes senior correspondent, *Chicago Tribune*'s Red Eye magazine; 2005, becomes columnist for *Chicago Tribune*'s Sunday magazine.
Interview, 2007

Watson, Jerome R. *(1960)*
1978: 40 years old, reporter, *Chicago Sun-Times*; 1981, becomes White House correspondent; 1987, becomes bureau chief.
1993: died (*Washington Post,* December 20, 1993).
Interview, 1978

Weaver Jr., Warren *(1947)*
1978: 55 years old, reporter, *New York Times.*
1989: retires.
1997: died (*New York Times,* February 20, 1997).

Wehr, Elizabeth *(1974)**
1978: 37 years old, reporter, *CQ*; rises to senior writer.
1989: leaves journalism; becomes legislative director, Senator Nancy Kassebaum (R-Ks.).
1990: studies law, University of California, Berkeley; receives degree.
1993: becomes research scientist, School of Public Health, George Washington University.
2003: becomes public health analyst at National Institutes of Health.
Interview, 2007

Wellborn, Stanley N. *(1969)**
1978: 33 years old, associate editor, *U.S. News & World Report;* 1978, becomes higher education writer.
1987: leaves journalism; becomes speechwriter, Bob Dole's presidential campaign.
1988: becomes director of public affairs, Brookings Institution; 1999, becomes director of external affairs.
2004: becomes director of communications, then public affairs director, Resources for the Future.
Interview, 2006

Wells, Betty *(1973)*
1978: 24 years old, regional correspondent, *Wichita Eagle* (Knight Ridder).
1988: Moves to Gary, Indiana, and becomes managing editor and future executive editor, *Post-Tribune.*
1993: returns to Kansas; works as freelancer.
1996: moves to Indiana; directs fundraising for PBS station; becomes political strategist for the mayor of Crown Point.
2004: moves to Florida; becomes digital editor for *News-Press,* Naples.
Interview, 2007

Wermiel, Stephen *(1972)**
1978: 28 years old, reporter, *Boston Globe;* part-time law student, American University.
1979: becomes Supreme Court reporter, *Wall Street Journal.*
1991: leaves journalism; becomes law professor, College of William and Mary.
1992: becomes law professor, Georgia State University.
1998: becomes law professor, American University.
Interview, 2006

Westlein, Patricia Rose *(1959)*
1978: 43 years old, managing editor, BNA.
1996: retires, remains as volunteer corporate historian and newsletter producer.
2008: died (*Washington Post,* August 31, 2008).

Wiese Jr., Arthur E. *(1967)**
1978: 32 years old, bureau chief, *Houston Post.*
1982: leaves journalism; becomes director of public relations, American Petroleum Institute; 1990, becomes vice president of public affairs.
2000: becomes vice president for corporate communications, Entergy Corporation.
Interview, 2007

Wilkie, Curtis *(1963)*
1978: 37 years old, reporter, *Boston Globe;* 1984, becomes Jerusalem bureau chief; 1987, becomes national reporter; 1993, becomes traveling reporter based in New Orleans.
2000: retires.
2001: becomes professor of journalism, University of Mississippi.
Interview, 2007

Williams, Betty Anne *(1973)*
1978: 26 years old, reporter, AP.
1984: becomes assistant managing editor, *Democrat and Chronicle* (Rochester, N.Y.)
1988: becomes assignment editor, *USA Today*, Washington; 1995, becomes recruiter.
2000: works for Black College Wire.
2005: becomes a managing editor, *Gazette-Star* (Prince George's County, Maryland); becomes adjunct professor, Howard University.
2008: becomes director of communications, Joint Center for Political and Economic Studies, Washington.
Interview, 2007

Wolman, Jonathan *(1973)*
1978: 27 years old, national writer, AP; 1979, becomes assistant news editor; 1981, becomes news editor; 1984, becomes assistant bureau chief; 1989, becomes bureau chief; 1998, becomes managing editor in New York; 2000, becomes vice president and executive editor; 2002, becomes senior vice president.
2004: becomes editorial page editor, *Denver Post.*
2007: becomes editor and publisher, *Detroit News.*
Interview, 2008

Woodruff, Judy *(1968)*
1978: 31 years old, White House correspondent, NBC News; 1982, becomes interview reporter, *Today*, NBC.
1983: becomes Washington correspondent, *NewsHour* and *Frontline*, PBS.
1993: becomes news anchor, CNN.
2005: becomes visiting fellow, Shorenstein Center, Harvard
2007: becomes senior correspondent, *NewsHour*, PBS; anchors weekly interview program, Bloomberg TV.
Interview, 2005

Wordham, Bill *(1961)**
1978: 47 years old, correspondent, ABC News.
1980s: leaves journalism; becomes spokesman, American Petroleum Institute.
1990s: becomes spokesman, Tobacco Institute; writes Civil War novels.

Yoder, Allan
1978: 29 years old, correspondent, *The Record* (Bergen County, N.J.); returns to Bergen as assignment editor.
1992: died (*Editor & Publisher*, August 15, 1992).

Young, Leah R.
1978: 35 years old, reporter, *Journal of Commerce.*
1988: leaves journalism; becomes press director, House of Representatives Small Business Committee.
1991: becomes freelance writer, including as part-time columnist, *Crane's Chicago Business.*
1996: becomes director of media services, Substance and Mental Health Services Administration.
Interview, 2006

Young, Robert C. *(1936)*
1978: 63 years old, *Chicago Tribune.*
1979: retires.
2000: died (*Washington Post*, June 12, 2000).

Zimmerman, Bill *(1961)*
1978: 38 years old, reporter, ABC News.
1980: becomes prime time anchor, CNN, Atlanta.
1984: becomes anchor, executive producer, and senior correspondent, Cablevision, New York.
1994: retires; does public relations part-time.
Interview, 2007

Zimmerman, Richard *(1960)*
1978: 43 years old, reporter, *Cleveland Plain Dealer.*
1985: retires.
2008: died (*Cleveland Plain Dealer,* January 12, 2008).

Zuckerman, Edward *(1963)*
1978: 35 years old, reporter, Knight Ridder
1980: starts newsletter, *The Political Finance & Lobby Reporter,* and reference book, *The Almanac of Federal PACs.*
2005: closes newsletter; sells reference book to *CQ.*
Interview, 2011

Listed below are journalists surveyed in 1978 who could not be located for the follow-up survey. Age and employer are as given in 1978.

Anderson, Helen: 40s, "Texas newspapers"
Barton, Salley: 29, newsletter
Blount, Charlotte: 26, Mutual Black Network
Bowne, Thomas: 28, AP Radio
Carlson, Herbert P.: 51, F-D-C Reports
Christy, Jeffrey B.: 26, F-D-C Reports
Clayton, William: 42, UPI
Connover, Lynn: 29, *American Banker*
Conway, Bill: 32, CCH
Deschenes, Michele: 24, F-D-C Reports
Diamond, Tom: 39, *Washington Star*
Earle, G.: 25, F-D-C Reports
Edwards, Tom: 38, F-D-C Reports
Fassberg, Benjamin C.: 52, BNA
Flanagan, Mike: 38, *Tulsa World*
Foster, James: 46, Scripps Howard
Hanna, Sam: 51, *New Orleans State-Item, Youngstown Vindicator*
Harris, Emily: 49, Capitol Publications
Hickling, Lee: 48, Gannett
Hildreth, James: 34, UPI
Hoover, Dan: 28, Mutual Broadcasting
Hughes, Thomas: 58, *U.S. News & World Report*
Jackson, Stuart: 28, McGraw-Hill

Kelly, Daniel: 24, Prentice-Hall
Law, Lou: 28, Mutual Black Network
Long, Steven: 35, Fairchild Publications
Maxfield, David M.: 35, *CQ*
McCarthy, Jim: 42, CBS Radio
McClain, Wallace: 35, Plus Publications
McGuire, Frank: 46, Kimberly Newspapers
Miller, Peter G.: 32, freelancer
Mills, Jeffrey: 33, AP
Morris, James: 44, Morris Associates newsletter
Parker, Rich: 42, Donray Newspapers
Rubin, B. J.: 32, BNA
Singer, James: 42, *National Journal*
Steele, Sally: 60, "regional papers"
Strickland, Jean V.: 32, Chilton Publications
Taft, Dale R.: 49, Kiplinger
Thompson, Alan R.: 36, Scripps Howard
Thompson, Stephen: 34, Kiplinger
Tuthill, Mary: 48, Booth Newspapers
Verbrycke, Pamela P.: 32, CCH
Waters, Robert: 52, *Hartford Courant*
Wiper, Roberta: 29, Fairchild Publications.

NOTES

Newswork: How I Got There

1. Leo C. Rosten , *The Washington Correspondents* (1937; reprint, Arno Press, 1974).
2. Dan D. Nimmo, *Newsgathering in Washington: A Study in Political Communication* (Atherton, 1964).
3. Stephen Hess, *The Washington Reporters* (Brookings, 1981), p. 124.

Chapter 1

Note: For journalists who were guests in the classes that I taught at George Washington University, the interviewer is listed as "GWU class." When no interviewer is identified, I was the interviewer.

1. Bernard Kalb, CBS, interviewed by GWU class, October 3, 2007.
2. Corbin Gwaltney, *Chronicle of Higher Education*, interviewed March 25, 1977, and by GWU class, October 10, 2007.
3. "Journalist James H. McCartney Dies at 85," *Washington Post*, May 7, 2011.
4. Richard Boyce, *Scripps Howard News Service*; Jerry Baulch, *Associated Press*; Jim Free, *Birmingham News*; Lloyd Norman, *Chicago Tribune*; David Kelso, *Bureau of National Affairs*; Daniel Gilmore, *UPI*; Robert Heinl, *Detroit News*; John Averill, *Los Angeles Times*; James Roper, *freelance*; Charlotte Moulton, *UPI*. Obituary research was done by Michelle Begnoche, Caryl Ann McAleer, and Christine Wallace. Obituary sources are as follows: John Averill, *Los Angeles Times*, January 11, 1984; Jerry Baulch, AP, February 7, 1985; Richard Boyce, Scripps Howard News Service, January 25, 2000; James Free, *Congressional Record* (Senate), April 18, 1996; Daniel Gilmore, *Washington Post*, August 9, 1988; Robert Heinl, *Washington Post*, May 7, 1979; David Kelso, *Washington Post*, October 19, 1992; Charlotte Moulton, UPI, May 7, 2004; Lloyd Norman, *Chicago Tribune*, November 16, 1987; James Roper, *Washington Post*, November 13, 1998.
5. Amherst: Warren Weaver, *New York Times*; Dartmouth: George Herman, *CBS*; Harvard (6): David Barnett, *U.S. News & World Report*, Edward Behr, *Wall Street Journal*, Juan Cameron, *Fortune*, Alan Emory, *Watertown (N.Y.) Daily Times*, Richard Strout, *Christian Science Monitor*, and Sidney Sulkin, *Changing Times (Kiplinger)*; Johns Hopkins: Corbin Gwaltney, *Chronicle of Higher Education*; Princeton (2): Bob Abernethy, *NBC*, and Don Irwin, *Los Angeles Times*; University of Pennsylvania: David Dear, *Dear Publications*; Stanford (3): John Averill, *Los Angeles Times*, Don Shannon, *Los Angeles Times*, and William Steif, *Scripps Howard News Service*; Yale (2): Wilson Hall, *NBC*, and Robert Heinl, *Detroit News*.

6. Oklahoma: Seth King, *New York Times;* Michigan State: James McCartney, *Knight-Ridder;* Utah: Hays Gorey, *Time.*

7. Glenn Everett, letter to author, April 22, 1978.

8. Orr Kelly, interviewed by Caryl Ann McAleer, January 21, 2008.

9. Donald Larrabee interview, April 19, 1977.

10. Hugh Sidey interview, March 10, 1977.

11. "Simmons Fentress, 56; Correspondent at *Time*," *New York Times,* August 12, 1981.

12. James Cary, interviewed by Lynda Marlow, October 15, 2007.

13. Adam Bernstein, "Darwin Olofson, 81, Dies," *Washington Post,* October 22, 2002.

14. William Steif interview, July 18, 1978; interviewed by Nathaniel Lubin, August 9, 2007.

15. Robert Boyd interview, March 14, 1977.

16. Sidney Hurlburt interview, January 25, 1978.

17. Ernest (Pat) Furgurson interview, April 1, 1977.

18. Jack Germond interview, April 14, 1977.

19. Morton Mintz, interviewed by Sarah Lovenheim, May 26, 2006.

20. David Dear interview, February 2, 2007.

21. Morton Paulson, interviewed by Michelle Begnoche, February 14, 2008.

22. A. Robert Smith had a varied career for a journalist of this generation. After working in Washington for the *Washington Star, Portland Oregonian,* and King Broadcasting (Seattle) between 1950 and 1978, he moved to Virginia Beach to be an editorial writer for the *Virginian Pilot* and later started a magazine for psychic Edgar Cayce's organization. Interviewed by Lynda Marlow, November 19, 2007.

23. Richard Maloy interview, May 26, 1977; interview by Sarah Lovenheim, July 11, 2006.

24. Don Shannon, interviewed by Lynda Marlow, November 6, 2007.

25. "Frank Cormier, 66; Covered 5 Presidents for Associated Press," *New York Times,* February 11, 1994.

26. Helen Thomas, interviewed by Riki Parikh, September 9, 2005.

27. Fred Taylor interview, May 9, 1978.

28. David Kraslow interview, April 6, 1977.

29. See Stephen Hess, *The Washington Reporters* (Brookings, 1981), pp. 79–80.

30. Alan Emory interview, April 22, 1977.

31. Corbin Gwaltney interview, March 25, 1977.

32. Robert Abernethy, interviewed by Michelle Begnoche, September 7, 2007.

33. Seth King interview, March 7, 2007.

34. Dale Nelson, interviewed by Nathaniel Lubin, August 8, 2007.

35. Dale Nelson, *Gin before Breakfast* (Syracuse University Press, 2007), p. xix. The book's title is from Archibald MacLeish's warning to young poets "to avoid the practice of journalism as they would wet socks and gin before breakfast." The poet-journalists include Coleridge, Whitman, Kipling, Edgar Allen Poe, Stephen Crane, and Carl Sandburg.

36. Jon Margolis, interviewed by Nathaniel Lubin, July 24, 2007.

Chapter 2

1. Thomas Fiedler, interviewed by Lynda Marlow, October 2, 2007.

2. Rich Jaroslovsky, interviewed by GWU class, February 13, 2008.

3. Jack Fuller, interviewed by Elizabeth Krevsky, August 4, 2009.

4. The boomer journalists with law degrees are Cynthia Bolbach, Richard Carelli, Stan Crock, Richard Cohen, Jack Fuller, Cully Irving, Urban Lehrer, Peter Segall, Glenn Waggoner, and Stephen Wermeil.

5. See "In the Niche," chapter 8 in this book. The niche publications proved especially hospitable to women boomers, including Nancy Aldrich (BPI), Cynthia Bolbach (BNA),

Paula Cruickshank (CCH), Kathleen Gill (BNA), Vicky Mason (*Telecommunications Report*), and Deanne Neumann (BNA).

6. Ann Devroy, interviewed by Amy B. McIntosh, June 16, 1978.

7. Quoted in Gina Duwe, "Ann's Story" (www.uwec.edu/cj/devroy/story.htm).

8. Ibid.

9. Quoted in "Ann Devroy, 49, Reporter for the *Post*," *Washington Times*, October 27, 1997.

10. Walter Mossberg, interviewed by Richard Martinelli, November 16, 2007.

11. Kim Masters, interviewed by Nathaniel Lubin, July 31, 2007.

12. Joe Flint, "Hollywood Reporter Hires Kim Masters," *Los Angeles Times*, June 1, 2010.

13. Jim Fattibene, interviewed by Sarah Lovenheim, May 30, 2006.

14. Ira Allen, interviewed by Sarah Lovenheim, May 30, 2006.

15. Becky Bailey, interviewed by Jeffrey Rayport, June 29, 1978, and by Lynda Marlow, November 7, 2007.

16. Lisa Myers, interviewed by Elizabeth Krevsky, August 14, 2009.

17. See Stephen Hess, *International News and Foreign Correspondents* (Brookings, 1996), p. 69.

18. Macculloch Irving, interviewed by Richard V. Nalley, June 2, 1978, and by Elizabeth Krevsky, July 7, 2009.

19. Jonathan Bernstein, interviewed by Richard V. Nalley, June 8, 1978, and by Nathaniel Lubin, August 1, 2007.

20. Steven Parkhurst, interviewed by Richard V. Nalley, July 12, 1978, and by Nathaniel Lubin, August 3, 2007.

21. Mary Lord, interviewed by Richard V. Nalley, June 5, 1978, and by Elizabeth Krevsky, July 10, 2009.

22. Russell Dawson, interviewed by Samantha Barry, March 5, 2007. Among other boomers making journalism-to-government moves: Jay Rosenstein, a 23-year-old reporter with the *American Banker* in 1978, has spent a long career as a writer/editor with the Federal Deposit Insurance Corporation; Sue Mathis, Cox Broadcasting, became a special assistant to President Ronald Reagan and later deputy associate administrator for NASA's Office of Communication. She died in 2002 at the age of 53.

23. William Lanouette, interviewed by Sarah Lovenheim, June 1, 2006.

24. Joanne Collings, "Strobe Talbott: Experimenting with History," *The Examiner*, January 20, 2008.

25. Kathy Patterson, interviewed by Lesley H. Bruno, March 5, 2007.

26. Edward Alwood, interviewed by Daniel Reilly, September 18, 2006.

27. Douglas Lowenstein, interviewed by GWU class, October 24, 2007.

28. See Hillary Canada, "Speculation about Lowenstein's Resignation," *Private Equity Beat*, WSJ Blogs, August 25, 2011.

29. Rod Kuckro, interviewed by Amy B. McIntosh, June 16, 1978, and by Sarah Lovenheim, June 21, 2006. 30. Robert Gettlin, interviewed by Sarah Lovenheim, June 5, 2006.

31. Robert Cunningham, interviewed by Nathaniel Lubin, July 31, 2007.

32. Robert Cullen, interviewed by Helen Graham, August 7, 1978, and by Nathaniel Lubin, July 16, 2007.

33. Lucy Knight, interviewed by Helen Graham, July 25, 1978, and by Lesley H. Bruno, February 22, 2007.

34. Ellen Warren, interviewed by Nathaniel Lubin, July 24, 2007.

35. Patricia Mochel, interviewed by Richard V. Nalley, June 13, 1978, and by Elizabeth Krevsky, July 15, 2009.

36. James H. McCartney, interviewed by Lynda Marlow, September 11, 2007.

37. Merrilee Cox, interviewed by Helen Graham, July 14, 1978, and by Austin Dillon, May 28, 2009.

38. Bill Choyke, interviewed by Sarah Lovenheim, June 16, 2006.

39. Anthony Barbieri, interviewed by Amy B. McIntosh, June 26, 1978, and Michelle Begnoche, October 8, 2007. He became managing editor of the *Baltimore Sun* in 2000 and retired in 2004. He is now Foster Professor of Writing and Editing at Penn State.

40. Thomas Fiedler was executive editor of the *Miami Herald* from 2001 to 2007 and is now dean of the College of Communication, Boston University.

41. Jack Fuller became CEO of the *Chicago Tribune* in 1993 and president of Tribune Publishing Company in 1997; he retired in 2004.

42. Dean Reed interview, June 16, 1977.

43. Bill Keller, interviewed by Richard V. Nalley, July 3, 1978. Keller's subsequent positions after Washington: Moscow (1986–91); Johannesburg (1992–95); and New York as foreign editor (1995–97), managing editor (1997–2001), columnist (2001–03), executive editor (2003–11), and columnist (2011–).

44. Karen Elliott House, interviewed by Richard V. Nalley, July 27, 1978, and by Elizabeth Krevsky, July 20, 2009. A summary of House's career is found in chapter 3.

45. Jonathan Wolman, interviewed by Michelle Begnoche, February 21, 2008. Wolman was in New York from 1998 to 2004 as AP managing editor, vice president and executive editor, and senior vice president. After retirement in 2004 he became editorial page editor of the *Denver Post* and in 2007 editor and publisher of the *Detroit News.*

46. Roy E. Bode, interviewed by Nathaniel Lubin, July 13, 2007.

Chapter 3

1. The interview with Charlotte Moulton was conducted by Anne S. Kasper, 1991, for the Washington Press Club Foundation.

2. See Kay Mills, *A Place in the News* (Dodd, Mead, 1988), p. 36.

3. See Irvin Molotsky, "Marjorie Hunter, 78, a Pioneering Washington Correspondent for *The Times,*" *New York Times,* April 11, 2001.

4. See Leo C. Rosten, *The Washington Correspondents* (1937; reprinted by Arno Press, 1974), pp. 312–23.

5. Quoted in Mills, *A Place in the News,* p. 51, and in Nan Robertson, *The Girls in the Balcony* (Random House, 1992), pp. 111–12.

6. Deborah Howell, interviewed by GWU class, March 2, 2005.

7. Judy Woodruff, interviewed by GWU class, September 7, 2005.

8. Nina Totenberg, interviewed by Jeremy Holden, February 2, 2006.

9. Alicia Shepard, interviewed by Lesley Bruno, March 15, 2007.

10. Jo Thomas, interviewed by Lesley Bruno, March 7, 2007.

11. Lisa Myers, interviewed by Elizabeth Krevsky, August 14, 2009.

12. Robin Sproul, interviewed by GWU class, January 25, 2006.

13. Robert Pierpoint, White House correspondent for CBS, 1958–1980, interviewed by Michelle Begnoche, March 18, 2008.

14. Don Shannon, who reported from Paris and Tokyo for the *Los Angeles Times* before becoming a Washington correspondent, interviewed by Lynda Marlow, November 6, 2007.

15. Georgie Anne Geyer, *Buying the Night Flight* (Delacorte Press, 1983), p. 9.

16. See Adam Bernstein, "Mal Johnson, Cox Employee," *Washington Post,* November 9, 2007.

17. Judlyne Lilly, interviewed by Caryl Ann McAleer, January 21, 2008.

18. Lee Thornton, interviewed by Lesley Bruno, March 2, 2007.

19. Jean Heller, interviewed by Nathaniel Lubin, August 6, 2007.

20. Richard Roth, interviewed by Lynda Marlow, October 11, 2007.

21. Carol Falk, interviewed by Lesley Bruno, February 22, 2007.

22. Nancy Koran, interviewed by Heather Kleba, September 11, 2007.

23. Judy Rutter, interviewed by Lynda Marlow, September 12, 2007.

24. Don Campbell, interviewed by Nathaniel Lubin, July 20, 2007.

25. Quoted in Stephen Hess, *International News and Foreign Correspondents* (Brookings, 1996), p. 20.

26. Patricia Fanning, interviewed by Lynda Marlow, September 18, 2007.

27. Anne Davenport, interviewed by Sarah Lovenheim, February 8, 2005.

28. Mary Kay Quinlan, interviewed by Lynda Marlow, September 17, 2007. This also concerned Carol Richards, who went from the founding editorial board of *USA Today* in Washington to "a family-oriented community" when she joined *Newsday* on Long Island, New York. "I have two great kids, and I think it was good that they grew up here." Interviewed by Lynda Marlow, October 18, 2007.

29. Gloria Borger and her husband, Lance Morgan, a former journalist who became a leading crisis management specialist, from a joint interview with the GWU class, October 19, 2005.

30. The other woman journalist who would become anchor of primetime network news at CBS, Katie Couric, was born in 1957, graduated from the University of Virginia in 1979, and became a Washington correspondent at NBC in 1989.

31. A tragic exception was Jessica Savitch, who died in 1983 at 36 years of age when the car she was riding in fell into a shallow canal, landed upside down, and sank into deep mud that sealed the doors shut.

32. Candy Crowley, interviewed by Sarah Lovenheim, February 15, 2005.

33. Ann Compton, interviewed by Sarah Lovenheim, July 10, 2006.

34. E-mail from Linda Douglass, January 23, 2007.

35. Hale Boggs (D-La.) was killed in a plane crash and was succeeded in Congress by his wife, Lindy Boggs, Cokie's mother.

36. Adam Bernstein, "Charles W. Bailey II, 82, Co-wrote Bestseller 'Seven Days in May,'" *Washington Post,* January 5, 2012.

37. Cheryl Arvidson, interviewed by Sarah Lovenheim, June 19, 2006.

38. Ellen Warren, interviewed by Nathaniel Lubin, July 24, 2007.

39. Susan Page, interviewed by GWU class, January 26, 2005.

40. Karen Elliott House, interviewed by Elizabeth Krevsky, July 20, 2009; Judith Miller, interviewed by Amy B. McIntoch, July 19, 1978.

41. Franklin Foer, "The Source of the Trouble," *New York,* May 31, 2004.

42. See Stephen Hess, *Live from Capitol Hill!* (Brookings,1991), pp. 110–30, especially pages 116–21, 161–70.

43. See David H. Weaver, Randal A. Beam, Bonnie J. Brownlee, Paul S. Voakes, and G. Cleveland Wilhoit, *The American Journalist in the 21st Century* (Lawrence Erlbaum Associates, 2007), especially chapter 5, pp. 182–96.

44. U.S. Bureau of the Census, *Statistical Abstract of the United States 2001,* p. 380.

45. Laura Meckler, interviewed by Sarah Halzack, February 15, 2006.

46. Christine Brennan, interviewed by Clare Lloyd Jones, February 2005.

47. Elisabeth Bumiller, interviewed by Rick Barry, January 25, 2005.

48. Lisa Meyer, interviewed by Gillian McHale, February 7, 2006.

49. Martha Derthick's notes on a conversation, April 26, 1979.

50. Joan Biskupic, interviewed by Jeremy Holden, March 24, 2006.

51. Anne Hawke, interviewed by Jennifer Puckett, January 30, 2005.

52. Brooke Hart, interviewed by Carly Cooperman, October 24, 2005.

53. Donna Cassata, interviewed by Sarah Spooner, December 13, 2005.

54. Susan Feeney and Steve Hirsh, interviewed by GWU class, April 19, 2006.

55. June Kronholz, interviewed by Christine Grimaldi, April 24, 2006.

Chapter 4

1. Hal Logan, interviewed by Nathaniel Lubin, August 14, 2007. Logan is now CEO of BuyBook Technologies Inc.
2. Carole Simpson, interviewed by Donita Moorhus, 1992–94, for the Washington Press Club Foundation.
3. Warren Brown, interviewed by Richard Martinelli, November 20, 2007; additional interview, May 5, 2011.
4. James Adams, interviewed by Michelle Begnoche, November 8, 2007.
5. Roy Betts, interviewed by Elizabeth Richardson, November 2, 2007.
6. Betty Anne Williams, interviewed by Lesley Bruno, March 23, 2007.
7. Karen DeWitt interview, September 26, 2006.
8. The ASNE survey reports that the number of Hispanic journalists declined less than the national average for all journalists and that the number of Asian American journalists actually increased. Our 1978 survey included one Hispanic and one Asian American.
9. Bob Papper, quoted in RTDNA news release, September 22, 2010.
10. Emily Guskin, Mahvish Shahid Khan, and Amy Mitchell, "A Study of African Americans in U.S. News Coverage" (Pew Research Center Project for Excellence in Journalism, July 26, 2010).
11. Barbara Reynolds interview, April 4, 1978.
12. Metro staffers do get opportunities to go beyond the city limits as, for example, when Theola Labbe-DeBose, whose beat was crime and public safety, had an extended assignment in Iraq and also in Haiti, reporting on the 2010 earthquake.
13. See Paul Farhi, "Obama Opts for Low-Key Reveal on Major Issue," *Washington Post,* May 10, 2012.
14. See Brian Stelter, "60 Minutes Gets Younger," *New York Times,* May 6, 2012.
15. Vicki Walton-James, interviewed by GWU class, April 12, 2006.
16. Ellyn Ferguson, interviewed by Sarah Lovenheim, April 26, 2005. Ferguson became agriculture reporter for *CQ Roll Call* in 2009.
17. Emily Guskin, Paul Moore, and Amy Mitchell, "African American Media: Evolving in the New Era" (Pew Research Center Project for Excellence in Journalism, 2011). There were two weekend talk shows, *Weekly with Ed Gordon* (BET) and *Washington Week with Roland Martin* (TV One).
18. Robin Sproul, interviewed by GWU class, January 25, 2006.
19. Terry Neal, interviewed by GWU class, October 26, 2005.
20. Frank James, interviewed by Jerah R. Cordova, April 18, 2005.

Chapter 5

1. No other newspaper's journalists have written as many books recounting the history of their organization or their place in it. See Gerald M. Boyd, *My Times in Black and White: Race and Power at the* New York Times (Lawrence Hill Books, 2010); Max Frankel, *The Times of My Life and My Life with* The Times (Random House, 1999); Arthur Krock, *Memoirs: 60 Years on the Firing Line* (Funk and Wagnalls, 1968); Robert H. Phelps, *God and the Editor: My Search for Meaning at* The New York Times (Syracuse University Press, 2009); Howell Raines, *The One that Got Away: A Memoir* (Simon and Schuster, 2006); James Reston, *Deadline: A Memoir* (Random House, 1991); Tom Wicker, *On Press* (Viking, 1978). Also see David Halberstam, *The Powers That Be* (Knopf, 1979) and Gay Talese, *The Kingdom and the Power* (NAL Book, World Publishing, 1969).
2. Tom Wicker interview, July 21, 1978.
3. Joseph Kraft, *Profiles in Power* (New American Library, 1966), p. 78.

4. Frankel, *The Times of My Life and My Life with* The Times, p. 219.

5. See Bill Lawrence, *Six Presidents, Too Many Wars* (Saturday Review Press, 1972), pp. 257–58.

6. See "Milestones," *Time*, July 15, 2002. Foreman and Cianfrani later married.

7. Boyd, *My Times in Black and White*, p. 119. Boyd rose to managing editor until forced out by collateral damage from the Jayson Blair scandal in 2003.

8. Russell Baker, "A Bad Morning at the *New York Times*," *New York Review*, April 29, 2010, p. 4.

9. Edward Cowan interview, June 29, 2011.

10. Howell Raines, *The One That Got Away*, p. 33.

11 Talese, *The Kingdom and the Power*, p. 385; also see David S. Broder, *Behind the Front Page* (Simon and Schuster, 1987), pp. 333–334.

12. There are many versions of the Wicker-Greenfield struggle. I have chosen to rely on Susan E. Tifft and Alex S. Jones, *The Trust: The Private and Powerful Family behind* The New York Times (Little, Brown, 1999), p. 422–26.

13. Bill Kovach interview, April 19, 2010.

14. Hedrick Smith, interviewed by the GWU class, October 31, 2007.

15. Nancy Hicks interview, March 24, 1977.

16. Marjorie Hunter interview, April 28, 1977; for notable retirements, see David Binder, "William Blair, 83, Reporter for *Times* on the Environment," *New York Times*, January 20, 1995, and David E. Rosenbaum, "E. W. Kenworthy, 83, Reporter Who Covered Capital with Flair," *New York Times*, January 26, 1993.

17. Anthony Ripley interview, April 14, 1977.

18. For Judith Miller, see chapter 3. Steven Rattner went from Washington to the London bureau, quit journalism, and joined the Wall Street firms Morgan Stanley and Lazard before co-founding Quadrangle Group in 2000. As a dealmaker, he specialized in the media and communications sector. In 2009 President Obama put him in charge of the auto task force that essentially dictated the reorganization of Chrysler and General Motors. At the time, Rattner's financial disclosure statement showed a net worth of at least $188 million. See Jonathan D. Salant and Justin Blum, "Obama Automobile Adviser Worth at Least $188 Million," *Bloomberg.com*, May 28, 2009.

19. See Tifft and Jones, *The Trust*, p. 560. Confirmed in Kovach interview.

20. Richard Burt, interviewed by GWU class, November 7, 2007.

21. Steven V. Roberts, interviewed by Jeremy Holden, August 8, 1978, and by GWU class, September 19, 2007.

22. Martin Tolchin interviewed October 19, 1978, and by GWU class, September 12, 2007.

23. Bernard Gwertzman, interviewed by Sarah Lovenheim, June 5, 2006, supplemented with Pranay Gupte, "Bernard Gwertzman: Born with Ink in His Blood," *New York Sun*, April 5, 2005; Emily C. Graff, "Bernard M. Gwertzman '57: A Journalist with a Global Reach," *Harvard Crimson*, June 1, 2007; Mark Glaser, "Online News Pioneers See Lots of Changes in the First 10 Years," *USC Annenberg Online Journalism Review*, September 9, 2003.

24. Hedrick Smith interview, April 7, 2010.

25. Seth King, interviewed by Amy B. McIntosh, June 7, 1978, and by Samantha Barry, March 7, 2007.

26. Philip Shabecoff, interviewed by Michelle Begnoche, January 22, 2008.

27. Jo Thomas, interviewed by Helen Graham, July 10, 1978, and by Lesley Bruno, March 7, 2007.

28. Anthony Marro, interviewed by Nathaniel Lubin, July 17, 2007; the others, according to Marro, were Nick Horrock and Wendall Rawls.

29. Founded in 1977, the Institute for Journalism Education was renamed the Maynard Institute for Journalism Education to honor Bob Maynard after his death in 1993. Maynard

and Hicks bought the *Oakland Tribune* in 1983, making them the first African Americans to own a major metropolitan newspaper.

30. Hedrick Smith interview, April 28, 1977. The number did not include support staff or columnists.

Chapter 6

1. Bob Schieffer, interviewed by GWU class, February 9, 2005.

2. Quoted in Desmond Smith, "The Small World of NBC News," *New York Magazine,* June 29, 1981, p. 24.

3. Bernard Kalb and Marvin Kalb, interviewed by GWU class, October 3, 2007; also Marvin Kalb, July 26, 2006, and Bernard Kalb, July 31, 2006, interviewed by Sarah Lovenheim.

4. Roger Mudd, *The Place to Be* (Public Affairs, 2008), pp. 55 and 77. After leaving NBC, Mudd became an essayist on the *MacNeil-Lehrer NewsHour,* PBS, and a longtime anchor with the History Channel.

5. For his account of the dispute with CBS, see Daniel Schorr, *Clearing the Air* (Houghton Mifflin, 1977).

6. Robert Pierpoint, interviewed by Michelle Begnoche, March 18, 2008.

7. See Ted Koppel and Kyle Gibson, *Nightline: History in the Making and the Making of Television* (Times Books, 1996), p. 48.

8. Bernard Kalb left NBC to become the State Department spokesman, as described in chapter 1.

9. Brit Hume, interviewed by GWU class, October 17, 2007, and by Lauren Melvin, November 1, 2005.

10. For their White House recollections, see Dan Rather with Mickey Herskowitz, *The Camera Never Blinks* (William Morrow, 1977); Sam Donaldson, *Hold On, Mr. President!* (Random House, 1987).

11. Bill Plante, interviewed by Samantha Vizer, February 17, 2006.

12. Judy Woodruff interviewed by GWU class, July 9, 2005. She reflects on the White House beat in Judy Woodruff with Kathleen Maxa, *"This is Judy Woodruff at the White House"* (Addison-Wesley, 1982).

13. Russell Baker, *An American in Washington* (Knopf, 1961), pp. 198–99.

14. See Marvin Kalb and Ted Koppel, *In the National Interest* (Simon and Schuster, 1977).

15. See Stephen Hess, *International News and Foreign Correspondents* (Brookings, 1996), p.33.

16. Barry Dunsmore, interviewed by Nathaniel Lubin, July 17, 2007.

17. Carl Stern, interviewed by GWU class, April 10, 2007.

18. Fred Graham, interviewed by GWU class, April 16, 2008.

19. Tim O'Brien, interviewed by Jenner Gibson, July 28, 2010.

20. Bruce Weber, "Irving R. Levine, NBC News Correspondent, Dies at 86," *New York Times,* March 28, 2009.

21. Robert Bazell, interviewed by Helen Graham, June 28, 1978.

22. Robert Bazell, interviewed by Lynda Marlow, October 9, 2007.

23. Jed Duvall, interviewed by Caryl Ann McAleer, February 19, 2008.

24. Richard Roth had been a CBS correspondent for 22 years when his contract was not renewed in 1994, and he switched to NBC in London. "After 4 years at NBC, CBS asked me to come back and I agreed. That was in 1998, and I've been a London-based correspondent for CBS since then." Interview with Lynda Marlow, October 11, 2007. Harry Reasoner (CBS-ABC-CBS) provides another example of "coming home again."

25. Walter Rogers, interviewed by Lynda Marlow, October 1, 2007.

26. Bill Zimmerman, interviewed by Lynda Marlow, October 8, 2007.

27. Don Farmer, interviewed by Sarah Lovenheim, May 30, 2006.

28. David Garcia, interviewed by Nathaniel Lubin, July 11, 2007.

29. Gail Shister, "One Name Draws Steve Bell out of Academe: Koppel," *Philadelphia Inquirer*, November 22, 2005; also see AP, "Former ABC News Correspondent Steve Bell Retiring from Teaching Post at Ball State University," April 27, 2007.

30. "Journalist Wilson Hall Dies at 69," *Commercial Appeal* [Memphis], January 12, 1991.

31. Jackson Bain, interviewed by Nathaniel Lubin, July 26, 2007.

32. Dominic Mariani, "Connecticut Q & A: Richard Valeriani; The Word on Getting Out the Word," *New York Times*, August 14, 1994.

33. Charles Quinn, interviewed by Samantha Barry, February 13, 2007.

34. See "Los Angeles Panel Backs Restaurant Smoking Ban," *New York Times*, June 24, 1993.

35. Ike Pappas was interviewed by Heather Kleba, October 4 and 22, 2007. Roger Peterson "left ABC News in 1988 to establish a video production company. His clients included the Air Force, the Social Security Administration, and the Justice Department," obituary, *Washington Post*, April 24, 2004.

36. Patricia Sullivan, "Ike Pappas, 75; Newsman Covered Vietnam, Kent State," *Washington Post*, September 3, 2008.

37. Herb Kaplow, interviewed by Christine Wallace, February 28, 2008.

38. Bruce Morton, interviewed by Emily Hochberg, November 28, 2005.

Chapter 7

1. Roberta Hornig-Draper, interviewed by Lesley Bruno, April 6, 2007.

2. John Fialka, interviewed by the GWU class, February 13, 2008, and by Sarah Lovenheim, May 25, 2006.

3. Barbara Cochran, interviewed by the GWU class, November 16, 2005.

4. Ed Pound, interviewed by Heather Kleba, September 13, 2007.

5. See Lisa Myers's move to TV in chapter 3.

6. Stephen Aug, interviewed by Richard Martinelli, October 8, 2007.

7. Lyle Denniston, interviewed by Samantha Barry, March 14, 2007.

8. Lance Gay, e-mail to author, May 12, 2006.

9. Dan Poole, interviewed by Samantha Barry, March 30, 2007.

10. Henry Bradsher, interviewed by David Pupkin, October 2, 2009.

11. James Dickenson, interviewed by Michelle Begnoche, October 12, 2007.

12. John Goshko, interviewed by Elizabeth Krevsky, July 30, 2009.

13. William Claiborne, interviewed by Lynda Marlow, September 27, 2007.

14. E-mail to author, April 5, 2011.

15. Don Oberdorfer, interviewed by Sarah Lovenheim, July 12, 2006.

16. T. R. Reid, interviewed by Lynda Marlow, September 6, 2007.

17. Walter Pincus, interviewed by Sarah Lovenheim, July 25, 2006.

18. See Hal Logan in chapter 4; Bill Richards, interviewed by Nathaniel Lubin, August 8, 2007; Carole Shifrin, interviewed by Michelle Begnoche, November 1, 2007.

19. Helen Thomas, interviewed by Riki Parikh, September 9, 2005.

20. Grant Dillman interview, July 14, 1977.

21. See Joe Holley, "Pye Chamberlayne, 68; UPI Radio Correspondent," *Washington Post*, November 7, 2006. The other two radio reporters were Merrilee Cox and Tom Foty, who has been with all-news WTOP in Washington since 1997. The other two retirees were Daniel Gilmore and Charlotte Moulton (see chapter 1).

22. Jim Anderson, interviewed by Daniel Reilly, October 8, 2002.

23. Mike Feinsilber, interviewed by Richard Martinelli, September 24, 2007.

24. Nicholas Daniloff, interviewed by Lynda Marlow, October 5, 2007.

25. John Barton, interviewed by Elizabeth Krevsky, August 6, 2009.

26. Ira Allen, interviewed by Sarah Lovenheim, May 30, 2006.

27. John Milne, interviewed by Michelle Begnoche, January 31, 2008.

28. Bob Kaylor, interviewed by Lynda Marlow, September 24, 2007.

29. Greg Gordon, interviewed by Ilana Weinberg, January 30, 2005, and by Infinite McCloud, January 29, 2008. For Cheryl Arvidon's post-UPI career, see chapter 3.

30. Dale Nelson, interviewed by Nathaniel Lubin, August 8, 2007; also see chapter 1.

31. Walter Mears, interviewed by Sarah Lovenheim, June 8, 2006; also see career of Jonathan Wolman, chapter 2.

32. James Adams, interviewed by Samantha Barry, February 2, 2007.

33. Bob Cullen, interviewed by Nathaniel Lubin, July 16, 2007; also see chapter 2.

34. Brian King, interviewed by Christine Wallace, January 28, 2008.

35. Brooks Jackson, interviewed by Jake Sherman, March 14 and April 4, 2007. Others who left AP for other journalism jobs are James Gerstenzang (AP, 1970–84), who went to the *LA Times;* Michael Putzel (AP, 1967–91), to the *Boston Globe;* Marc Rosenwasser (AP, 1975–82), to ABC News; and Betty Ann Williams (AP, 1973–84) to Gannett.

36. Mark Knoller, interviewed by Heather Kleba, September 18, 2007.

37. Walter Rogers, interviewed by Lynda Marlow, October 1, 2007; see chapter 6.

38. Bob Berkowitz, interviewed by Nathaniel Lubin, July 23, 2007.

39. Kirsten Lindquist, interviewed by Elizabeth Krevsky, July 15, 2009.

40. Ike Pappas, interviewed by Heather Kleba, October 4 and 22, 2007; also see chapter 10.

41. Tom Fiedler, interviewed by Lynda Marlow, October 2, 2007; also see chapter 10.

42. Bill Richards, interviewed by Nathaniel Lubin, August 8, 2007.

Chapter 8

1. See Stephen Hess, "The Washington Reporters Redux: 1978–98," in *Media Power, Professionals, and Policies,* edited by Howard Tumber (Routledge, 2000), pp. 225–35. The 1998 resurvey of congressional news coverage included the three television networks and five major newspapers.

2. See Jim Marshall, "Newsletter & Electronic Publishers Association Marks 25th Anniversary," *Newsletter on Newsletters,* May 31, 2001.

3. Interviewed by GWU class, December 5, 2007.

4. Robert Cazalas, interviewed by Nathaniel Lubin, July 30, 2007.

5. Edward Zuckerman interview, July 5, 2011.

6. Nancy Aldrich, interviewed by Michelle Begnoche, October 5, 2007.

7. Martin Sibley, interviewed by Jeffrey Rayport, June 26, 1978.

8. Nancy Koran, interviewed by Heather Kleba, September 11, 2007.

9. Janet Walker, interviewed by Sarah Lovenheim, July 21, 2006.

10. Mark LaPedus, "Iconic Electronics Journalist Jack Robertson Dies," *EE Times,* October 21, 2010; Adam Bernstein, "Jack Robertson, Reporter," *Washington Post,* November 5, 2010.

11. Karen Haas Smith interview, July 11, 1978.

12. Karen Haas Smith, interviewed by David Pupkin, November 24, 2009.

13. Morris A. Ward, interviewed by Nathaniel Lubin, July 27, 2007.

14. Judith Dobrzynski, interviewed by Nathaniel Lubin, July 20, 2007.

15. See Hess, *International News and Foreign Correspondents* (Brookings, 1996), pp. 21–23.

16. Richard Smolka, interviewed by Sarah Lovenheim, July 26, 2006.

17. "Jonathan Eberhart: Scientist as Journalist: In Memoriam," *Science News*, March 1, 2003."

18. Claudia Levy, "Jonathan Eberhart Dies; Space Editor, Folk Singer," *Washington Post*, February 26, 2003.

19. See *The Washington Reporters* (Brookings, 1981), p. 141. Note the response of Robert Bazell, NBC's longtime science correspondent, in chapter 7. When asked whether he was satisfied with his career, he replied, "Yes, indeed. I can't imagine anything else I would have rather done."

20. Paula Lazor Cruickshank, interviewed by Lesley Bruno, March 2, 2007.

21. Vicky Mason, interviewed by Amy B. McIntosh, August 10, 1978, and by Lesley Bruno, April 12, 2007.

22. Oliver Patton, interviewed by Curtis Raye, February 9, 2005.

23. Mary Bruce Batte interview, March 11, 1977.

24. Charles Aldrich, interviewed by Richard Martinelli, September 21, 2007.

25. Charles Raab, interviewed by Richard Nalley, June 27, 1978.

26. Bill Hickman, interviewed by Caryl Ann McAleer, February 4, 2008.

27. Judy Haberek, interviewed May 9, 2007.

28. Lucy Knight, interviewed by Lesley Bruno, February 22, 2007.

29. Phil Battey, interviewed by Richard Martinelli, September 10, 2007.

30. Mort Paulson, interviewed by Michelle Begnoche, February 14, 2008.

31. Cynthia Bolbach, interviewed by Michelle Begnoche, October 22, 2007.

32. Deanne Neumann, interviewed by Heather Kleba, 2007.

33. Robert Merry, interviewed by GWU class, November 28, 2007.

34. Wayne Kelley interview, May 16, 1979.

35. Christopher Buchanan, interviewed by Caryl Ann McAleer, February 1, 2008.

36. Irwin Arieff, interviewed by Elizabeth Krevsky, July 31, 2009.

37. Elizabeth Wehr, interviewed by Elizabeth Richardson, October 2, 2007.

38. E-mail to author, March 28, 2009.

39. Kathryn Gest, interviewed by Sarah Lovenheim, July 6, 2006.

40. Rhodes Cook, interviewed by Sarah Lovenheim, May 25, 2006.

41. Bruce Weber, "Thomas N. Schroth, Influential Washington Editor, Is Dead at 88," *New York Times*, August 5, 2009.

42. Dom Bonafede interview, March 24, 1978.

43. Dick Kirschten, interviewed by David Pupkin, October 1, 2009.

44. John Fox Sullivan interview, May 17, 1978.

45. Rochelle Stanfield, interviewed by Sarah Lovenheim, June 1, 2006.

46. John F. Harris and Jim VandeHei, "Happy Birthday, POLITICO," *POLITICO*, January 23, 2012. Also see Jodi Enda, "POLITICO, Act II," *American Journalism Review* (Winter 2011), pp. 14–21.

47. See Russell Adams, "Bloomberg Hatches Big Deal," *Wall Street Journal*, August 26, 2011; see also Harold W. Pskowski interview, September 15, 2011.

Chapter 9

1. The organization's official name is Gridiron Club and Foundation. The foundation is a $1 million fund for charitable purposes. The club throws a small black-tie party in December, restricted to members and their spouses, where speakers sometimes cause a buzz, as did Sarah Palin in 2010. For archival material and their insights, the author thanks *Dallas Morning News* columnist Carl Leubsdorf, the club's secretary, and *Politico* contributing editor Andrew Glass, the fund's administrator.

2. Andrew Glass, "Cheney Yuks It Up with the Press," *Politico*, April 1, 2007.

3. Robert D. Novak, *The Prince of Darkness: 50 Years Reporting in Washington* (Crown Forum, 2007), pp. 545–46. Novak is also responsible for calling the program "soft-core satire," p. 375.

4. Frank A. Aukofer, *Never a Slow Day: Adventures of a 20th-Century Newspaper Reporter* (Marquette University Press, 2009), pp. 226–27.

5. See Linton Weeks, "Stand-Up Comity, One Night Only," *Washington Post,* April 1, 2007.

6. See Donald A. Ritchie, *Reporting from Washington: The History of the Washington Press Corps* (Oxford University Press, 2005), pp. 180-181.

7. Pulitzer Prize winners were Robert Boyd, David Broder, Clark Hoyt, Haynes Johnson, Walter Mears, Clarence Page, William Raspberry, James Risser (twice), David Shribman, Patrick Sloyan, Hedrick Smith, and Tom Toles.

8. Andrew Alexander, interviewed by GWU class, February 6, 2008, and by Samantha Vizer, April 11, 2006.

9. Letter to author, August 29, 2010.

10. Walter Mears, interviewed by Sarah Lovenheim, June 8, 2006.

11. James McCartney, interviewed by Lynda Marlow, September 11, 2007.

12. Leland (Lee) Bandy, interviewed by Sarah Lovenheim, June 1, 2006.

13. Arthur Wiese Jr., interviewed by Heather Kleba, November 20, 2007, and letter to author, October 3, 2006.

14. Twelve percent of the mainstream journalists in the 1978 survey continued as journalists after leaving Washington, but only three of the active members of the Gridiron in 1978 did so. When journalists from niche publications are included, a third of the 1978 reporters left journalism.

15. See David H. Weaver and colleagues, *The American Journalist in the 21st Century* (Lawrence Erlbaum Associates, 2007), p. 134.

16. Richard Dudman interview, April 5, 1977.

17. The estate created the Herb Block Foundation, which gives grants and scholarships in "the spirit of . . . his lifelong fight against abuses by the powerful."

18. Interview with Gil Bailey, February 15, 2007.

19. Interview with Bill Broom, Ridder bureau chief, March 14, 1977. The bureau also included Walter Ridder, who wrote a column, and his wife Marie, who was described as covering "spot news."

20. Robert Boyd interview, March 14, 1977.

21. Dean Reed interview, June 16, 1977.

22. Deborah Howell, interviewed by GWU class, March 2, 2005.

23. See Matt Schudel, "Former Post Ombudsman Helped Break Glass Ceiling," *Washington Post,* January 3, 2010.

24. John Curley interview, May 16, 1977.

25. John Curley, interviewed by Elizabeth Krevsky, August 3, 2009.

26. See Peter S. Prichard, *The Making of McPaper: The Inside Story of How USA Today Made It* (Spotlight Press, 1987).

27. The company, which began with the 1898 purchase of a foundering newspaper in Dayton, Ohio, by 28-year-old James Middleton Cox, grew to more than 77,000 employees and 300 separate businesses, including Cox Cable, Valpak, Manheim, and AutoTrader.com.

28. David Kraslow interview, April 6, 1977.

29. The *Miami News* folded on December 31, 1988. Kraslow wrote on its last front page: "It hurts when any newspaper with a rich and proud history dies. But this is not just another newspaper. Not to me. And not to this town."

30. Andrew Glass interview, February 6, 2008.

31. Letter to author, August 19, 2010.

32. Andrew Alexander, interviewed by Samantha Vizer, April 11, 2006.

33. Andrew Alexander interview, April 1, 2009.

34. Finlay Lewis interview, April 5, 1977.

35. Finlay Lewis, interviewed by Sarah Lovenheim, June 12, 2006.

36. Carl M. Cannon, "If You See It in the Sun, It's So: A Christmas Wish for Newspapers," *Politics Daily*, December 20, 2009.

37. Letter from Finlay Lewis to author, August 31, 2010.

38. Letter from George Condon to author, August 31, 2010.

39. Richard Wilson won his Pulitzer in 1954 for the exclusive publication of the FBI report to the White House in the Harry Dexter White spying case (Wilson retired from the paper in 1970); the winner in 1958 was Clark Mollenhoff, for a series exposing racketeering and fraud in the Teamsters Union (Mollenhoff joined the Nixon White House staff in 1969); Nick Kotz won in 1968 for a report on unsanitary conditions in many meat packing plants (Kotz left newspapering to become an author and historian).

40. James Risser interview, April 4, 1977.

41. James Risser, interviewed by Nathaniel Lubin, August 13, 2007.

42. Letter to author, August 31, 2010.

43. See Jennifer Dorroh, "Endangered Species," *American Journalism Review*, December/January 2009.

44. See David Carr, "At Flagging Tribune, Tales of a Bankrupt Culture," *New York Times*, October 6, 2010.

45. See Jack Shafer, "What Happens to Tribune after Bankruptcy?" Reuters.com, June 11, 2012 (http://blogs.reuters.com/jackshafer/2012/06/11/what-happens-to-tribune-after-bankruptcy/).

46. Albert Hunt, interviewed by GWU class, February 23, 2005.

47. See Jodi Enda, "The Bloomberg Juggernaut," *American Journalism Review*, Spring 2011.

48. Opening Gridiron membership to TV and radio journalists was not a defining factor in advancing membership of women. Only five women of the sixty-five active members had careers that have been exclusively in electronic media: Candy Crowley (CNN), Mara Liasson (NPR), Andrea Mitchell (NBC), Robin Sproul (ABC), and Judy Woodruff (PBS). Overall, the careers of the women mirror those of the male members.

49. The figures from the 1978 survey show that 74.7 percent had only one Washington employer; 73.1 percent went from print to print if they changed jobs, and 17.9 percent went from broadcast to broadcast. See *The Washington Reporters*, p. 150.

50. Candy Crowley, interviewed by Sarah Lovenheim, February 15, 2005.

51. Tom Rosenstiel, "In Memoriam, A Reporter First," *National Journal*, March 13, 2011, p. 6.

52. David S. Broder, interviewed by GWU class, March 30, 2005.

Chapter 10

1. Stanley Degler, interviewed by Helen Graham, July 3, 1978, and by Elizabeth Richardson, November 12, 2007.

2. Vicky Mason, interviewed by Amy McIntosh, August 10, 1978, and by Lesley Bruno, April 12, 2007.

3. Todd Kiplinger, interviewed by Richard Nalley, June 7, 1978; *Washington Post* obituary by Patricia Sullivan, October 8, 2008.

4. Helen Dewar, interviewed by Amy McIntosh, July 11, 1978; *Washington Post* obituary by Patricia Sullivan, November 5, 2006.

5. Hays Gorey, interviewed by Amy McIntosh, June 8, 1978; *Washington Post* obituary by Adam Bernstein, April 14, 2011.

6. Judith Dobrzynski, interviewed by Richard Nalley, July 18, 1978, and by Nathaniel Lubin, July 20, 2007.

7. Richard Nalley interview with Karen Elliott House, July 27, 1978, and Sam Donaldson, June 26, 1978.

8. Jack Fuller, interviewed by Elizabeth Krevsky, August 4, 2009.

9. Thomas Fiedler, interviewed by Lynda Marlow, October 2, 2007.

10. See Meryl Aldridge and Julia Evetts, "Rethinking the Concept of Professionalism: The Case of Journalism," *British Journal of Sociology* (December 2003), p. 560.

11. John Fialka, interviewed by Sarah Lovenheim, May 25, 2006.

12. Jeff Lubar, interviewed by Sarah Lovenheim, June 16, 2006. Lubar left journalism to become vice president of public affairs at the National Association of Realtors.

13. Donald Bacon, interviewed by Samantha Barry, February 23, 2007.

14. Greg Conderacci, interviewed by Nathaniel Lubin, July 17, 2007.

15. Cheryl Arvidson, interviewed by Sarah Lovenheim, June 19, 2006.

16. While the question of career patterns has drawn only modest attention in the United States, there are excellent studies on the British press. See Jeremy Tunstall, *The Westminster Lobby Correspondents* (London: Routledge and Kegan Paul, 1970) and *Journalists at Work* (Sage, 1971).

17. They were Allan Blanchard, 49; Ann Devroy, 48; James Herzog, 39; John Holliman, 49; Bill Peterson, 47; Marilyn Robinson, 44; and Allan Yoder, 43.

18. We estimated the dropouts as under 30 years old; TJs, from 30 to 44; lifers, at 45-plus. Unlike the national surveys of journalists, our survey also includes those working for niche publications. Using the same age criterion for guessing the status of the "not located," we estimate that 45 percent of those who were niche journalists in 1978 became lifers.

19. J. Peter Segall, interviewed July 7, 2011.

20. John McClure, interviewed by Michelle Begnoche, November 20, 2007.

21. Susan Fogg Braaten, interviewed by Lesley Bruno, March 2, 2007.

22. Lynne Olson, interviewed by GWU class, February 27, 2008.

23. Stanley Karnow interview, October 14, 1977.

24. Cindy Parmenter, interviewed by Sarah Lovenheim, June 7, 2007.

25. Doug Underwood, interviewed by Michelle Begnoche, December 11, 2007.

26. Kathy Burns interview, June 19, 2011.

27. Ferrel Guillory, interviewed by Sarah Lovenheim, June 18, 2006.

28. See Paul Lewis, "John Wallach, 59, Who Fought Hatred with Youth Camp," *New York Times,* July 12, 2002.

29. Stephen Aug, interviewed by Richard Martinelli, October 8, 2007.

30. John Bascom, interviewed by Lynda Marlow, November 19, 2007.

31. Jim Coates, interviewed by Nathaniel Lubin, July 20, 2007.

32. Berl Schwartz, interviewed by Lynda Marlow, October 16, 2007.

33. Carol Richards, interviewed by Lynda Marlow, October 18, 2007. Or Anthony Barbieri, managing editor, on leaving the *Baltimore Sun:* "*I really didn't think that I would be happy helping to dismantle the paper that I had known and that I helped build. So it was an easy decision.*" Interviewed by Michelle Begnoche, October 8, 2007. Also see James O'Shea, *The Deal from Hell* (Public Affairs, 2011).

34. Stan Benjamin, interviewed by Michelle Begnoche, September 26, 2007.

35. Mary Kay Quinlan, interviewed by Lynda Marlow, September 17, 2007.

36. Christopher Bonner, interviewed by Sarah Lovenheim, June 14, 2006.

37. Christopher Conte, interviewed by Nathaniel Lubin, July 16, 2007.

38. Mary Leonard, interviewed by Lynda Marlow, November 2, 2007.

39. Frank Greve, interviewed by Sarah Lovenheim, June 6, 2006.

40. Elaine Shannon, interviewed by Sarah Lovenheim, June 5, 2006.

41. Bill Choyke, interviewed by Sarah Lovenheim, June 16, 2006.

42. Norman Kempster interview, July 6, 2011.

43. Marlene Cimons, interviewed by Sarah Lovenheim, June 10, 2006; e-mail exchange with author, July 18, 2011.

44. Staying in journalism did not seem to be influenced by having studied journalism, which might have indicated early interest. When categorizing the "not located," we estimated that 47 percent of the dropouts and 49 percent of the TJs had been journalism majors.

45. Richard Carelli, interviewed by Richard Martinelli, September 24, 2007. Another reporter who went to Georgetown Law School at night, Urban Lehner (*Wall Street Journal*), said he learned from the experience "not to be intimidated by lawyers, which I think is a big thing for a journalist." Lehner, interviewed by Nathaniel Lubin, August 2, 2007.

46. Stan Crock, interviewed by Elizabeth Krevsky, July 29, 2009.

47. James Roper's 60 years were spent with United Press, *Washington Star,* and Newhouse; Edgar Allen Poe spent 64 years with the *New Orleans Times-Picayune;* Richard Strout's remarkable 65-year career is noted in chapter 1.

48. The labor force participation rate of those ages 65 and older increased from 12.9 percent in 2000 to 16.8 percent in 2008. Contributing to this trend are the recent recession, the switch from defined-benefit to defined-contribution retirement plans, and changes in Social Security legislation that have increased the incentives to work at older ages. See Rich Morin, "Most Middle-Aged Adults Are Rethinking Retirement Plans," May 28, 2009, Pew Research Center Publications (http://pewresearch.org/pubs/1234/the-threshold-generation).

49. See the appendix for Lee Bandy's career; see chapter 1 and the appendix for Ellen Warren's.

50. Jeff Antevil, interviewed by Michelle Begnoche, September 17, 2007.

51. Richard Ryan, interviewed by Elizabeth Richardson, October 22, 2007.

52. Richard Roth, interviewed by Lynda Marlow, October 11, 2007.

53. "Guild Releases Details on Post Salaries," July 9, 2008 (www.wbng.org/post/bulletins/2008/08-0709PostSalary.pdf).

54. Robert Pierpoint, interviewed by Michelle Begnoche, March 18, 2008.

55. Walter Rogers, interviewed by Lynda Marlow, October 1, 2007.

56. See James Fallows, *Breaking the News* (Pantheon, 1996), pp. 84–88.

57. Richard Cohen, interviewed by Sarah Lovenheim, August 1, 2006.

58. Andrew Alexander, interviewed by GWU class, February 6, 2008.

59. Andrew Glass, interviewed by GWU class, February 6, 2008.

60. James Doyle, interviewed by Elizabeth Krevsky, August 7, 2009.

61. William D. Hickman, interviewed by Caryl Ann McAleer, February 4, 2008.

62. Christopher Ogden, interviewed by Heather Kleba, September 20, 2007.

63. Ike Pappas, interviewed by Heather Kleba, October 4 and 22, 2007.

64. David Garcia, interviewed by Nathaniel Lubin, July 11, 2007.

65. Walter Rogers, interviewed by Lynda Marlow, October 1, 2007.

66. James Adams, interviewed by Samantha Barry, February 2, 2007.

67. See Stephen Hess, *Through Their Eyes* (Brookings, 2005), pp. 29–30.

68. Robert Rankin, interviewed by Sarah Lovenheim, May 25, 2006.

69. Bill Zimmerman, interviewed by Lynda Marlow, October 8, 2007.

70. Jed Duvall, interviewed by Caryl Ann McAleer, February 19, 2008.

71. Eleanor Randolph, interviewed by Michelle Begnoche, November 30, 2007.

72. James Adams, interviewed by Michelle Begnoche, November 8, 2007.

73. Dale Nelson, interviewed by Nathaniel Lubin, August 8, 2007.

74. Robert Abernethy, interviewed by Michelle Begnoche, September 7, 2007.

75. Rudy Abramson, interviewed by Richard Martinelli, October 12 and October 22, 2007.

76. Judlyne Lilly, interviewed by Caryl Ann McAleer, January 21, 2008.

77. James Canan, interviewed by Michelle Begnoche, September 19, 2007.

78 . Edward Behr, interviewed by Michele Begnoche, October 12, 2007.

79. Andrew Alexander, interviewed by Samantha Vizer, April 11, 2006.

80. James McCartney, interviewed by Lynda Marlow, September 11, 2007.

INDEX

ABC, 24, 32, 37–38, 46, 51, 53, 71, 72, 76, 79, 80, 85, 134, 140
Abernethy, Bob, 10–11, 78, 82, 135, 143, 191n5
Abramson, Rudy, 143
Acheson, Dean, 11
Adams, James, 92–93, 140, 143
Adams, James M., 48, 143
Adams, Robert, 144
African American publications, 52–53
African American reporters: bias and discrimination, 45, 46, 47–48; career paths, *xxi,* 44–49; coverage of African American issues, 50, 52–53; employment trends, *xxi,* 45, 50, 52, 53–54; Gridiron Club membership, 109; at *New York Times,* 58; prominent national journalists, *xxi,* 50–52; in television, 51; women, 34, 46, 48
Ailes, Roger, 74–75
Albright, Joseph, 144
Aldrich, Charles, 101, 144
Aldrich, Nancy, 97–98, 144, 192n5
Alexander, Andrew, 109, 116–17, 137, 144
Allen, Ira, 17, 91, 144
Allison, Graham, 73
All Things Considered (NPR), 38
Alwood, Edward, 21, 128, 144
American Petroleum Institute, 81, 110
Anderson, Helen, 189
Anderson, Jack, 18
Anderson, James, 90, 144
Angle, James, 122
Annenberg Public Policy Center, *xvi,* 93
Antevil, Jeffrey H., 145
Arehart-Treichel, Joan, 145

Arieff, Irwin, 104, 145
Arkansas Gazette, 28
Arledge, Roone, 71, 76, 79
Arnett, Peter, 94
Arvidson, Cheryl, 39, 127, 145
Associated Press, 4, 14, 26, 27–28, 31, 33, 89, 92–94, 131
Atlantic, The, 106
Attkisson, Sharyl, 38
Aug, Stephen, 85, 145
Aukofer, Frank, 109
Averill, John, 2, 6, 145, 191n4

Baby boom generation reporters, *xxi;* backgrounds and education, 14; career paths, *xxi,* 14, 15–19; post-journalism careers, 18, 19–25; women among, 14–15, 31–33
Bacon, Donald, 126–27, 145
Bailey, Becky, 17, 19, 145
Bailey, Chuck, 38–39, 110
Bailey, Gil, 113, 146
Bain, C. Jackson, 80–81, 146
Baker, Russell, 56, 58, 75, 197n8, 198n13
Baltimore Evening Sun, 39
Baltimore Sun, 4, 25, 85–86, 121
Bandy, Leland, 110, 135, 146
Baquet, Dean, 50
Barbieri, Anthony, 25, 146, 194n39, 204n33
Barnett, David, 5, 146, 191n5
Baron, Stephen, 146
Barton, John, 91, 146
Barton, Salley, 189
Bascom, Jon, 146
Batte, Mary Bruce, 101
Battey, Phil, 103, 146
Baulch, Jerry, 1, 92, 147, 191n4

207

CPSIA information can be obtained at www.ICGtesting.com
Printed in the USA
BVOW07s1049200713

326021BV00002B/12/P